D0392356

DIAMINDS:
DECODING THE MENTAL HABITS OF SUCCESSFUL THINKERS

MIHNEA MOLDOVEANU AND
ROGER MARTIN

Diaminds

Decoding the Mental Habits
of Successful Thinkers

UNIVERSITY OF TORONTO PRESS
Toronto Buffalo London

Rotman/UTP Publishing
University of Toronto Press Incorporated
Toronto Buffalo London
www.utppublishing.com
Printed in Canada

ISBN 978-0-8020-9991-4

Printed on acid-free, 100% post-consumer recycled paper with
vegetable-based inks.

Library and Archives Canada Cataloguing in Publication

Moldoveanu, Mihnea, 1968–
Diaminds : decoding the mental habits of successful thinkers /
Mihnea Moldoveanu, Roger Martin.

Includes bibliographical references and index.
ISBN 978-0-8020-9991-4

1. Thought and thinking. 2. Success – Psychological aspects.
3. Success in business – Psychological aspects.   I. Martin, Roger L.
II. Title

BF441.M64 2009   153   C2009-904968-6

University of Toronto Press acknowledges the financial assistance to its
publishing program of the Canada Council for the Arts and the Ontario
Arts Council.

 Canada Council   Conseil des Arts   ONTARIO ARTS COUNCIL
for the Arts   du Canada   CONSEIL DES ARTS DE L'ONTARIO

University of Toronto Press acknowledges the financial support for its
publishing activities of the Government of Canada through the Book
Publishing Industry Development Program (BPIDP).

To the diaminds, and to our students. May it function as a bridge …

Contents

Preface

Ceci n'est pas une pipe.

René Magritte

This is not a book. It is a hook. Its purpose is to hook you into a relationship with your own thinking that is un-ordinary. The *ordinary* way of thinking about thinking is to ask: *What* do you think? (The answer is usually some belief about the world.) The un-ordinary way of thinking that we will attempt to sketch rests with asking, rather, *How* do you think? (The answer is not going to be a belief any more, but rather a description of some way of *forming* beliefs.)

This book (a.k.a. 'hook') asks: *How* do successful thinkers think? And *how* is it that their ways of thinking make it more likely that they will succeed than fail in the cauldron of business *and* life – this complex, messy, ambivalent, and often irretrievably ambiguous life? One cannot ask such a question without having some sort of intuition or premonition about what counts for an answer. That is because most people, when you ask them *how* they think, will give you a look that blends incomprehension with suspicion. '*What* do you think?' is a much 'tamer' question – the answer is already embedded in it. By contrast, '*How* do you think?' is a *wild* question. One cannot be certain in advance what would count as an answer.

So in order to ask, of the remarkable thinkers, doers, and thinking doers whom we portray in what follows, '*How* do you think?' we must first come up with some sort of *descriptive language* for thinking, some way of making explicit what is meant by the question. Which is precisely what we do. This book (or hook) you hold in your hands attempts to describe thinking in such a way that you can build a *template* that will allow you to learn from the 'diaminds' – to transfer from their (dia) minds to your own not what they know (which is far less relevant than is commonly assumed) but *how* they know what they know, and *how* they interact with the world through their senses in such a way that they transform raw feelings into ideas, concepts, prescriptions, what have you.

By the end of the proceedings, we – and you – should be in a position to *wink* at questions such as 'What do you think?' and to see them as far less interesting than questions such as 'How do you think?' … as unintelligible and possibly annoying as that question might seem right now. And you should, by the end, realize that thinking about thinking about the world is as important as is thinking about the world, *tout court*.

We have, like all authors, incurred many debts in the production of this piece. First and foremost is our debt to those Diaminds who allowed us to probe their minds, who shared with us fragments of their being and of their memory of their being, and who were patient with our dead ends and wrong turns in providing interpretations for our 'findings.' Second and equally foremost is our debt to the man who made endeavours such as this one possible: Marcel Desautels, whose endowment of the Desautels Centre for Integrative Thinking was as far-sighted as it was audacious and generous. Third, we would like to thank those who have taken the time and given of their mindshare to comment on the ideas in this book in its earlier embodiments: Olivier Leclerc, Keith Oatley, Jordan Peterson, Ato Quayson, and Jennifer Riel.

We are also grateful to Jennifer DiDomenico, our editor at University of Toronto Press, for her patient help and guidance in the creation and production of the manuscript; to Sally Smith of the Desautels Centre and Noelle Hindi of Tampold Architects for their work on creating and refining the figures in the manuscript; and to each other, for the dialogue.

A quick stylistic note on the use of the pronouns 'he' and 'she' throughout the book. The 'he/she' or 'he or she' construction is cumbersome. Whenever we use a general example, we choose the protagonist to be either 'he' or 'she' and trust the reader will trust that all such nameless 'he's' could have been 'she's' and vice versa. We know the reader will likely know this. But now she will also know that we know he knows it.

DIAMINDS:
DECODING THE MENTAL HABITS OF SUCCESSFUL THINKERS

Praeludium: Invitation to a Journey and the Beckoning of a Destination

Imagine a mind so confident, nimble, and adaptive that it can tackle any practical problem you throw its way and come up with several ways of approaching it. So powerful that it can cause the body within which it resides to take action that is consistent with the best possible solution, regardless of immediate temptations and entrenched habits. So broad that it can justify that course of action to large numbers of people, each of whom has a different set of wishes, wants, desires, interests, principles, and ways of looking at the world and understanding its workings. So tough that it can turn on a dime if 'the world' supplies it with evidence that it has erred. So resilient and courageous that it can persist in thinking through conflict, ambiguity, and uncertainty even in the face of impending disaster. Would you not want this mind on your team? In your organization? Indeed, would you not want to *be* that mind?

Imagine a mind with the logical depth of a star computer engineer and the breadth and flexibility of a great saleswoman; with the rigour of a financial auditor and the improvisational skills of a master negotiator; with the capacity of a great private investigator to discern others' motives and strategies on the fly; with the discipline of a senior clinician at developing a comprehensive diagnosis of any ailment; with the nimbleness and emotional mobility of a seasoned actor and the vision of a master playwright. Would you not be setting out to cultivate and train such a mind if you were designing a program of study for a leader of the future?

Imagine – if you are philosophically inclined – a mind that combines the depth, subtlety, and expansiveness of a Socrates with the pragmatism of a C.S. Peirce; a Kantian commitment to responsiveness and autonomy – hallmarks of reason – with the technical proficiency of a Russell or a Reichenbach; a Humean capacity to doubt, radically and truthfully, with a Cartesian capacity to probe knowledge to its very limits; the sensitivity to the tenuousness with which words glom onto objects and events of a Wittgenstein with a Heideggerian awareness that reasoning and representation depend on mood and attunement; the all-encompassing ambition of a Hegel with the technical precision of a Willard Quine; the logical depth of a Hintikka with the cognitive breadth of a Rorty; the sensitivity to meaning and feeling of a Merleau-Ponty with the awareness of the consequences and pragmatics of assertion of a Searle; and that turns all of these qualities into precise, imaginative, constructive action predicated on an Aristotelian commitment to feeling the right sentiment at the right time, towards the right person, for the right reasons, through a properly sequenced chain of causes and effects. Would you not be attempting to train such a mind, if you were building the university for developing the thinkers of the future?

The book you are about to read is an attempt to capture this sort of mind in action. It is not, to be clear, about people who sit inside philosophy departments – or other departments as they presently exist. It is not an excursus on the intricacies of meaning and mental causation. It is not a treatise on experimental ontology and applied epistemology. It is a book about *real* minds – the ones that are working this very day in our world, doing business, making money, creating value of all kinds, energizing others to more productive visions of the world and more constructive ways of being in this world. It is an attempt to portray a certain kind of intelligence that has gone unnoticed by intelligence hunters, IQ measure peddlers, and theorists of human capacity. It is also an attempt to understand situated, pragmatic, reflective, adaptive intelligence *from within* through a set of directed exercises and thought experiments aimed at capturing the salient features of this mind.

Now, what is a 'salient feature'? Try this: You watch in awe as Usain Bolt shatters the 100 metre and the 200 metre world records at the Beijing Olympics of 2008. You wonder: How does he do it? Now rephrase that question: What would the world look like in which *I* could do that? What would I or someone else, more highly gifted but still *a person more or less like me,* have to do to achieve the seemingly magical combination of thrust and drive of 'the Bolt'?

Enter a well-trained sports physiologist. She tells you: 'I know that looking at the replay of Bolt's race is mesmerizing, but if you want to know *how* rather than *that* it happened, you have to train your sights on *the right part* of it. So look at Bolt's *rate-limiting step* – that is, isolate the muscle group that is *in the way* of the Bolt being *even faster* than he is. Look for the *critical link* in the chain of muscular thrusts that, taken together, form a *step* in that world-breaking sprint. And that step is, as it turns out, discernible and isolatable. It is the *flexion of the hip joint* – the movement by which one leg is swung in front of the other, which involves the weakest muscles of the ensemble that sprinters train. Focus on that movement. Study it. Design exercises for it. Practise them with discipline and perseverance. *Then*, perhaps, even if you won't bolt like the Bolt, you will at least see your way to a *path* for getting there. The rest will be only a matter of more work.'

And that is our project, in a nutshell. In this book we set out to isolate a few of the key *mechanisms* in the minds of successful thinkers –mechanisms that seem to account for enormous differences in individual outcomes. We attempt to describe those mechanisms precisely enough that readers will see how they themselves can absorb and develop them.

Unlike many of our 'normal social science' counterparts, we have little interest in achieving – for now, at least – a statistically reliable description of the 'twenty-nine mental habits of outliers.' We are more interested in describing vividly those two or three mechanisms or mental habits that, when assembled, explain much of the 'tail' of the distribution of successful intelligence in the Age of Knowledge. And that distribution is not Gaussian, as many textbooks would have you and us believe – often so that their authors can shift their focus to 'tame' features such as mean and standard deviation. The tail is in fact *unknown* and may even be *unknowable;* but in the worlds we will be examining, it is more important than the mean. The tail, after all, is the realm of extremes, of exceptionality, of 'the Bolt.'

The study of extremes is a 'strange new world' in conventional science. This should be no surprise – after all, the point of normal science is to describe means and small departures from them – not extremes. Conventional science is built on premises of normality, in both the 'normal' and the 'Gaussian' sense of *normal*. A normal (or Gaussian) distribution is one in which remote extremes are so improbable as to be reasonably considered impossible. Which legitimates, of course, our not having to worry about them. In light of recent world events, this is clearly one of those 'necessary illusions' that Nietzsche wrote about – one of those illusions that, though false, is life enhancing (career enhancing, if one is feeling malicious) for those countless social scientists who are attempting to achieve the security that comes with tenure. As Douglas Hofstadter has pointed out, 'the way forward' in the 'normal' cognitive-scientific approach to the study of the mind has long been to develop a program or algorithm that explains what 'most people' would do in a given situation.

'Most people'! Which is to say, not Richard Feynman, or Andrew Viterbi, or Charlie Munger, or John Doerr, or Steve Jobs. 'Most people.' This particular algorithm for the study of minds has long been employed as a reliable heuristic for pushing 'normal science' forward. Question: Forward towards *what?* At the current rate, given the state of the art in the field, it could take us 10,000 years to reach the level of insight comparable to that of Plato 2,400 years ago. Hofstadter has suggested that we focus instead, and in painstaking detail, on building models of *remarkable* minds – that is, on out-of-the-way mental habits and on the turns of thought they exemplify. That we isolate these models' characteristics and test them against tough new problems. That is the approach we will be taking in the following chapters.

We want to focus on a particular feature of remarkable minds, the 'dia' feature, in reference to both *dia*lectical (à la Hegel) and *dia*-logical (à la Bakhtin). Simply put, the 'diamind' is a way of being in the world that marshals differences and complexities to the task of building better solutions to problems. The diamind is not *comfortable* with difference, ambiguity, conflict, and tension – *comfortable*, here, is an insipid euphemism that betrays just how *un*comfortable these demons make us feel. The diamind, rather, *embraces* difference, ambiguity, conflict, and tension – indeed, it treats those things as signposts to better solutions and better problems. Which in turn suggests that the diamind is more awake, more conscious, and more aware of its own states, and more able, as a result, to reject old habits and proclivities that consign most minds to the clutches of familiarity, simplicity, and 'the one right way' of seeing and feeling.

By the time our journey is finished, you will have seen a number of these diaminds in action. We have interviewed and analysed some of them ourselves. Others we have 'filmed' at work in their writing and speaking. Our focus is on finding the *crux* of the diamind, the rate-limiting step, the flexion of the diamind's hip. We start off slowly, focusing first on the diamind's ability to experience radically different thoughts, perceptions, and ideas; and then on the diamind's ability to expand the window through which it perceives the world in order to deepen and broaden its understanding. We study, in slow motion, the *what* and the *how* of the diamind's flexion of the hip. At each step we pause for some exercises, which are aimed at stimulating more thinking about both the *what* and the *how*. Then we dive into a fast-paced coda that aims to build a far more detailed portrait of the diamind, using some of the precise vernacular that fifty years of computation theory and artificial intelligence (AI) have brought us. This move turns AI as we know it on its head: we do not use our case studies to build computer models of highly successful minds; rather, we use the language of computer modelling to render our portrait of the diamind more precise and thereby more teachable, more transferable. We turn AI on its head because, as it turns out, we have a lot to learn from the mind-emulating machines we have been trying to build – or, more precisely, from those of us who have been trying to build those machines. In this way *AI* becomes *IA* – 'intelligent artificiality,' the discipline that allows us to figure out what remarkable minds do by pinpointing their inner dynamics with algorithmic precision. All to the end of being able to *learn* from those minds – to transfer their dynamics, which have long eluded practitioners of normal science.

A warning. We will be asking you to do something quite different from what other books or programs of study have expected of you. We will be asking you to take a different perspective from the one that seems customary or comfortable. We will be asking you to shift from the normal perspective wherein you are trying to figure out *what* someone is saying, what he is trying to get across, to the *meta*perspective of trying to figure out *how someone thinks* in order to be able to say what he or she is saying. The difference is more easily enunciated than instantiated. When you read a *Forbes, Maclean's, Walrus, Fortune,* or *Harvard Business Review* article or op-ed piece, when you listen to a colleague or a friend try to make a point, your attention is focused on the *what* and the *who*: on *what* the writer, the colleague, the friend is trying to say, and on *who* that person is when he or she says or writes the way he or she does ('friend or foe?' is probably both the most common and simple-minded categorization of possible who's). You are less likely to be paying heed to *how they think,* or on *how you think* through *what they say*. Which brings to the fore the perspectival shift we are trying to bring: from the 'what–who?' space to the 'how?' space, and, in particular, to the 'how do they think?' space. You will find that in that space you will be far less worried about what our characters *do;* about the parents to whom they were born; about the people they *know;* and about the networks, clubs, and cliques they belong to; and far more concerned with how they use language; and about how they categorize people, things, events, theories, what have you. With the *ways* they search rather than with the end results of their searches; with the type of logic they use to reach certain conclusions rather than with the conclusions themselves; with the ways they frame problems rather than with the precise problems they have solved.

All of this is unavoidably tricky – for some, it will be downright uncomfortable. Yet doing well and feeling good are only infrequently aligned, and many of the mental habits of the diaminds we are about to describe do not instantaneously feel good. This encourages us to tell our readers, 'Try this – give it a shot, and see what happens *within* you as a result.'

1 Introduction to Thinking about Thinking While Continuing to Think

Does thinking matter to success in business? If so, how? Before reading on, take a moment to pose these questions to yourself.

Try bringing to mind a successful business person – a Jack Welch, a Michael Dell, a Charlie Munger, a Steve Jobs, an Ann Mulcahy, an Indra Nooyi, a Rob McEwen – and figuring out whether that person's thinking style or pattern is in any way unique, whether something sets that person's thinking apart from the thought processes of others who have not succeeded as greatly.

You will immediately run into several problems. First, how do you even know *what* they think, let alone *how* they think? It's much easier to figure out what accounts for a great tennis player's success – a devastating forehand, a versatile backhand, or a lethal serve – because you can *see* the effects of these shots on the opponent's actions and on the outcome of the match. But *thinking*? That's a different matter altogether. We have no way of observing *thoughts*. We can only infer them from their effects on actions. We have to start with what the successful performer said and did and then try to map that person's behaviours in various predicaments onto plausible mental causes of their behaviours. Tough, no?

You could *ask* them, of course: 'How do you think, and what is it about how you think that is unique, robust, and valuable?' Here you run into two more difficulties.

First, *most thinkers* – even highly successful ones – *do not know how they think*. It is simply not part of one's training or life preparation – in our age, at least – to think carefully about how one thinks. Thinking about thinking is not something one does naturally. Second, even if the person you ask *does* give you an answer better than 'I don't know,' you still have to factor in that most people have a perverse incentive to attribute their success to their personal characteristics rather than to chance events or the positive influences of others. And since our culture prizes intelligence and other thinking capacities as personal character-istics, the perverse incentive that results makes it likely that the answer we get back will be a self-enhancing rationalization, a story that feels good to its teller. For the person being asked, this amounts to a form of self-therapy and, sometimes, a means of validating success. So you will have to somehow figure out a way to see through the webs of deception and self-deception – webs that can lead a successful business person to perceive a series of random events as directly attributable to his or her way of thinking.

Suppose you could somehow steer clear of these difficulties and fig-ure out a way to unobtrusively probe the thinking styles of the success-ful. You would still be faced with the problem of what to make of your findings: How could you *know* that the way this person thinks is *really* relevant to his success? How could you know that the characteristic in question is not spurious, irrelevant, or (even worse) counterproductive, and therefore that success came to the successful one despite her ways of thinking rather than because of them?

The nearest cognitive psychologist, if consulted, would caution that you are being unscientific: to make valid inferences, you should be looking at the thinking styles of unsuccessful people as well, and of people who have succeeded even though they lack the characteristic you believe to be the key to their success. For any one feature of think-ing that you believe to be related to business success, you should be looking at successful people who possess it, unsuccessful people who possess it, successful people who do not possess it, and unsuccessful people who do not possess it. Only if the successful possess it, the un-successful do not possess it, and there is no other thinking pattern the successful exhibit that can be tied to their success, can you – still with some caution – infer that there is a meaningful correlation between that particular characteristic and success in business.

Potentially meaningful, that is, because there could always be some *other* characteristic – one that you did not think about (such as self-discipline, presence, or, some uncanny and hard-to-verbalize ability to 'read situations') that is actually responsible for the successful behav-iour you have observed but that you did not consider during your in-vestigation – because, after all, you were concentrating on thinking, not feeling, doing, or sensing.

Faced with all these difficulties, you might experience a sudden loss of interest in the question: 'Why bother?' Our answer: It is worth the bother because thinking is too important an activity to be left unscrutinized and unexplored. The opportunity cost of forgoing opportunities to learn to produce more successful patterns of thought is too high, because thinking shapes action, and action shapes outcomes, and the resulting outcomes are what make up our 'lives' and destinies. Also, thinking is something that – however covert – we do all the time: try to not think at all for a moment and you'll see what we mean. Because we do it habitually and it is of great consequence to our actions, thinking – like living – is worth trying to do better. That is a key premise of this book.

But in the realm of thinking, there is still the problem of figuring out what 'better' means. Once again, the nearest cognitive psychologist offers her services: standardized tests of intelligence, rules for thinking more reliably in uncertain situations, and interventions and training programs to help you become a 'better thinker.' To buy or not to buy? – that is the question. 'If you're so smart, why aren't *you* rich?' So you will be tempted to ask her. A good question, which in this case has a good answer: taken together, the 'toolkit' of standard psychological science (IQ, EQ, and all the other Q's and personality measures) does not explain more than 35 per cent of the variance in outcomes (i.e., 'success in business'). The thinking virtues that psychologists have come up with so far have provided only weak results – results that in most cases can't be acted on anyway, because they most often have to do with genes, upbringing, early life experiences, and other things you cannot change.

So: how to design a training program for making yourself smarter, even in a purely IQ sense? How can you get yourself to pay more heed to the frequency with which certain kinds of events happen? And having done that, how can you judge how likely they are to recur – especially when the need to act is pressing and the stakes are high? How do you become less automatic in your patterns of reasoning – less constrained by mindless, knee-jerk (or brain-jerk) 'tics of the mind'? To be actionable, the answers to such 'how' questions have to spell out activities that you, whoever you are, can engage in tomorrow with the expectation of seeing desired results after some finite period of time; and 'can' means 'truly able to in practice,' the same way you can go to the corner store and buy bottled water.

By now, frustration will have reared its head, as it did for us when we started the work that culminated in the writing of this book. *Productive* frustration, to be sure, of the sort that announces a new path, but what is this new path?

That new path is to *bite the bullet*, whatever the warnings of normal science. It is to seek out successful business people and study their thinking through structured interviews and detailed observations of their thought patterns. This is a high-risk approach. We risk mistaking what we want to see for what is in fact the case. We risk making our prototypical thinkers too smart, too nimble, or just too good in some other way. We risk missing certain characteristics of their patterns of thinking that we did not think to include in our inquiry. In sum, we run the risk of too much subjectivity so that we end up telling 'just so' stories from which nothing of general value can be learned.

These risks are real. They are the risks that any new attempt to capture a human phenomenon or characteristic will face. They faced Spearman in 1904 when he declared that he had 'objectively measured' general intelligence, and Binet in the 1910s when he articulated his first intelligence tests. They faced the architects of the cognitive 'revolution' in psychology (such as Herbert Simon), who studied mental entities – such as concepts, categories, metaphors and reasoning protocols – that were suspect to the rest of the psychological profession because they were, well, *mental* and therefore not as *real* as more 'tangible' entities, such as human behaviour and sense perception. They will continue to face every new articulator of a new phenomenon – but they are well worth facing when the result might be a description of *a better way to think*.

Of course, we will be making full use of the conceptual toolkit of cognitive science and epistemology. We will use it to make sense of what we have observed and to turn these observations into actionable models for new ways to think. Just as we use *grammar* as an implicit theory of someone's language in order to make sense of what someone says when finding it difficult to understand him or her, we will utilize the conceptual repertoire developed by those who study minds for a living in order make sense of the patterns of thinking that we observe in our subjects.

The result of this detailed mind mapping will be a new 'logic of successful thinking' that is friendly to psychological insight and at the same time open to the new and remarkable patterns of practical thought that have long gone unnoticed precisely because they are so difficult to express verbally. A 'logic,' then, and not necessarily a *science* – in the same way that game theory, the craft of optimization, and the discipline of design are 'logics': things that enable the intelligent design of new behaviour. And what behaviour is more worth learning to design intelligently than *thinking?* This, then, is our project. And, with these words, let us proceed.

The Mental Habits of Successful Thinkers

We begin with a first cut at this question: 'What kind of thinking leads to better outcomes in business for the thinker?' This seems innocuous. The world is complex and indeterminate, and there are many ways of seeing, experiencing, and representing it, which we will call *models.* Successful thinking *integrates* several radically different models while preserving the thinker's ability to act decisively. The successful thinker is an integrator who can quickly and effectively abstract the best qualities of radically different ways of seeing and representing; in doing so, that person develops 'a better lens' on the bewildering phenomenon we call the 'world.'

What does the integrator *do?* He – who will often turn out to be a *she* – sees his way clear to successful action in situations where others see only a choice among poor or mediocre outcomes. His is a dialectical mind: a *dia*mind, that is, a mind that beholds at least two often contradictory ways of seeing the world, gives each its full due, and instead of fearing and fleeing the resulting tension, lives it, embraces it, and comes up with a better way – one that does violence to neither but improves on both.

The experience of radical tension can be conceived of as a *limit point* in the thinker's existence. Karl Jaspers defined limit points as situations that are inescapable and unresolvable. Death – Jaspers's example – is a limit point of human life. None of us can escape or avoid it. Most of us try to 'resolve' it as a problem of existence, one that sometimes shapes life itself.

Executive choice is another limit point: the clock ticks on the money in the bank; the Board of Directors will exercise its decision-making rights in ways that are often complicated and unpredictable; analysts will distort the information given to them to their own ends; competitors will attack undefended market segments; suppliers will ship late and request early payment; customers will ask for early shipments and – in exchange – pay late for them. As all of this unfolds, the future opens like a chasm. 'How now?' the future asks us. 'Given this situation, what is to be done?' Everything one does in this predicament has rising opportunity and marginal costs, and no word, no action, no gesture can be taken back. Feeling the heat yet?

There are options, to be sure. Management theory often provides the executive with a generic set of alternatives: profit from the core by building products and services that arise from core capabilities; diversify in other markets and businesses to hedge cyclical risks; integrate vertically to minimize the uncertainty of supply chain management; integrate horizontally to increase monopoly power; cut costs to increase profitability and save cash; invest in R&D to develop new features that can lead to monopoly positions in a product market; create joint ventures and other alliances to minimize the cost of that development; leverage diverse approaches and skills to solve problems; invest in marketing to increase demand and differentiation ... There is a soothing, almost therapeutic quality to the language in which these options are couched. That is part of their appeal. But the executive faced with a high-stakes decision – which is effectively a limit point – is not deceived: the fact that these options are *generic* in his industry means that the moment he has conceptualized his options in the language of business, his work has just begun, for now he has to give precise and actionable meaning to the generic words of management theories by asking these questions: 'What *is* "the core" of my business? What *is* the value chain of activities I am trying to reverse engineer? What *is* the right way to think about the cost structure of my business?' And the answers he seeks cannot themselves be generic.

The diamind makes new meanings: she re-engineers unattractive problem statements and strategic options into attractive ones. She turns trade-offs into synergies, local peaks into global optima, paradoxes into mere difficulties, and obstacles into opportunities, and she does so – as we will show – by engaging in an identifiable and *learnable* pattern of thinking.

Mind Design: The Engineering of Successful Mental Habits

Like much of behaviour, thinking is habitual. It is made up of habits, or automatisms – that is, repetitive and recurrent units of mental behaviour that occur on very short time scales.

Most mental habits *close off* opportunities for further thought and perception. This may or may not be useful, depending on the context. 'If you see a lion, run towards water' is a useful 'closure-oriented' mental routine when you're alone in the wilds of the savannah, but not at the local zoo. Of course, the trick here is to figure out *quickly* whether you are in the wild or at the local zoo, and act accordingly. But in the realm of organizations, savannahs and zoos do not come pre-labelled. It is easy to mistake one for the other, with disastrous consequences, so you have to figure out quickly and effectively the ecological value of your own thinking routines.

Because they are habits, the basic units of our mental behaviour are often less sensitive than they should be to changes of context. 'One plus one?' asked in a social setting begets 'two' as the immediate, 'thoughtless' answer. You could instead ask, 'One plus one *what*?' treating the *one* not as an indexical term referring to the number '1,' but rather as a qualifier: one clump of clay added to another clump of clay in the right way makes *one* larger clump of clay, not two. Or you could ask, 'In what base?' Here, 'two' would be the answer in base 10; whereas in base 2, the answer would be 'one.'

And why would someone ask this question in the first place? To what end? How does the answer matter to the end goal? Perhaps they were trying to make a stupid joke, or to drive home an obvious point, in which case a cooperative – albeit self-defeating – strategy would simply prolong a mediocre situation for everyone present. Similarly, a question such as 'Why did you fire her?' almost immediately inspires a *because* reply, which typically not does not actually refer to a *cause* (for instance, 'It *caused me* to get rid of the constant resentment which feeling envious of her caused me') but rather to a *reason* ('*Because* she was not a good fit with the rest of the group').

Of course, not all mental habits and routines are counterproductive. Want to see *your own brain* engage in a really productive one, live? 'Read' the following:

I cdnuolt blveiee that I cluod aulactlty uesdnatnrd what I was rdanieg. The phaomneal pweor of the haumn mind! It deo'nst mtater in what order the ltteers in a word are, the only iprmotnt thing is that the frist and lsat ltter be in the rghit pclae. And, you tuohgt slpleing was ipmorantt!

Neat – no? Decoding the text 'explicitly' would take way too long, relative to the amount of time in which 'real' minds – like yours – do it, which seems closer to 'implicitly.' Some mental habit must be at play, one that has long left conscious awareness and controlled processing and become, at some point, an automatism – a sort of 'error-correcting decoder' of the type you pay Qualcomm, Inc., predatory licensing fees for – discreetly lumped into your cellular phone bills, of course. So, what is the habit?

To be sure, it is hard to say, right away. That is why we need to *model* the mind as it does what it does. To say something worthwhile about how it 'does its thing,' we need to be able to 'name the thing' we believe it does. A bit of modelling, in this situation, comes in very handy. One quick and dirty model of the way the mind turns *I cdnuolt blveiee that I cluod aulactlty uesdnatnrd* into 'I couldn't believe that I could actually understand' is to assume that, when it sees, for instance, *cdnuolt*, it begins to parse through all of the seven-letter words in its vocabulary that begin with *c* and end with *t*, and look for resemblances between the letters in each word on the list and the middle letters of *cdnuolt*.

Okay, but how do you look for a resemblance? Well, you take each letter that occurs between the *c* and the *t* in *cdnuolt* and you compare it with every middle letter in the words on the list you have brought up. One problem: this is horrendously time consuming! Human creatures just cannot compare random lists of strings that quickly to one another. There must be a better way.

Another approach is to *build some trees* – not real ones, of course, only some treelike structures that can organize the search and make it more efficient. For instance, at the root of the tree (Figure 1.1) that is supposed to model 'the way the mind works' when it 'processes' *cdnuolt* as *couldn't* at such speeds, we could place the first letter of the word, *c*. At the level of the first branches we could place each of the other middle letters – *d, n, u, o, l* – since we do not, after all, know *which* letter goes second, only *that* the second letter is *one* of the set *d, n, u, o, l*. We could repeat the same manoeuvre for the second, third, fourth, and fifth-level branches – and then, we know that the word ends in a 't' – so all is well there.

Now, when your mind uses the tree of Figure 0.1 to process *cdnuolt* as *couldn't*, it just 'leafs through its branches' and quickly prunes the ones that don't make sense at first sight. The magic of the tree structure is that the pruning is done *quickly*: you don't need to consider the *entire* branch of the tree corresponding to *cndoult* in order to eliminate it: you just cut it off when you get to the first branch, *cn*, because it doesn't look like the beginning of any familiar word. So instead of having to search through $5 \times 5 \times 5 \times 5 \times 5 = 3,125$ words representing all possible combinations, you can get away with performing as few as five to ten 'pruning' operations that will take you right to the answer. Mental habits don't have to be a burden – indeed, quite often they make thinking *bearably* simple.

And how, you might ask, does your mind *know* there is no word in the English language that begins with *cn*? It doesn't (and actually, there

Figure 1.1 Tree-structure search aimed at unscrambling 'cdnuolt' into 'couldn't'

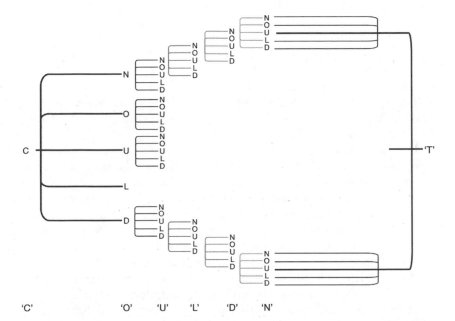

is at least one: 'cnoidal'). But *knowing* is not the problem your mind is trying to solve here – let alone achieving certainty. The real problem is how to maximize the probability of getting a good enough answer, given sometimes severe time constraints. And in such conditions, taking the seven-letter English words that begin with *c* that you know – or the first that come to mind – as representative of all the English words that begin with *c* is not a bad place to start. It leads to an efficient way to search a tree-structured memory. Understanding mental habits as *procedures* that have been engineered for specific applications is one key to mental habit detection, creation, and procreation.

Of course, one could argue that there are several such 'decoding loops' at play in understanding the pseudo-cryptic message above – loops that entail classifying the context in which the text appears (you 'expected' some sort of puzzle, as you are reading a text published by a university press), the relative difficulty of the task being proposed (you 'kind of knew' that the task was not going to be either totally and uninterestingly trivial or certifiably impossible to perform, as either would defeat the purpose of the project of writing this text, and so on. But the point remains: fast, tree-structured encoding and decoding – the key mental habits that allow us to deploy and use concepts and symbols – is 'in play' in all of these cases.

Unlike behavioural habits, *mental* habits are difficult to spot, name, and describe. Partly because they're covert, and partly because they sneak up on us in moments of unawareness, they're also difficult to eliminate or change. This is why we need a *new kind of language* for describing patterns of mental behaviour: we need to learn to speak *mentalese*, a language that will allow us to figure out quickly and effectively how we and others think.

That is the first and best use we will make of the formal, academic languages inherited from twenty-five centuries of theorizing about the mind. We prize them for their *precision*. As Tom Stewart once pointed out to us, all academic theories are best thought of as *languages*, in the same way that English, French, German, C++, and LISP are languages. All of them have specific signs that represent the objects that you as the speaker want to refer to, along with specific rules for putting these signs together correctly. Our natural languages are great at referring to the world of objects and events we experience first-hand, but not so great at referring to the *inner world* of thoughts and mental habits. That is why we will focus on developing a language for representing patterns of thought – a language that will allow us to think more transparently about thinking.

Mental habits work in conjunction with one another to make up patterns of thinking, which are analogous to patterns of behaviour in that they are reliably reproducible and yield predictable results in similar circumstances. It is a commonplace that 'marketing people' and 'engineering people' process information in different ways. But *in what ways are they different?* and what difference do their differences make?

This is where the language of cognitive science comes in handy as a *language for describing patterns of thought*. Thus one finds that 'marketing people' pay attention to a lot of information – they are informationally *broad* in their thinking patterns. They are constantly foraging the world for new bits of information and comparing that new information with parts of their existing database – which they keep around in working memory – in order to arrive at action prescriptions or decision rules. But they spend less time than engineers thinking about each piece of information and about how the various pieces fit together. In other words, compared to engineers, marketers are logically *shallower* in their thinking approach.

By contrast, one finds that 'engineering people' are informationally narrower but *logically deeper* in their thinking styles. They seek out far less information than do their marketing counterparts; then, having gathered it, they strive for logical consistency among the various pieces of information they deem relevant. For instance, they look for ways in which what they *believe* connects to what they *know*. They look for the logical implications of what they already know or believe in order decide what new beliefs to hold out for testing. They look for connections of the logical and causal type among facts and quasi-facts, rather than just associations and correlations.

Aware of this difference, we can ask: In what circumstances should logical depth dominate informational breadth and, vice versa? In what situations is *more thinking* better than *more foraging* or *more asking*, given that one can only think (or forage) more if one forages (or thinks) less?

Having answered these questions, we can then ask: How can we get 'marketing people' and 'engineering people' to think together? How can we *integrate* the thinking patterns of informationally broad thinkers (the marketers) with those of logically deep thinkers (the engineers) in order to create *better* thinkers ('better' as in 'better than either')? At last, we have come to a sharply posed question, one we can hope to answer in a way that would not have been possible without some way of representing the patterns of thinking of 'marketing people' and 'engineering people.'

But why, you might ask, do you think that successful business people are sophisticated, reflective thinkers who actually *think about thinking* to the extent you believe is necessary or useful to produce integrative outcomes? The answer: We *don't*. We *emphatically* do not. In fact, many of the people we will be introducing and trying to understand *don't know how they think*. Indeed, that is precisely why they most often cannot *teach* their modes of thinking to others.

Thinking happens in silence and solitude and often far outside the realm of explicit language. You do not have to think about thinking in order to think in a new way, but you do have to think about thinking in order to learn how to think in a *specific* new way. *Making things explicit is a learning tool*. An explicit understanding of what one does when one thinks integratively is not a prerequisite for thinking integratively. So we will be making things explicit here not because the subjects of our study do, but rather because making explicit what they do is a bridge to figuring out how they do it.

An example of the difference between pure cognitive intelligence on the one hand and embodied intelligence on the other should make this point clear. Let's start with the cognitive part: Sherlock Holmes, the master sleuth, and Moriarty, the criminal mastermind, are playing a mind game that can have serious consequences. Holmes is on the train from Oxford to London, and Moriarty is trying to meet the sleuth at the train station and kill him. Moriarty knows that Holmes has two options – he can get off the train at Charing Cross, or at Waterloo – so he must choose one station to wait for his prey. Moriarty thinks that Holmes will likely get off at Charing Cross, but he also knows that Holmes – being Holmes – will think about what Moriarty thinks he will do, and instead of getting off at Charing Cross, will get off at Waterloo. Of course, Holmes, being Holmes, may think about *this* as well, which would make him get off at Charing Cross … and so on.

What, then, should Moriarty do? That is the standard question posed to eager students of game theory as a way of teaching the concept of a *mixed strategy Nash equilibrium*, a funny name for a simple concept: Moriarty should *toss a coin* in order to decide where to wait for his intended victim.

A daring and literal-minded student in attendance might venture this question: 'What does Moriarty do if he does not have a coin in hand?' To see just how clever a question this is, consider that most people, when told 'it does not matter, just pick a number,' will not toss an *actual* coin to determine the number, but rather will pick the first number that comes to mind – which is, of course, a good way to make sure the number is not truly random, as it is likely correlated with the last thought they had, which, if someone knows how they think … And consider, also, that most people, when told 'it's a coin toss,' will hear 'it does not matter' and therefore will 'pick a number.' So, the question, then, is: How does Moriarty go about *mentally* tossing a coin?

Now suppose that Moriarty and Holmes play this little game every Friday night – perhaps because their existence is somehow too monotonous without such a stimulus. Then our game theorist's advice to Moriarty will be to 'randomize' his choice of where to wait for Holmes. 'Randomization' is a difficult thing, however: the alternating sequence (*Waterloo, Charing Cross, Waterloo, Charing Cross* …) is hardly random; nor is the more clever elaboration (*Waterloo, Charing Cross, Charing Cross, Waterloo, Waterloo, Charing Cross, Charing Cross, Charing Cross, Waterloo* …). The point is that getting a *random* sequence right requires *a lot* of intelligence – more intelligence than getting the *most complex imaginable pattern* right. So Moriarty has to be *a very complex creature* in order to play the perfect complex strategy against Holmes (which is the best strategy, given that Moriarty expects Holmes to play *his* best strategy).

Lots of thinking, no? To be sure. But the question is: Can you do all this thinking *without thinking?* If someone whom we can't expect to consciously understand the principle of randomization turns out to *actually* randomize in games of the Moriarty–Holmes type, then *that* would be an example of a situation in which *embodying* an intelligent behaviour does not necessarily rest on conscious understanding. Two economists from the University of Arizona showed that the talented John McEnroe actually did randomize his tennis serves.[1] When serving in either the deuce (left) or the ad (right) court, a player who can accurately place his shot has a choice: he can go to the opponent's forehand side or to his opponent's backhand side. Against a serve of the calibre of McEnroe's, an opponent will try to anticipate the ball's direction and lean either to the left or to the right, depending on where he feels the server will go. Against returners of serve of the calibre of a Jimmy Connors or an Ivan Lendl – two of McEnroe's regular late-round match-ups at Wimbledon and the U.S. Open – a server like McEnroe will try to use *surprise* to his best advantage, and serve to the forehand when the opponent expects the ball to come to his backhand and to the backhand when the opponent expects the ball to come to his forehand. In a typical match, this mind game – albeit one with very real consequences – gets played out between one hundred and two hundred times. The two economists found that McEnroe's serving patterns revealed him to be playing consistently with the mixed Nash equilibrium of strategies; moreover, he did it *without* thinking about it. *Behaviour does not have to be conscious to be intelligent*. In the same way, the diamind often *thinks and acts* without *thinking about thinking*. It is only we – who *stalk* and *track* the diamind for the purpose of *understanding* his moves and *teaching* them – who have to think about the diamind's thinking.

Mental Habits: A Deep(er) Dive

A mental habit is a pattern of thought that is so entrenched and feels so natural that it has become unconscious and therefore goes unnoticed. If asked to supply a one-sentence explanation for being ten minutes late to a board meeting, many will cite traffic congestion, some unforeseen personal emergency, a mix-up over the room number, or similar. What we look for when looking for a mental *habit* is a consistently recurring way in which these explanations are produced, a guiding *rule or principle* that remains unchanged no matter what the specific explanation. A good candidate principle for this example is 'place responsibility for the delay elsewhere' – either in something that is itself *uncontrollable* ('traffic patterns,' 'unforeseen personal emergency') or in something that, though controllable, is *not controllable by me* (I was given the wrong room number).

All of this suggests that the main characteristics of a mental habit are as follows:

First, it is *unconscious:* the precise reasons for the delay will vary from situation from situation, and unless you are open to scrutinizing the *patterns* of the reason-giving behaviours, you will not detect the underlying mental habit. You will merely *produce* the thinking required to produce the excuse, without *thinking through* your thinking.

Second, it *feels natural:* basically, we are saying here that excuses come easily and do not feel effortful. To drive the point home, imagine that you have adopted the 'counter-habit' of always taking responsibility for delays, saying things such as 'I was late because I did not leave home ten minutes early' (which would have allowed a time cushion), or 'I was late because I did not double-check the room number for the meeting last night, when checking other e-mail' (making precise the reason for the delay and placing blameworthiness squarely on oneself). Systematically producing *responsible* (rather than *defensible*) causes for one's behaviour – even when it would be easy to produce irresponsible ones – is likely to feel effortful and to require an exercise of the will.

Mental habits can also colour how we feel about facts and figures – that is, the very ways in which we *believe our beliefs*. Consider:

- CEO to CFO: 'Are you sure about the data you have produced?' CFO to CEO: 'No.' [CEO to himself: 'Then either you are incompetent or we need more data.']
- CEO to VP Engineering: 'How certain are you of hitting the development deadline?' VP Engineering to CEO: 'Ninety per cent.' CEO to VP Engineering: 'What can we do to drive to hundred percent certainty?'

What's the mental habit here? Try this one: 'Certainty entails truth, and truth entails certainty.' This mental tic is potentially disastrous: the CFO of our first example may be a hard-nosed number cruncher who is never certain of anything and, *precisely because of that*, usually gets things right. The CEO of the second example needs to drive to a point of certainty *so that she can stop thinking* – or obsessing – about the product delivery schedule (and everything that hinges on it); thus she confuses the VP's level of *certainty* with the objective *likelihood* that the product will arrive on time. Mental habits are *hidden* from direct observation by how familiar we are with their overt signs. They can also be based on local 'feel-good' motives: certainty *feels good*.

Other mental habits constrain the kinds of problems that humans try to solve in a given situation by mechanically associating *good* and *bad* with particular qualities, which then *become* good or bad in themselves: 'Is this a fair outcome?' – when asked in the right tone – presupposes the habitual mapping 'fair is good, unfair is bad.' 'Is this an efficient outcome?' – when asked in the right tone – presupposes the habitual mapping 'efficient is good, inefficient is bad.' But: *Is it efficient to be fair?* And for that matter, *Is it fair to always strive for efficiency?* These questions are often dismissed by (yet another) brain spasm that we have encountered in the business world – namely, 'That is too abstract' or (worse) 'That is too philosophical.' What shall we call *this* habit?

How about the *'eliminate-thinking-that-does-not-relate-in-an-obvious-way-to-a-decision-that-has-to-be-made-today'* habit, or, the *'why-do-you-have-to-complicate-things-so-much?'* habit, or – more incisively but less precisely – the *shrinking-mind* habit. Like the others – like the habitual mappings of good and bad to 'fair' and 'unfair' – it sneaks up on you to the point of becoming something *you just do*, to the point that engaging in it *feels good*.

But is it good *for* you? Merely asking this question is worth at least as much as achieving a definitive answer to it, because having asked it, we become aware that more effective mental habits are possible and that it may also be possible to develop such habits intelligently. The 'tricks' we will be trying to uncover in patterns of successful thinking relate to the successful re-engineering of habitual patterns of thinking, to exercises in *mind design*.

Many readers will be quick to retort that a mind is an impossibly difficult thing to design – and point with a superior smile to the failures of AI to build an object that produces behaviour that we cannot distinguish from that of humans.

And they will be correct to have pointed this out, if the starting point is a *piece of immutable hardware* (an electronic 'brain'); but not, however, if the starting point is an *already existing mind* (yours). The *mind design* principle we will be invoking throughout this book is a principle of *transformation*, not of creation. It posits thinking as behaviour, behaviour as habituation, and habituation as something one can *change*, or transform. But how do you *change* your own patterns of thinking when it is so hard to *see* them to begin with?

How to Tinker with Your 'Thinker': The Panopticon Effect

In his study of the origins of the prison, Michel Foucault made much of an invention that he believed altered the very nature of incarceration when it was put into flesh-and-blood practice.[2] The panopticon was (or *is*, if it is still in use at Guantanamo Bay) an optical device that allowed the prison guard to see any and all of the inmates in his charge (it was always a 'he' in the times Foucault speaks of) without himself being seen by them. In this way the guard could monitor the prisoners; detect whether they at any time were engaging in forbidden practices such as masturbation, vandalism, and violence against and sexual intercourse with other inmates; and punish the transgressors using the customary methods. Guards in panopticon-type prisons discovered that, after a period of ubiquitous and omniscient monitoring and prompt sanctions against observed perpetrators, the inmates began to regulate their own behaviour, *internalizing* the observer so that each became his or her own monitor. They behaved as if they were being observed even when they knew there was no guard watching them. External constraints on behaviour had been *taken inside* and become *habits*.

Thinking – especially thinking in words and sentences – is a form of internal communication. In thinking, you-in-the-present communicates with you-in-the-future. But though thinking is a private and covert activity, it is influenced by external interactions – in particular, by how you communicate with others. Communicative patterns become mental habits. The implication is that counterproductive – closed, oblivious, disconnected, narrow, hermetic, rigid – ways of communicating are thereby internalized and become counterproductive ways of thinking.

If this simple model is valid, the implications for our prospects for *designing minds* are significant, for now we can hope to detect a person's mental habits by observing her patterns of communication – which is the route we have taken to analyse successful business thinkers. We can also hope to bring about *changes* in thinking by prescribing and motivating changes in the ways we communicate. The backbone of the 'mental habits design program,' then, is a simple model that takes seriously the metaphor of thought as internal conversation and in this way makes conversation the lever for changing thought. As Heinz von Foerster put it: 'If you want to *think* differently, first learn to *act* differently'[3] – in particular, to *communicate* differently, we would add.

How does this work in practice? Take the 'place responsibility for negative effects elsewhere' habit we described earlier. What makes it a mental habit rather than a social habit is the fact that the shirker of systematic responsibility comes to *believe* in the validity of her own explanations and does not produce them simply for the purpose of easing out of tricky social situations. This is precisely what makes the habit so dangerous to begin with: the fact that it has become part of the way one *thinks*, not just the way one *speaks*. How does the panopticon effect help us make sense of how the habit became a habit – and suggest, perhaps, how to go about undoing it?

The panopticon effect tells us that how one thinks is an internalized version of how one communicates – indeed, it sheds light on how one communicates. The systematic placing of responsibility elsewhere for ills and mishaps is a *locally effective* social strategy – one that is often rewarded by nods of understanding and (potentially false, but who looks that closely?) expressions of sympathy. It also helps one avoid being placed on the spot by difficult 'why?' questions. It *feels* good to get understanding from others and to avoid such difficult moments. In time, this way of communicating becomes a script.

There is one problem: it is difficult to produce the message convincingly without at least half-believing it. Most humans are reasonably good at identifying liars and dissimulators, even if they are not professionally trained to do so. As every good salesman knows, there is no substitute for genuine enthusiasm. But a solution is at hand: make a habit of the way you communicate part of the very fabric of thinking. 'Place responsibility for ills elsewhere' thus becomes a mental habit, not just a social and communicative habit. Here, the panopticon effect explains the *genesis of a mental habit*. Later on we will see that it can also be used as a device for *discovering* mental habits – and as an engineering device to *undo* and *replace* or *modify* mental habits deemed counterproductive – because it suggests and harnesses ways of talking and ways of thinking that are interconnected.

The systematic shirker in our example can – if she chooses – *train* herself to think differently by modifying the way she accounts for mishaps and errors in social settings. By systematically morphing her 'I-was-late-because-of-the-traffic'-type accounts into 'I-was-late-because-I-did-not-leave-early-enough'-type accounts in situations in which the 'excuse' is clearly the locally easy thing for her to produce, she will also be changing her *thinking* about situations in which responsibility is ambiguous. Our 'mind design principle' for new and more success-ful mental habits is thus a simple one: because thinking is self-talk, talk and thought are linked. To change patterns of thinking, change patterns of talking. The panopticon mechanism allows us to study how success-ful thinkers think through careful observation of how they talk; it also allows us to *design* interventions aimed at *changing* patterns of thinking. It is both a lens and a design tool.

With our measurement and design toolkit in hand – a way of map-ping mental habits, a lens for discerning those habits in the ways peo-ple speak, and a tool for designing new ways of thinking – we are ready to face the beast in its natural habitat.

The Integrator's Way of Being-in-the-World: The Diamind's Stance

'What does my mind want to do with the world?' Here is the question that you, dear reader, should be asking yourself as we begin to ponder the nature of the diamind together. Not, to be sure, 'What do *I* want to do with the world?' but rather, 'What does my *mind* want to do with it?' Note that by asking this question you have established a distance between yourself and your mind so that you now have a chance to hold out your mind as an object of inquiry.

Now, you have good reason to be sceptical of such a *koan*-esque ques-tion: academics love to ask questions that sound sophisticated – doing so maximizes their freedom to frame answers that make them seem intelligent, informed, and credible. Here, however, the question cuts to the core of the diamind, for it singles out the mental phenomena we are aiming to study.

Example: You are bidding to buy a new house, which you have al-ready identified as 'the one that is right for me.' There is you, and there is the 'other one' – the seller. But the world does not consist merely of the two of you: you do not directly 'talk' to the seller (not even by e-mail); rather, you talk to your agent, who in turn talks to the seller's agent, who in turn talks to the seller. Your agent is young and attrac-tive, not only in a sexual way but also in an interpersonal one: articulate and educated, she advertises her degree in philosophy from Yale on her business card (it even says: 'BA, Yale'!) as a 'credential' for her job.

When talking to her, you find your resolve slackening to stick to a ceiling price for the house: you focus on the upper end of the range of possible returns on your mutual fund holdings. You cannot even think straight about all of the provisos and quids pro quo that have to be specified in the agreement of purchase and sale. Positive emotions spontaneously gush out of you, and you find it hard to 'check' them.

Late at night, however, you get the sinking feeling – why does it always have to be late at night? – that you are being led down a path of financial overstretch and decreased autonomy – especially as your mind focuses on your boss, on whose capricious goodwill you will depend even more now that you are overleveraged. When morning arrives and *she* calls, however, these concerns evaporate: she, after all, specializes in concern evaporation, but that is not a thought that your mind can behold while she is speaking to you.

Enter an economist – also trained at Yale – who specializes in the study of bargaining theory and bargaining behaviour. He exposes what he refers to as the core of the situation for you: all those involved are trying to maximize their own take from the transaction: you, your agent, 'the other one,' and her agent. Everyone knows this, and everyone knows everyone knows this, and at the 'end of the day' the sucker is likely to be he or she who has 'temporarily' forgotten it – or who has acted *as if* he or she has forgotten it.

After talking to him – and in this case it *is* most often a *he* – you sense a 'distance' from the transaction, one that feels at once peaceful and slightly depressing. The adrenalin rushes are gone, the neocortex takes over from the 'lizard brain,' and the cartoonlike picture that emerges from all of this is that of a linked set of transactions among a bunch of people each of whom wants to end up with as much cash as possible after the deed is signed: the PacMan model of behaviour. *She* is all of a sudden caricatured by your inner eye as a pure maximizer. You seem to be able to 'see through' her apparently authentic behaviours – like her 'Rembrandt' smile – as scripted attempts to induce in you the psychological, and – why not? – even physiological state that will serve her own ends.

However, you find that you have difficulty 'holding on' to this lucid state of mind: after about ten minutes of interacting with your agent in a poker-faced manner, you notice your facial expression beginning to loosen and you begin producing flirtatious behaviours that have the uncanny effect of blurring your mental model of her behaviours. Not that you believe in this model any less: if interviewed by your friendly neighbourhood social psychologist, you no doubt would say: 'She is a dissembler whose body language is orchestrated to maximize the chances of the transaction.'

But 'in the heat of conversation' this mental model is no longer a blueprint for your own behaviour, over which your mind seems to have lost its sway. Under the seductive influence of the Rembrandt smile, your mind wanders again to the attractive features of the new property and the accelerating rate of increase of mean property prices – rather than the spread of error in predictions. If you are among those who notice such mental wanderings, you may try to 'correct' your mind's errant behaviour by suppressing alluring thoughts about the property. But as Daniel Wegner argued in his experimental work, trying to suppress thoughts can be a tricky business, because in order to suppress a thought you have to behold, in your mind's eye, the very thought you are trying to suppress.[4] Why is this?

It's because to wilfully *suppress* something, you have to know *what* it is you're trying to suppress, in the same way that carrying out a 'search and destroy' mission requires the unit commander to know what the unit is searching for. But this means – you've guessed it! – that you have to *think* the thought you are trying to suppress, which in turn means that you haven't suppressed it at all. With your mind focused on all this inner turmoil, you aren't likely to give more than cursory thought to all the details that actually do make a difference to the total cost of the house – the conditions on the purchase that could make the seller do more work and save you time and money over the coming year.

The Uncontrollable Organ

All of which hints at what an answer to 'What does my mind want to do with the world?' might look like. The mind goes its own way in constructing scenarios and looking for evidence, and it simplifies and analyses the data presented to it in ways that are hidden from ongoing introspection. Most of the time the mind is *already doing* something before you can either register an awareness of what it is doing or foment a plan for what you would rather it did. This, incidentally, is one reason why a computer's operations are often not a good model for the workings of the mind: you can always hit your computer's 'stop' and 'run' buttons, but – *try this!* – you can only rarely and with great difficulty do so on the 'interface' to your own mind.

There are many operations the mind wants to perform – *simplify* its contents by discarding some of them, or *encode* those contents so as to render them more accessible, or *calculate* the relevance of the contents it holds to what it wants to achieve, or *forage* for more sense data, and so on, and so on – and each of these operations influences what the mind does in the moments that immediately follow. It is hard to stop focusing on the growing tendency in mean house prices in the chosen area in the midst of a 'positive spiral,' even if one 'knows' – somewhere, in a tucked-away spot – that thoughts of the positive spiral were triggered by the Rembrandt smile, which in turn was carefully structured to trigger the spiral …

It is also difficult to wean the mind off the 'maximizer' model that the economist gladly feeds it once *this* model has taken shape and begun to hold sway. Mental images and models resemble moods in that they recruit new mental energy to their aims. The mind naturally looks for *verifying* or *confirming* instances for whatever the dominant picture of 'reality' happens to be at the time: it will interpret the Rembrandt smile as a slightly distasteful fake when in the 'economist mode,' but (in spite of itself) as an alluring gesture when in the 'everyday' mode of being. And because the mind 'thinks all the time,' the effects of its habits and ways of being compound much more rapidly, perhaps, than those of any pure behaviour that you engage in. They become 'you.'

A Slim Chance: The Prospect of Reconfiguring the Mind

Yet the very possibility that we can – alone, it seems, among living creatures – examine and adjust the goings-on in our own minds in order to achieve different results, the very possibility of engineering and re-engineering our patterns of thought, suggests that many of our thought processes are not *necessary* – that is, they aren't 'hard-wired' either literally or figuratively. And if this possibility is alive in the sense that we can conduct mind design at least *some* of the time, then the nascent art and science of mind design will have a leg to stand on.

You *can* think your way through the house-buying process differently – you *can* break with the yo-yo dynamic of being seduced by the Rembrandt smile, racked by guilt and anxiety in the wee hours, and comforted by the economist's PacMan approach, without any convergence or Archimedean point for all of this rumination. You can *integrate* across these different ways of being and achieve what Aristotle thought (erroneously) that all human intellects can do naturally (though only few succeed).

For instance, a Machiavelli-type integration will have you apply the

economist's model *everywhere:* to your own moods (which want to maximize their hold on you); to the Rembrandt woman, who has learned to
summon the smile at will in order to secure goodwill, which she then
uses for economic ends, *but* – and here is the stroke of genius – who has
persuaded herself that her smile is authentic (which, of course, helps
it *look* authentic!); and to the economist himself, who wants to recruit
minds to ways of thinking that have become so established in the profession that none of his brethren stop to ask, 'Why do we believe this?'
– and all find comfort in the fact that all find comfort … in the fact that
none *will*, in fact, ask such questions. Of course, the *temporary* result of
such an image of how the world works is something that resembles
panic or anxiety; but if weathered, the result can be spectacular, for you
have arrived at a picture of the world that can weather any mood: there
is no more comfort in the economist's model than there is in the Rembrandt smile.

There is no more pain in the anguish of the night's visions than there
is in the cool understanding that the *consequences* of the agent's behaviour are, in fact, identical to the *goals* of her behaviour. No longer are
you subject to the yo-yo effects that have come to seem so much like
rumination and that a wily and clever speculator could easily use to
build all sorts of money pumps from your bank account to hers. You
have achieved a vantage point from which you can *globally optimize*
across your emotional states and local models. You can now choose
the behaviours that make the most sense, given *all that you know to be
the case*. You can write down a *ranking* of all possible worlds that does
not change with variations in local context and then *design* intelligent
behaviour optimally suited to bringing about your favourite possible
world, one that is based on a global understanding of the payoff landscape that your mind is navigating.

Not that Machiavellianism is the only path to achieving an integration across the moods and impulses that pull you in different directions
and that lead to the feeling of 'stuckness.' You could also, for example,
attempt a *self-therapeutic* integration – one that attempts to maximize
the chances that, no matter what happens with the sale of the house
(and to the selling price), *all will be well inside*. To do so, you could build
a model of the total amount of pain, suffering, contentment, and elation
that the negotiation process will bring you by carefully examining how
you feel (a) when talking to your economist friend and internalizing
his view of the world, (b) when ruminating about the potentially too-
high mortgage you are about to commit to, (c) when chattering with

the Rembrandt woman and playing along with the stories she tells you, and (d) when finding out that you have paid too much for the house – and what the odds of finding this out were, and then (e) optimizing across *this* larger landscape in such a way as to maximize your total happiness throughout the negotiation process. You could choose the parameters of the optimization process so that, for instance, you set bounds on the maximum discomfort you are willing to feel at any one time ('no psychic crises'), or bounds on the *average* discomfort you are willing to feel over the entire period of the negotiation ('total amount of misery').

The net result of this broader optimization process is another integration – one that straddles various moods, images, scripts, and impulses – a broadening of the mind to include your entire predicament so that you are not blinded by your own automatisms. Behaviour becomes more intelligent, more adaptive, in proportion to the inclusiveness of the predictive *model* you have built from the situation at hand.

No matter which route you take, the important point is that an integration requires an *integrator* – that is, a powerful, versatile *model* of the situation that can explain, contain, and comfortably accommodate the various impulses you feel. It also requires a *will* to weather the temporary discomfort of this larger model in order to bring about the integration in question. Our claim is that the integrator's skill set can be traced back to a set of habitual ways of being, of *habits of the mind*.

If You Want to Know 'How Useful Is a Good Mental Habit?'
Ask Yourself, 'How Dense Is a Human Life'?

The problem for us diamind hunters is to show how the mind's habitual ways of being can be re-engineered to the end of producing more successful behaviour – which is our aim in this book. 'More successful' does not, of course, always mean 'perfectly successful' in the sense of always being able to achieve that which you have willed. More successful means that, *on average*, diaminds do better in conditions that mirror the social and business worlds. They may *sometimes* do worse, but because the world just keeps on happening to us and the sequence of events that get strung together into a life in business is dense, *on average* they can enjoy spectacular results.

An example will help make this point. Psychologists have for many decades attempted to predict the effects of individual characteristics on 'personal success.' They are natural-born data miners, so they try to look at *everything* – or at least, at everything they believe they can objectively measure: IQ, EQ, MQ, 'empathy,' what have you. Unfortunately, they cannot predict with a probability of much better than 0.5 whether a person possessing any combination of these characteristics will be successful – which is not significantly better than flipping a coin after all of these thousands of man years of careful experimental work! How bad is this?

The answer: 'Not as bad as it looks.' For as Bob Rosenthal has suggested, even a *small* positive correlation between possessing a certain trait (IQ) and success *compounds* over time to very high effective rates of return, *provided that the interactions that make use of the trait are dense!*[5] So if you interact *a lot* with other humans in ways that make use of the proclivities and abilities that IQ measures measure, a *small* difference in IQ will come to matter *a lot* in the long run. The world is *dense:* small advantages will compound!

Think of a manager's life as a long series of connected activities, such as assertions, questions, paraphrases, and the like – as *meaningful speech acts*, to be precise. If a manager participates in, say, 10 meetings a week and commits 10 such speech acts per meeting, then in a 50-week year she will engage in 5,000 such serially correlated activities, and in a 30-year managerial career, 150,000 of them. Now, if she possesses or develops some characteristic that makes her even 1 per cent of 1 per cent (0.0001) more effective at bringing about constructive effects by what she says and how she thinks, then over course of her career that advantage will compound to a multiplier of 3.2×10^6 – that is, her overall effectiveness will go up by a factor of 3 million! A 1 per cent effectiveness improvement on a per interaction basis will compound to an unimaginably high 1.6×10^{48} advantage – provided, of course, that such advantages compound.

Do they? Well, that is precisely the function of *reputation and trust effects* in the (new) market for talent, which provides a 'social memory' of the manager's actions and their consequences, with a measure of future value added. Thus, especially in the 'hyperdense' interaction environment that characterizes both early chimpanzee societies and postmodern high capitalism, the positive effects of effective habits can compound quickly to spectacularly high levels. (Of course, not all densities are created equal: Google, Facebook, and Twitter attempt to do for tradition-bound human societies roughly what sexual promiscuity and emotional unhingedness accomplish in chimpanzee societies, but the social amplification effects in the former case far exceed those in the latter).

We want to discover not only how thinking matters in business, but also the mental microbehaviours of the diamind. Thinking is habitual. It is as much of a habit as personal hygiene routines, facial tics, and recurring slips of the tongue. For this very reason, small changes in the basic building blocks of thinking lead to what Charlie Munger has called 'lollapalooza' effects: large, before-the-fact inconceivable and after-the-fact self-evident consequences of small and seemingly innocuous changes in behaviour.

And, with this motivational foreword, let us dive into some mind-mapping.

2 Mental Choicefulness: Choosing to Believe (and to Dis-believe) and the Suspension of Resolution

Tell me what the truth is so I can decide whether or not to believe it.

Elizabeth I

Within the paradoxical, reality appears. He who confronts the paradoxical exposes himself to reality.

Friedrich Durrenmatt

We begin by considering the view that diaminds take of their own contents, and of the relationship they have to the world. We are interested in getting precise about the diamind's *stance*, its way of being-in-the-world.

To get a feel for what a stance might look like, don't ask yourself 'What do I believe?' but rather 'How *do* I believe my beliefs and how *should* I believe them?' There are, to be sure, some facile answers to this question: 'I believe something *because* it is true – and that is why I *should* be believing it.'

To see how facile – and false – a view this is, consider the word 'because' in the above sentence. If *A* happens *because of* B, then in the absence of *A*, B should not happen. So if you believe something because it is true, you should not believe it if it is not true. You should only believe beliefs that *are* true, in other words.

As an empirical fact about how you believe your beliefs, chances are that this is completely false: human minds have cherished and defended false beliefs ever since believing became possible for them. 'The earth is round'? No it is not: it is a slightly oblate sphere, or an oblate spheroid. 'Markets are efficient processors of decentralized information'? No they are not efficient on the time scales on which John Simons and Rennaissance Technology have made their consistently anomalous returns over the past twenty years – the era of 'high frequency' finance. 'Time is linear sequence'? No, it is not 'really' a linear sequence according to the latest thinking in the physical sciences, though it is convenient or expedient for us to think of it as such.

Truth, then – actual, literal truth – is not an accurate and complete yardstick for measuring the believability of our beliefs. However, our examples suggest a potentially useful modification of the answer to the question: 'How do we believe our beliefs?' It is: 'Truth serves a purpose.' In other words, say, *for the purpose* of writing a paper for the *American Economic Review* or the *Journal of Finance*, 'markets are efficient' is true in the sense that after writing down something like '… assuming that markets are efficient …' in a paper sent to the reviewers of these journals, one is not called on to justify oneself any further, to give reasons for the assumption. One does not have to answer nagging questions from academic reviewers, even though one would be laughed right out of a sophisticated traders' gathering. Similarly, 'the earth is round' is true *for the purpose* of passing a grade-school geography test, or *for the purpose* of getting a coarse estimate of the distance between Stockholm and Baghdad, but *not for the purpose* of calculating the trajectory of a low-earth-orbiting satellite that provides video surveillance of an American-led terrorist operation in the Middle East.

Moreover, what you believe is not *determined* by what 'the data are' and by your purpose – rather, it is *under*determined. It is not completely free, but not totally constrained, either. Consider the data points showing share price as a function of time in Figure 2.1a. They are, collectively, 'the data.' Suppose you believe the data are valid – by no means an obvious leap, given that the subtle yet undeniable distortion of information is showing signs of becoming *the* 'hot specialty' of the new millennium across all industries. Nevertheless, let's grant the validity of the data.

The problem for you – the 'person of action' – is to figure out what happens in the all-important future; in other words, it is to answer the $69K question: 'What line should I be drawing through these points?'

The econometrician entices you with a straight line (Figure 2.1b), citing some fourteenth-century English philosopher he has not read (but was told about in first-year university), who maintained that we should go for the *simplest* explanation consistent with the data points. But why? What reason do we have for always going with the simplest explana-

Figure 2.1 Share price

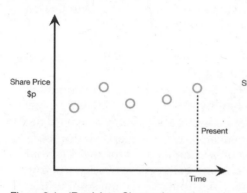

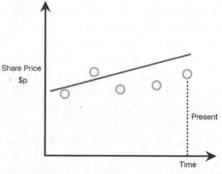

Figure 2.1a 'Raw' data: Share price measured as a function of time

Figure 2.1b 'Straight line' interpolation and resulting extrapolation of share price as a function of time

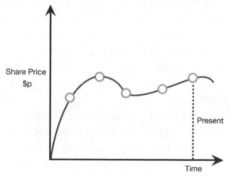

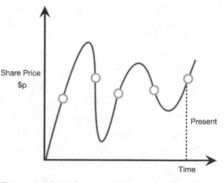

Figure 2.1c Polynomial interpolation and resulting extrapolation of share price as a function of time

Figure 2.1d Higher-order (more complicated) polynomial interpolation and resulting extrapolation of share price as a function of time

tion? Is the general theory of relativity *simple?* Is it *simpler* than was suggested by a seventeenth-century freemason by the name of Isaac Newton? The econometrician blinks at you, stunned.

Had he done a bit more reading in graduate school, he might have encountered the argument – made by Quine and Ullian[1] – that the human preference for simpler beliefs over more complex ones was developed through an evolutionary process: holding beliefs that are *valid* confers a survival advantage on those who hold them; therefore, the fact that we have come to *prefer* simpler beliefs to more complicated ones indicates that simpler beliefs are more likely to be the valid ones. The survivors favoured them, and the survivors were precisely the ones who possessed the greatest number of true beliefs.

Of course, the econometrician will light up when you give her this *out*, even if *she* did not think of it. Clever … But still, you think about this word – 'simple' – for a little while longer, and ask: 'You mean, like the belief in the Gaussian distribution of stock returns, nose sizes, IQs, and so on? The one that led to the demise of many traders and "name" hedge funds like Long-Term Capital Management? Was *that* belief true because it was simple, or was it false because it was *too* simple? And while we're at it, this belief in the evolution of preferences for simple beliefs – is *it* also a simple belief? It seems kind of complicated.' The econometrician blinks again …

Now, the more complicated curve of Figure 2.1c looks like a potentially good candidate for your predictive arsenal. So does the even more complicated curve of Figure 2.1d. How now?

As with figures, so with gestalts. Look hard at a close friend or co-worker the next time he's near you, and ask yourself: 'What evidence do I have that he really has a *mind?*' He will *look* human in the biological sense, but a *mind? That* seems like a tall assumption to make, given the evidence at your disposal.

Picture him, instead, as an exclusively *biological* and *physical* entity – as a *brain* connected to muscles, nerves, viscera, and bones. As an 'it.' Think about your interactions with *it* as interactions with a brain: you are simply trying to get this brain to get the motor neurons attached to it to do something, instead of trying to co-reason with a mind. Picture your own behaviours – a smile, a smirk, a frown – as means of *putting its brain in some state* that is more favourable to its agreeing with you, supporting you, giving you affection, respect, support, whatever …

Far-fetched? Consider, though: psychologists consistently find that humans' *attitudes* are *not* responsive to facts or reasons. Supporters of capital punishment who justify their commitment to it by stating that capital punishment saves lives by deterring future would-be murderers do not change their position on capital punishment when informed of empirical studies indicating that the threat of capital punishment has no deterrent value. Many salespeople wear Armani suits, apply expensive colognes, and flash Rembrandt smiles in order to dazzle their would-be clients into buying sophisticated products, instead of trying to tap into their clients' mental models of the causal link between buying the products and their own welfare. Typical corporate boardroom 'etiquette' is oriented towards keeping difficult questions from public airing, even though these are precisely the questions that directors have a fiduciary obligation to their shareholders to raise and discuss. What are these, if not clear instances of 'managing the brain' by selectively pressing its 'pain' and 'pleasure' buttons? What are they, if not clear evidence that the *Other-as-a-brain* gestalt is not only *not* far-fetched, but rather *the very way we do business?*

Changing this 'animal management' gestalt does not specifically require that we *suppress* mental images of the 'other guy' as a mere organism and *picture* that person as having as much of a mind as you believe yourself to have. Rather, it requires *acting* in ways that are consistent with *reasoning your way through* to closure of an argument in a public setting, even if this feels awkward and leads to that abysmal interpersonal state of 'stuckness' in which no closure seems possible. Or, it requires *changing* your own stated position – publicly and explicitly – in response to arguments that refute the reasons for which you believe your beliefs. Only then will the 'mind' model kick in and trump the 'brain' model as a predictive model of behaviour. Get it? Treating another as a mind may require you to treat that person more, not less, harshly than would treating him as a brain-in-a-body. It is our ability to 'flip back and forth' unconsciously that keeps things running smoothly.

... All the Way Down ... : Beliefs Rest on Turtles

During a tour of North America, at the end of one of his lectures, the philosopher Bertrand Russell was confronted by an old lady who told him she believed that the scientific view of the world was incorrect – that the earth truly did rest on the back of a turtle. Russell blinked at her, then smiled: 'And what does that turtle rest on?' he asked. 'Oh, come on, Professor,' she shot back. 'Don't you know? It's turtles *all the way down!*'

Science – and social science in particular – is great at creating its own turtles, which are then insulated from challenge by turtles-all-the-way-down kinds of arguments. Linearity, Gaussianity, and rationality are, for our 'scientific' ways of talking, what Friedrich Nietzsche referred to as *necessary fictions*. It is *rational* to believe that others are rational (so, *just do it, okay?*); it is reasonable to *be* rational yourself, given that you (rationally) believe others to be both rational and reasonable (so, *just be that way, all right?*); 'most people' (reasonably) believe that stock-return distributions – along with the distributions of just about all naturally occurring 'events' or 'properties' – are Gaussian (so, *just believe it!*); and 'pick the simplest model' is the simplest model that predicts why people pick the simplest model (so, *just pick Figure 2.1b over Figures 2.1c or 2.1d as predictive models consistent with the data of Figure 2.1a*). 'Why do you have to make it so complicated?' one often hears, as if 'simpler is better' is a foregone conclusion. But it isn't: it is, though, a simple-*minded* one. It's turtles all the way down!

Seeing Past the Turtles: NNT and His Black Swans

Nassim Nicholas Taleb (NNT) 'is' not a trader, certainly not in the sense of 'is' used by an executive who says: 'I am a senior VP of product development at Intel.' Yes, he trades, and he does so very successfully: the founder of Empirica, LLC has likely made enough trading profits over the past five years to cover all of his trading positions for the next ten. But that, according to him, is his day job: 'Trading is for the Philistines,' he snarls.[2] He describes himself as an epistemologist of uncertainty, a 'Black Swan hunter.' A Black Swan is an event or object that is, beforehand, unpredictable (even inconceivable) but that we afterwards convince ourselves is a 'normal' occurrence (part and parcel of the furniture of the universe) through a feat of self-therapy that is peculiar to the human mind, a feat that has to do with making up stories and inventing models and theories that rationalize away discontinuities and surprises – presumably in order to tame the horror of unpredictability and the terror of the unnameable. How does this diamind work? That is the question we have set for ourselves.

To start, we could ask: 'What does NNT know – and what does he believe he knows?' What NNT believes he 'really knows' about is not 'trading' or 'mathematical finance' – though he writes competently about various exotic probability-distribution functions and their effects on the stochastic models that underlie options-pricing models, such as the Black-Scholes model, the credit for which, with his historical sense and precise erudition, he restores to his intellectual precursors, Thorpe and Bachelier. What NNT *believes* he knows about is French literature – from Diderot to Proust and beyond – and the writings of hardcore empiricists who take reality seriously, from Sextus Empiricus through Hume to Popper and Quine. He underscores the importance of a scarce resource, one that human beings can scarcely deploy at will: the faculty of *doubt* – of *radical* doubt in particular.

How Much Can I Doubt?

NNT's mind applies itself not to 'reasonably doubting,' not to 'doubting for the purpose of showing off my open-mindedness,' but to *'really doubting.'* NNT doubts with his viscera, brain, muscles, and hormones, as well as with what we call 'mind.' But what do we mean by *doubt?* Well, that depends on what you take yourself to 'know' —*really* know, again, in the visceral sense. 'Your beliefs can hurt you,' 'a little knowledge is a dangerous thing' … Make up your own cliché. The point is that such bits of 'common wisdom' cover up a fundamental human frailty. They are boilerplate provisos which acknowledge that we as a species 'suck at doubting.' They are *not* genuine road signs of the sort we obey because we feel their utility deep in our gizzards. Paradoxically, by skirting the truth they distort rather than reveal it. That is, they disguise it in ways that are reminiscent of the 'skilled incompetence' that Chris Argyris – the hunter of human defences – has described in relation to humans who attempt to shield their faces and egos in intricate, clever, and covert ways.

'I am open-minded' may, in fact, be a telltale sign of closed-mindedness: How do you know you're open-minded? Surely, if you do know it, you must be closed-minded about this fact, which means that you are not, after all, open-minded.

So the question is: 'How much can you doubt?' Can you doubt that *here is a hand* is true of the hand you hold out in front of you? That the sun will rise tomorrow? That your lovers and loved ones truly love you back? Before proceeding, take a moment (or more) to think these questions through: What do you need to know in order to be able to doubt these apparent certainties? And *why* do you need to know whatever it is you need to know in order to doubt what you know?

The (Underground) Discipline of Doubt

Here is where the work of those masters of the faculty of reasonable doubt – Hume, Popper, and Quine – and those masters of reasonable suspicion – Nietzsche, Bataille, Mannheim, and Foucault – come in handy (to say the least). Who are these guys? What do they have to do with achieving supernormal profits in trading? And what does all of this have to do with NNT's supernormal profits? What – more precisely – is the link between the mindscape of the Black Swan hunter and its owner's business success?

Well, 'these guys' are the ones who dared think through the platitudes of *their* eras and tried to see past the turtles – which, after all, go *all the way down* to the bottom of what we call 'contentment' – that pleasant, easy, contented state in which 'we just know it to be so.' But which platitudes did they think through, exactly?

Well, how about this one: the ages-old yet erroneous identification of truth with certainty. At this point you may be thinking we're talking gibberish or trying to pull a fast one: 'But surely truth is the same as certainty!' Is it not so that I am or should be certain of what is true and that whatever I am certain of is or should be true? *No.* It is, for instance, *true* that 'NNT is the author of the best-selling book *The Black Swan* and the founder of Empirica, LLC.' But if you had asked Karl Popper whether he was certain of it, he would have answered: 'No.'

So let's ask him: '*Why*, Sir Karl?' (He was awarded a knighthood for his labours – and, unfortunately, accepted). The answer: Well, because certainty means that *doubt is impossible* – which in this case it is not. It *is* possible that the whole 'NNT story' was concocted by a savvy media concern and 'packaged' ingeniously for public consumption. Consider that the public's gullibility – including your own – has been documented by the possibly ersatz NNT himself. So doubt is possible. We can accept a statement as true even if we aren't *certain* of its truth. The problems arise when we *need* to be certain of its truth.

That *the mind needs to believe stuff 'for sure'* is an uncomfortable insight, one that makes us feel unhinged and untethered. The diamind heeds – *truly heeds* – this insight, realizes that her mind craves certainty, and fights back by developing, honing, and applying its capacity to doubt. Not, to be sure, to the point of *dissing* everything she reads, thinks, or hears and giving up hope that competent predictions can be made (which would be the easy way out), but rather by regaining control of her own beliefs and realizing that *believing is an activity* – one that, like any other activity, can be understood as a sequence of *choices,* which she can make consciously, weighing costs and benefits and 'overriding' the 'lizard' part of her brain (the 'limbic system') in order to bring them under conscious scrutiny. The diamind takes an architect's view of her own 'states of mind' and asks not 'What am I certain of?' but rather 'What does it make sense for me to believe on an all-things-considered basis?'

Taking his cue from the masters of doubt, NNT launches his mind at some of the platitudes of *his* age – the ones that 'feel good' to believe. 'Which platitudes?' you ask? Well, how about our favourite trio – which, incidentally, serve as the creed of many economists and finance theorists: that cause–effect relationships are linear, that there is a 'normal' distribution of objects and events, and that oneself and others are rational beings?

Linearity? What linearity? The choice one makes between the shapes in Figures 2b, 2c, and 2d is not a choice *determined* by evidence. It is a choice precisely *because* evidence cannot determine it.

Normal? What normal? We have known for some time – from thinkers such as Herbert Simon and Benoit Mandelbrot – that firm sizes and stock returns are not normally distributed; rather, they have distributions with *fat tails*, such that the 'ten-sigma' events that brought down 'blue chip' hedge funds like Long-Term Capital Management – firms that, notwithstanding their Nobel-winning advisers and partners, are far more likely to fail than those who hold to Gaussian distributions of returns would have us believe.

Rationality? Whose rationality? Empirical psychologists have for the past thirty years generated an impressive body of work that can be interpreted to show that every single one of the axioms of rational choice theory – the rules that economists and finance theorists use to interpret the raw data of human behaviour – are empirically false. (Of course, if their findings are true 'of all humans' – as some of them claim – then they also apply to the psychologists themselves, placing their findings under a bright-red question mark.) On the other hand, if they are construed as true of 'some humans most of the time' or 'most humans some of the time,' or even 'most humans most of the time,' then we have a potentially valuable 'baseline model' of human thinking that encourages us to judiciously deploy doubt 'in the right place at the right time.' *Ahh … the priceless value of modesty in matters of studying the mind!* Yet in spite of all of these predictive failures, the mind often clings to the platitudes of the age, seeks shelter from the anxiety of unpredictability in false beliefs.

Mental Choicefulness: The Black Swan Hunter's 'Resting State'

A 'Black Swan' is not only a subversive idea but also a *self*-subverting idea, subversive of the very self of she who believes it, because it signals the presence of the unknown – and even of the inconceivable – in the realm of everyday human affairs. Coming to grips with the Black Swan phenomenon brings us to confront the future in a way that is – thus far – unfamiliar and alien to 'social science': by realizing that, when *believing,* we make choices among different models or representations of the world.

And you know what choice entails: that's right! – it entails taking *responsibility* for what you believe – a concept that is not foreign to the likes of Jean-Paul Sartre, who famously argued that we are responsible for the fact that we choose to forget that we truly are responsible for our emotions and beliefs, and not just our actions; and not foreign either to epistemologists like Popper, Quine, Kuhn, Feyerabend, Putnam, and Lakatos, who remind us of the degrees of freedom we have to formulate beliefs about the world; but *definitely* foreign to an unreflective lot of social scientists, who have flourished in business schools worldwide by preaching a tranquillizing creed based on – *you've got it!* – the three platitudes of our age.

The diamind, by contrast, sees through its own need for certainty and carefully cultivates the steely worm of inner doubt that bores its way through to the choices the believer must make. In so doing, *it looks the unknown in the face*. It knows that the unknown lurks everywhere, it knows that the very tools we use to make 'observations' are based on theories that may be false, and it senses the possibility – if not always the concrete presence – of the Black Swan everywhere; and for that reason it is more *vigilant*.

'Walk the Thought': Explanation is NOT Prediction in Reverse

What makes the diamind better at catching Black Swans?

The fact that it attempts to *live out its beliefs*, to act on them. The diamind becomes a diamind by *walking its thought*, not by 'sticking to its core values' or some such cant. That is, it becomes a diamind by basing its actions on its own *predictions*, by having a stake in the outcome of its own thinking. Like the engineer who builds a bridge across which cars, trains, and pedestrians will pass, so that people stand to lose their lives if the bridge collapses, the diamind is willing and able to *lay bets* on the validity of its beliefs. NNT – the self-designed Black Swan hunter – is not merely a critic of modern dogma in social sciences and management 'theory' – he is also a player, one who trades on the *basis* of his beliefs. The Black Swan's success in the realm of ideas is linked to the success of its proponent in the realm of capital flows.

But is the link *causal*? Will a Black Swan hunter be more successful *because he thinks himself to be a Black Swan hunter*? And if so, what *is* it about the Black Swan hunter's mind that makes success more likely? That is the hard question, and one whose answer NNT only implicitly addresses.

The question is tough because, as NNT himself points out, there are no rules for the sport of Black Swan hunting. When asked to make predictions for the end of proving that 'his rules' are better, he refuses with a snicker. A predictor without predictions to make: How good is *that?*

This move places his audience in a thorny spot, because 'rules' are precisely what the mind craves. Why? Because rules bring certainty, and certainty feels good – in the lukewarm ways that it *can* feel good: we *like* it. So, where are we with our little project – to lay bare the habits of the mind that lead to business success – if we can't even write down a rules-based model for the workings of the successful person's mind, in a way that allows us to test the hypothesis that these mental habits lead to better outcomes for those who exhibit them?

The answer is that the Black Swan hunter's mind is not to be described by a set of rules, but by a *stance* – by a way of being-in-the-world that allows it to feel comfortable in the normally uncomfortable space in which certainty is gone – as well as by a set of *experiences* that can be designed and sought rather than allowed to 'just happen.'

The stance is one of inner vigilance – one that attempts to clarify sharply all of the choices available to make *before* the mind comes to hold a belief. The Black Swan hunter's mind realizes that it has to *choose* to believe in the reality of the entities to which the beliefs refer ('rational agents,' 'volatility') – rather than in the realities of others (traders of no-greater-than-monkey intelligence typing orders on their computers). In the same way, it has to *choose* to believe in the methods for validating its own beliefs ('experiments,' statistical inferences) – rather than the methods of others ('introspection,' anecdote). And it realizes, too, that these choices are *live:* no one can make them for the Back Swan hunter (though he might *pretend* to believe that others can).

The Bi-Stable Mind: Building a Different Resting State

Having realized that this age's disciplines and dogmas have been erected on platitudes, and that the mind is free to choose (and free to lose) its own beliefs, the diamind achieves a different 'inner equilibrium,' one in which 'not knowing' feels as comfortable as 'knowing' once did.

Think of the state of your mind as a ball rolling around in a deep well (Figure 2.2a). Over time, the ball will come to a resting state at the bottom of the well. Call this state the 'feel good' state that certainty brings (Figure 2.2b). Next, suppose there are two other wells, equal in depth, whose bottoms are above the level of the first well's bottom, and suppose, too, that the ball can only get to those two other wells by leaping over a 'hump' (Figure 2.2c). Given enough kinetic energy – and no friction – the ball will bounce back and forth between the two wells and 'explore' them both.

Let bouncing around between the two less deep wells represent the state of *choicefulness* the mind enters when it realizes (a) that it has to choose among several possible models or belief sets in order to make sense of *the same* set of data points, and (b) that it has to do so without being able to sufficiently constrain the choice problem so that it looks like the choice between *$10,000* and *$1*. In this situation, jumping over the hump can be understood as going from a contented to a vigilant state of mind. In this vein, the state of the ball at the bottom of the deep well can be understood to represent a 'no-brainer' – the kind of choice that many seek to be able to make, presumably in order to economize on the use of 'the brain'.

What does 'jumping around,' or bi-stability, *feel* like? Want to see? Figure 2.3 shows a host of bi-stable figures, which could be 'either X or Y' in the sense that your mind can 'fall into' seeing either of two objects in them. Psychologists often use figures like these to exemplify the amount of preconception that is embedded even in the way we process purely *visual* information. Here, let's focus instead on the feeling of jumping from one way of seeing ('duck') to another way of seeing ('rabbit') *on cue*. Instead of 'falling into' the 'duck' well or the 'rabbit' well, *take yourself* back and forth, making the switch once every three seconds exactly. Experience the effort. Describe it to yourself or to a friend. Continue until the switch becomes comfortable – which it most likely *will*.

The sceptic might ask, 'What's the difference?' How can you argue that bouncing around *two* wells is better than bouncing around *one* well? Since we're dealing with metaphors, let's avail ourselves of some poetic licence: there's a reason why we've set the bottoms of the *two* wells above the bottom of the *single* well. If the bottoms of the higher wells were transparent – so that the ball modelling the vigilant mind could *see* its own previous ('stuck') state – then the higher-energy state would also be a more 'self-aware' state: it would know more about its own inner states. When having to make decisions among different possible predictions, which in turn hinge on different belief sets, and on which depend large future gains or losses, which well would you rather be in?

Before we answer that question, some disclaimers: this is not the same as the 'think or blink' question that Malcolm Gladwell has made famous.[3] Rather, it is a question of *how* to think, whether you blink or

Figure 2.2a Ball B bouncing around in a smooth-walled well ...

Figure 2.2b ... comes to rest after a finite period of time at the bottom of the well.

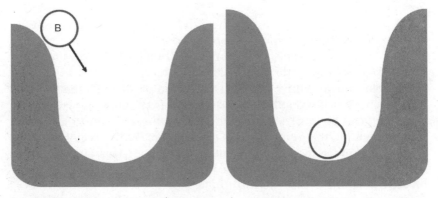

Figure 2.2c A metaphor for the 'bi-stable mind': the double well formed by ('well 2,' 'well 3') represents a state of 'mental choicefulness,' as the ball passes over barriers to explore both wells.

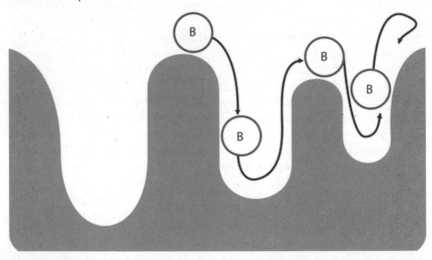

not. Do you 'lock and load' on to a single mental model in order to 'have peace of mind' while taking action based on that model being true? Or do you forgo that peace of mind in exchange for the 'vigilant state' we are trying to describe – a state that brings you to be of *at least two minds* about anything at any one time?

Figure 2.3 'Experiencing Bi-Stability.' Try ordering your mind to switch, at will, between the alternative and incommensurable ways in which it 'sees' these pictures. Practice helps. You might want to use a metronome to help you switch on faster and faster time scales.

Source: Figure 1-11 'duck and illusion,' figure D8 'Sara Nader,' and figure D9 'Wrangling Rungs' from *Mind-Sights* by Roger N. Shepard. Copyright © 1990 by Roger N. Shepard. Reprinted by arrangement with Henry Holt and Company, LLC.

For instance, when calculating your next play on the stock market, can you, while pressing the 'confirm buy selection' button on your keyboard – precisely at that moment – envision a world in which the business whose stock you are purchasing falls apart for reasons that can't be ignored (e.g., as a result of executive fraud)? *That* is the defining moment of the diamind, which can behold states of the world that have radically different implications for what you should do 'right now' even while it *retains the ability to act.*

I Believe, Therefore I See ... The Virtues of Intrapersonal Diversity

How does inner diversity help the Black Swan hunter? It's time for an-other metaphor: *Think of your mind as a fishnet and of the world as an ocean.* What you catch depends on the pattern of the net. Square-patterned nets are better at catching round-shaped fish of certain sizes (they can come in but have trouble getting out). Round-patterned nets are better if you are after square-shaped fish of certain sizes. The pattern of the fishnet represents the kinds of objects and events you see. A stable find-ing of the psychology of perception is that *you have to believe something in order to see it.*

Your thinking becomes embedded in your perception by a process very similar to that by which the fisherman's expectation of the shape of the fish he is after becomes embedded in the design of the pattern of the net he is about to cast out. Most people *fish with a standard net:* they look for Gaussian, linear patterns among the events that make up their lives and – *guess what?* – that is precisely what they detect. But they forget, of course, that what they detect is influenced by what they look for – by the pattern of the net they cast.

The diamind does not forget this: it casts *many nets*, each with a dif-ferent pattern, and in this way it equips its perceptual apparatus to 'ob-serve' many kinds of events. A Black Swan is the round-shaped fish that otters its way out of all round-patterned nets, or the square-shaped fish that otters its way out of square-shaped nets. But no fish is round and rectangular at the same time, which means that the more net pat-terns the mind casts into the world, the higher the chances that a Black Swan will be caught in at least one of them! If we think of perception and observation themselves as *problem-solving activities*, whereby the 'barely conscious' mind attempts to solve the problem of saying pre-cisely 'what *is* there, *there*?' then some recent insights about the value of diversity become readily applicable.

Scott Page has made precise the value of *inter*personal diversity to solving 'hard problems.' In his models, crowds of non-experts *necessar-ily* outperform experts in producing solutions.[4] *How*? The basic insight is simple enough to understand: crowds produce a *diversity* of both per-spectives (representations of the problem) and heuristics (local rule sets for driving forward to a solution), and if you can aggregate these ef-ficiently, you will arrive at a more precise answer for the same number of 'man hours' spent on solving the problem, and to a more accurate answer more of the time. That is, *if* ... as the Spartans would say. The problem of effectively culling useful insights from different sources is not as simple as it sounds once we introduce to our picture the normal proclivity that people have to hoard information, shield their insights from the gaze of others, and haggle over mutual recognition of authorship.

Cognitive diversity, as Page points out, often comes at the cost of interpersonal *conflict*, which is why he needs to write in a *prescriptive* vein: If you want the benefits of diversity, the argument goes, consider placing an explicit value *on* diversity and becoming more conflict-competent.

Here is a better approach: *bring the diversity inside*, by actively cultivating (a) a diverse *intrapersonal* repertoire of mental models and desires, and (b) the proclivity to deploy *many different ways* of seeing to the same problem. *Inner diversity* is the secret weapon of the diamind. NNT relishes *fin de siècle* French literature, listens to Rachmaninov's *morceaux de salon*, writes about the epistemology of uncertainty and the problems we run up against when trying to make inferences about quantities whose observed values are dependent on assumptions we have already made, and 'does' the buying and selling of assets with 'uncertain' levels of risk and returns. How does all of this work together to produce the better fishnet?

Here is a conjecture: a taste for the literary has sensitized NNT to the subtle ways in which 'experts' engage in the processes of deception and self-deception that come together into what they call 'careers' – careers that can in turn be analysed using tools that have been developed by epistemologists to try to answer this question: 'Can we really trust real flesh-and-blood scientists to safeguard the aims of science?' This is precisely what NNT is doing when he asks such questions as, 'What do you have to know about the properties of a population of events in order to make valid inferences about the population from a small sample thereof?' and 'To what extent and in what way do your inferences depend on assumptions about the distribution of events in the population in question?' Music gives him an appreciation for timing and rhythm as essential features of a trading strategy – which, unlike a purely 'contemplative' approach, is dependent on the rate at which you 'sample' reality. And the predicament he faces of having to *act* on his beliefs and premises – instead of merely writing papers about them – forces on him an intellectual honesty that is more characteristic of engineers than of scientists – for it is far harder to get monkeys to talk than it is to answer such questions as, 'Why can monkeys (theoretically) talk? – or not talk?'

Who cares, so long as the paper gets written and published?' His premise seems to be drawn from the Mass Mutual commercial: 'You can't predict, but you can prepare' – and he prepares by cultivating, simultaneously, several divergent ways of being.

But Will the Dogs Eat It? Intra-Personal Diversity in Action

How does this intrapersonal diversity work in the practice of trading? What should we see that is *different* in a trader who has internalized the admonishments of Quine, Popper, and Putnam, that we would not see in a trader who swears by the Hull–White option pricing model and the efficient markets hypothesis?

Well, what we should see is precisely a critical awareness of the 'implicit major premise' of the mental models on which the trader's actions are based. If you are a bettor, you want to *know* what you are betting on. 'Knowing' what you are betting on means, in this case, knowing the underlying probability distribution function for the events you are betting on. Most social scientists – including finance theorists – use Bernoulli processes to model *bounded* event spaces and Gaussian distributions to model *unbounded* event spaces; they also rely on a powerful and soothing result from statistics known as the central limit theorem, which states that the distribution of observed events converges more or less quickly on the assumed distribution for the entire event space.

This is, it *should* converge. But *will it*? Well, that depends on whether the probabilistic model you have chosen to represent the event space in the first place is the correct one. *That* is the implicit major premise of most statistical inference processes.

So, when you are making inferences about large event spaces from limited samples – the diamind reasons – you are really making at least *two* types of inference: the first about the kinds of processes that generate these events, processes that determine the distribution of the entire sample space; and the second about the *parameters* of the probability distribution in question. But of course, *this* mental model of the world only works if you *know* that the distribution of observed events converges on the actual distribution of events. But you *don't* know that – indeed, you *do* know that *some* probability distributions for events – like the Levy-Mandelbrot distributions – are such that you *cannot* make inferences about the probability distribution from observed samples of events drawn from the population described by it. The diamind is *lucid* about this predicament: that it cannot know 'for sure' what it would like to know 'for sure' in order to act 'with peace of mind.' What, then, does it do?

It forgoes the peace of mind that comes with self-deception, opting instead for a state of mental choicefulness in which *not knowing* does not necessarily lead to *not acting*. An example will help make the point. Suppose you have been given the opportunity to bet on the next toss of a coin, and suppose that coin has been tossed 1,000,000 times in the past. The 'bookie' – a respectable-looking fellow – has offered to let you look at the record of the past 1,000,000 coin tosses, and you find that heads has come up 921,502 times. Your bet will pay $1,000,000 if you guess right on the next toss, and will cost you $100,000 if you guess wrong. The bookie tells you the coin is 'fair,' but something in his eyes leads you to mistrust him on this point. You're mesmerized by the magnitude of the 921,502 heads outcomes and are about to bet heads, because you think – as any 'normal' human being would – that the distribution of observed events will converge rather quickly on the 'actual' distribution of heads and tails – which looks to be close to 0.8/0.2. So, would you bet $100,000 to win $1,000,000 with 90 per cent probability?

On an expected-value basis, it looks like a no-brainer. *But* … just as you're about to lay your bet, a mathematician (whom you know to be a mathematician because he went to the same university you went to) taps you on the shoulder and says: 'It might interest you to know that the record of coin tosses you're looking at shows that the coin comes up tails on all and only prime-numbered tosses. It 's also directly relevant to what you're about to do that the next toss is a prime-numbered one.' The mathematician seems to have nothing to sell you, and his words check out: tails does show up in the record of tosses that bear numbers you *know* to be prime: 13, 17, 19 … Of course, there are numbers on which you may have to take his word. For instance, is 53,573 a prime number or not? Time to take out your wireless connection device, go to Wikipedia, type 'distribution of primes,' and wait for the result … which comes back affirmative. The question for you is, 'Which way do you bet?' (Take a moment to think this over before reading on.)

Think. Who said you had to bet, or *when* you had to bet, or *on which toss* you had to bet? All the bookie can do is offer you the bet; he can't force you to make it. The mathematician's hypothesis changes your entire perception of what it is you're betting on: Is it an event drawn from the two possible events – heads or tails? Or is it a sequence of events drawn from the $2^{1,000,000}$ possible sequences of heads and tails that could have made up the first 1,000,000 tosses? Is there a way to turn his hypothesis into something with enough bite to justify an 'odds against' bet?

The problem your mind faces – or *should* face – whenever it yields to the seductive appeal of the mathematician's conjecture – which fits the data perfectly – is not that of figuring out how a coin can come to *know* the number of times it has been tossed in the past. Granted, it would be weird if it did, but, *weirdness* is not a good proxy for invalidity. The effects predicted by quantum mechanical theories, for instance, are *weird*, but physicists observe them nonetheless.

The problem, rather, is that the mathematician's 'theory' is *post-dictive*. It is an explanation of something that has already happened, and that is not necessarily a good thing for you. Explanation is the stuff that social science as we know it is made on; it has had a long and prosperous life under the cover of such platitudes as 'explanation is nothing but prediction in reverse.'[5] Being able to explain the past makes social scientists feel that they can predict the future; then, by a switch-eroo, feeling becomes 'knowledge.' Their minds substitute explanatory coverage with predictive power and then conspire to ignore the difference.

That there *is* a difference should be clear if you can imagine the persuasive force of the mathematician's conjecture had it been a *prediction* rather than an explanation – in other words, had he *predicted* that the 978,443rd toss would come up heads *before* the toss had been made, then produced a few more correct predictions of tosses consistent with his 'rule.' The 'pre/post' problem would have been significantly mitigated. 'Okay, I don't understand *how* you do this – or how the coin does it,' you might say, 'but still, you do *play it forward*.' Your confidence might be further boosted if you saw the *mathematician himself* bet a significant amount (relative to his net worth) on a coin toss, in agreement with his own theory, and win.[6]

Thus, instead of *betting*, you could buy the option to make the same bet on the 1,000,002nd to 1,000,005th tosses of the coin. This would allow you to witness the predictive power (or failure thereof) of the mathematician's theory *before* laying your bet. Alternatively, you could think of it as building a *stopping rule* into your betting strategy – that is, a predictive failure of the mathematician's theory would *stop* your betting strategy in its tracks. You have 'preordained' the fact that, should the outlandish 'heads on primes' theory be refuted even once by an observation of tails on a toss that should have come up heads, you will walk away from the belief that it is true.

All of which gives away the real use of the act of 'buying a well-defined option': it is not only a 'starting rule' of the form 'I will get involved in the trading game when the value of the stock reaches $v dollars,' but also – perhaps more important – a stopping rule of the form 'I will not get involved in the game until the value of the stock reaches $v' – which is much closer anyhow to the meaning of the word 'option.' An option is just that: an *affordance*, a condition that allows you to play but does not constrain you to play. Treated as a stopping rule rather than as a starting rule, an option serves as a value-self-disciplining tool for the diamind, by freeing it up to *do something else* – such as *look out for Black Swans*.

When you look at it in this light, NNT's definition of his own trading style as that of a naive falsificationist is telling: the Black Swan hunter knows the value of *stopping rules* because he understands that the mind has a proclivity to trick itself into seeking confirmations rather than disconfirmations of its beliefs, and a related proclivity to buy into overly general beliefs at the expense of more modest and restrictive ones – all to an end that is ultimately self-defeating, which is, to keep going in its habitual ways, which is, something it can do only if it can sweep the complications of particulars, anomalies, and exceptions under the great rugs of the mind.

The diaminded Black Swan hunter, then, *wires* stopping rules into its investment strategies, essentially saying: 'I do not know what a Black Swan looks like, *but* I *can* come to reliably guess when I have left a field of white swans. So I will build stopping rules that stop me from behaving as if I am dealing with white swans when, in fact, I may be dealing with Black Swans.' This practical wisdom comes not from a knowledge of the world, but rather from a knowledge of the mind. Just as 'the unexamined life is not worth living,' *the unexamined mind is not worth having.* Better to have no mind at all than to waste away tens of billions of dollars betting in ways that rule out the possibility of 'ten-sigma' events that are far more likely than our 'theorists' would have us believe.

Charlie Munger: Develop Your Chutzpah to Get Lollapalooza Effects

Inner diversity of experience and mindset can pay off in the cultivation of a stance towards the world that is vigilant and (at least) *bi*-stable rather than merely stable. This stance then allows us to cultivate the all-important but scarce faculty of *doubt*. It pays off by allowing one to create the requisite intrapersonal *cognitive diversity*, which in turn allows the mind to *see more:* to detect events that contradict its beliefs and to allow those beliefs to die *in its stead* – just as Karl Popper admonished. Yet savvy diaminds have been able to gaze even deeper than Sir Karl's insights and to realize that true inner openness actually *comes from* a dogged pursuit of intrapersonal diversity.

An aside should help make the point. Any person versed in success-fully ending difficult relationships knows that the best way to end an ongoing relationship is to start a new one.[7] The problem, of course, is how to navigate the period of inauthenticity, dissimulation, and out-right lying that is entailed when starting a new relationship without quite having finished another. But that is *not* a problem related to end-ing a relationship; rather, it is a problem related to one's unwillingness to have difficult discussions and weather difficult moments with other humans in general, and within the relationship that is about to end in particular.

Now, think of your beliefs and theories – especially the latter – as your *lovers*, with whom you have developed habit-based relationships that are dear to you precisely because they enforce and are enforced by familiar routines. Now, think of getting good at allowing beliefs to die on the anvil of reality as analogous to getting good at ending mutually destructive relationships: hard to do when there is no alternative, much easier if the alternative is at hand. One big difference between beliefs and lovers – who are, one hopes, other human beings – is that beliefs cannot suffer, and therefore feeling pity for them is not meaningful or useful. Knowing *this*, why not become a little more promiscuous in your *believing strategy* in order to become a little more open-minded in your strategy for facing the world and surviving it in prosperity? *Okay,* you might say, *but how?*

Meet Charlie Munger, Warren Buffet's partner in Berkshire Hatha-way and chairman of the Alfred Munger Foundation, a philanthropic organization named after his father. Let's allow a few words of intro-duction – his own, understated ones:

When Warren took over Berkshire, the market capitalization was about ten million dollars. And forty something years later, there are not many more shares outstanding now than there were then, and the market capi-talization is about a hundred billion dollars, ten thousand for one. And since that has happened, year after year, in kind of a grind-ahead fashion, with very few failures, it eventually drew some attention, indicating that maybe Warren and I know something useful in microeconomics.[8]

Focus on the word 'know,' above, and listen to Munger one step further: 'As I talk about my strengths and weaknesses in academic economics, one interesting fact you are entitled to know is that I never took a course in economics.' Red flag: Attention Required! 'Know' is not used here in its usual sense that is, in the sense in which one is trained to use it through out one's educational career. It is not the schoolhouse 'know.' It does not signal the kind of knowledge that carefully built theories give you, but rather something else: 'And with this striking lack of credentials, you may wonder why I have the chutzpah to be up here giving this talk. The answer is that I have a black belt in chutzpah. I was born with it.'[9]

Forget about 'born with it' for a moment (we will come back to it). Focus on *chutzpah*. Let's try to define it: it is the confidence to see through the platitudes of the age and bet on what you've seen. *Which platitudes?* Try 'the efficient markets hypothesis,' a staple of economic theory, one that claims that markets process information 'efficiently' – in other words, that the price system is such an effective (per unit of time) aggregator of information about buyers and sellers that no buyer or seller can beat the market except by sheer luck. How does one see through a platitude? By a counter-example, of course:

> It was always clear to me that the stock market couldn't be perfectly efficient, because as a teenager, I'd been to the racetrack in Omaha where they had the pari-mutuel system. And it was quite obvious to me that if the house takes the croupier's stake, which was 17%, some people lost a lot less than 17% of all of their bets, and other people consistently lost more than 17% of all of their bets. So, the pari-mutuel system in Omaha had no perfect efficiency. And so I didn't accept the argument that the stock market was always perfectly efficient in creating rational prices.

Counter-examples are ruthlessly efficient when dealing with platitudes couched in the language of the 'laws of nature': one counter-example disposes of an entire law – not a bad way to build a 'false-belief exterminator.'

But *merely* seeking negative rather than positive feedback for your beliefs is not enough, for this simple reason: you would end up with

no beliefs at all. Clearly, this would not be acting in an intelligent, purposive way. You cannot claim to have 'done X because you believed Y
would happen if you did' – because *then what*? *Something else* is needed,
something that turns mere scepticism or contrarianism or nihilism into
chutzpah, something that turns a Nietzsche into a Peirce.

Question: What could that something else be? Answer: Connected-
ness to a concrete problem, including all the realities surrounding it.
A *concrete* problem – note! – not a *textbook* problem but a *real* one.
To wit:

> Berkshire had this former savings and loan company, and it had made this
> loan on a hotel right opposite the Hollywood Park Racetrack. In due time
> the neighborhood changed and it was full of gangs, pimps, and dope deal-
> ers. They tore copper pipe out of the wall for dope fixes, and there were
> people hanging around the hotel with guns, and nobody would come. We
> foreclosed on it two or three times, and the loan value went down to noth-
> ing. We seemed to have an insolvable economic problem – a microeco-
> nomic problem. Now we could have gone to McKinsey, or maybe a bunch
> of professors from Harvard, and we would have gotten a report about
> 10 inches thick about the ways we could approach this failing hotel in
> this terrible neighborhood. But instead, we put a sign on the property that
> said: 'For sale or rent.' And in came, in response to that sign, a man who
> said, 'I'll spend $200,000 fixing up your hotel, and buy it at a high price
> on credit, if you can get zoning so I can turn the parking lot into a putting
> green.' 'You've got to have a parking lot in a hotel,' we said. 'What do you
> have in mind?' He said. 'No, my business is flying seniors in from Florida,
> putting them near the airport, and then letting them go out to Disneyland
> and various places by bus and coming back. And I don't care how bad the
> neighborhood is going to be because my people are self-contained behind
> walls. All they have to do is get on the bus in the morning and come home
> in the evening, and they don't need a parking lot; they need a putting
> green.' So we made the deal with the guy. The whole thing worked beauti-
> fully, and the loan got paid off.[10]

If you blinked, you might have missed it: 'the market' – with its 'imperfect information processing capabilities – made a star appearance
in this example. Munger *used* it, albeit with no illusions about its per-
fection. Clearly, 'imperfect' can still be a whole lot better than the alternatives. The diamind distrusts but does not disdain theory: on the
contrary, it embraces theory but takes from it what is useful. In this

case it was a 'design principle,' which is a mechanism that allows you to engineer more successful situations on the basis of a clear, synthetic understanding of disciplinary knowledge.

'Synthetic': there's another diaminded word for you. In the specialized worlds of academia and the professions, 'synthesis' is a *faux pas:* it just ain't happening. Listen to Munger again:

> The big general objection to economics was the one early described by Alfred North Whitehead when he spoke of the fatal unconnectedness of academic disciplines, wherein each professor didn't even know of the models of the other disciplines, much less try to synthesize those disciplines with his own ... The nature of this failure is that it creates what I always call 'man with a hammer' syndrome. To a man with only a hammer, every problem looks pretty much like a nail. And that works marvelously to gum up all professions, and all departments of academia, and indeed most practical life. So, what do we do, Charlie? The only antidote for being an absolute klutz due to the presence of a man with a hammer syndrome is to have a full kit of tools. You don't have just a hammer. You've got all the tools.[11]

Remember the fishnet metaphor? Munger has an even better one: models are *tools*. They allow you to do things with your mind so that you can act more competently upon the world. Like drugs, but unlike tools, models are *addictive:* they not only help you make predictions and generate explanations, but also become habitual ways of thinking about the world. You can get stuck *in* them and *with* them. The antidote is to reinterpret them as *tools*. And what is a tool? It is something you discard – or exchange for another tool – when it is no longer useful. All right, then the problem becomes: 'How do you know how to discard a model/tool when it is no longer useful?'

> You've got one more trick. You've got to use those tools checklist-style, because you'll miss a lot if you just hope that the right tool is going to pop up unaided whenever you need it. But if you've got a full list of tools, and go through them in your mind, checklist-style, you will find a lot of answers that you won't find any other way. So limiting this big general objection that so disturbed Alfred North Whitehead is very important, and there are mental tricks that help do the job.[12]

Don't think of 'economics' as a science or a discipline, then. Think of it, rather, as a bunch of *tools*, of *instruments* for designing more success-ful human interactions – something that only a few far-sighted econo-mists, like Al Roth, have only recently signalled. Game theory – as Tom Schelling, the guy who shared one of the Bank of Sweden Alfred Nobel Memorial Prizes for his work on it, has said – is *not* a theory: it is a *logic for thinking about situations in which outcomes depend not only on* my *deci-sions, but on* your *decisions as well*.[13] Knowing this, I have to think about *your* decisions, and if I think you're rational, then I'll realize that you in turn are thinking about my decisions, so: I have to think about what you think about my decisions ... and so forth. Game theory is a com-plexity *generator* as much as a complexity *annihilator* – which is what we are told most 'good theories' are (i.e., 'simplifications of reality'). It is, however, more than a logic: it is a *design tool* that allows me to design rules that constrain the moves of people who may be self-interested to the point of only caring about the results of their decisions on their own welfare. Like all tools, it needs to be put through one of the designer's favourite devices: the stress test.

The diamind will, like Munger, design *stress tests* for such design tools: it will ask itself, 'Under what conditions will this tool fail me?' and then watch out for *them* instead of watching out only for the condi-tions in which the tools will be useful. Just try using the hard logic of game theory on arguments with your lover about the proper division of labour around the household, or about the optimal allocation of 're-spect' or 'love signals' within the relationship. Figure out his or her set of strategies and payoffs, write them down, figure out your own, write those down as well, and choose, from this set, the strategy pairs from which no one can deviate without becoming worse off. To learn the use of the tool, *truly* learn it, try it, *really* try it, instead of just treating our invitation as a rhetorical device.

Now for the final step in the design of the mentally choiceful stance: the search engine, as in 'How did I solve these problems?' 'Obviously,' you will answer yourself, 'I was using a simple search engine in my mind to go through checklist style, and I was using some rough algo-rithms that work pretty well in many complex systems.' What does a search engine do? It searches. And how do you organize an efficient search? Well, algorithm designers tell us you have to have an efficient *organization* of the contents of whatever it is you are searching. And a *tree* structure allows you to search more efficiently than most alterna-tive structures (Figure 2.4).

Figure 2.4 How a tree structure helps simplify search: A detection algorithm for 'Fox.'

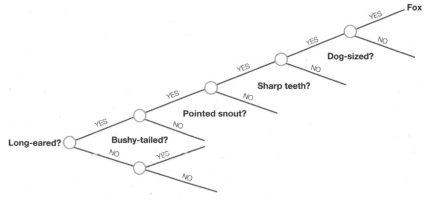

The reason is simple: with a tree, the search algorithm is simpler: it takes fewer steps. What is Munger's search algorithm? Here it is:

> Extreme success is likely to be caused by some combination of the following factors: a) Extreme maximization or minimization of one or two variables. Example[:] Costco, or, [Berkshire Hathaway's] furniture and appliance store. b) Adding success factors so that a bigger combination drives success, often in nonlinear fashion, as one is reminded of the concept of breakpoint or the concept of critical mass in physics. You get more mass, and you get a lollapalooza result. And of course I've been searching for lollapalooza results all my life, so I'm very interested in models that explain their occurrence. [Remember the Black Swan?] c) an extreme of good performance over many factors. Examples: Toyota or Les Schwab. d) Catching and riding some big wave.[14]

Figure 2.5 offers an efficient representation of Munger's search engine, in tree form.

A good search algorithm allows you to make your mental choices clear. It makes it easier for you to be *mentally choiceful* and to understand the reasons why you're making these mental choices.

Now, what should go on the branches of your tree of mental models? Well, how about basic mental models from a whole bunch of different disciplines? Such as: physics (non-linearity, criticality), economics (what Munger calls the 'super-power' of incentives), the multiplicative

Figure 2.5 Charlie Munger's lollapalooza detection algorithm, represented as a tree search.

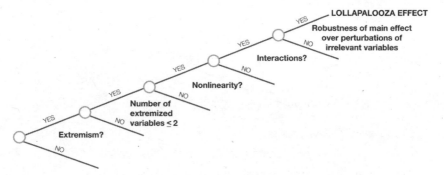

effects of several interacting causes (biophysics), and collective phenomena – or 'catching the wave' (plasma physics). How's *that* for a science that rocks, by placing at the disposal of the mind a *large library of forms* created by thinkers across hundreds of years and marshalling them for the purpose of detecting, building, and profiting from Black Swans?

The 'tree trick' has one more advantage – a big one: it lets you quickly visualize interactions among the various models and identify cumulative effects. Go *northwest* in your search, starting from the '0' node, and the interactions double with every step. Go southwest, on the other hand, and the interactions decrease in number at the same rate. Seen in this rather sketchy way, Black Swan hunting is no longer as daunting a sport as it might seem at first sight.

Reality does not come prepackaged in normally distributed populations. You have to figure out the distributions of the events you're recording, and *estimate the parameters of those distributions*. This is an 'underdetermined' problem – precisely the type of problem that Willard Quine and Pierre Duhem maintained that scientists have to solve all the time.[15] When a hypothesis is 'disconfirmed' by evidence – they argued – the scientist does not have to abandon her theory: she has many options and must get her mind to make choices. She can adjust the parameters of her theory, make changes to the apparatus used to make the measurements that produced the data points, or examine the data points more closely to determine whether they're systematically biased or distorted; and there are many ways she can do *each* of these. *Mental choices* are inevitable, so you might as well make them consciously and in ways that are responsive to the costs and benefits of each option.

NNT's diamind prizes the *ethos* of science even as it looks critically at 'scientists.' Thus NNT charts out, up front, the *cognitive choices* he will have to make so that he can stop betting on the dominated options more quickly. The Black Swan hunter knows that the biggest payoffs in his sport go to those who can shed most quickly the illusion that they are seeing nothing but *white* swans. So he defines as clearly and pre-cisely as possible, *up front*, what a non-white swan looks like – or what a white swan does *not* look like – so that he can *stop looking for it or betting on it once these criteria are met*. This is how, without being able to *describe* a Black Swan, he can nevertheless hope to catch one: whatever they are, Black Swans are *non-white swans*.

Accordingly, NNT writes down *stopping rules* for his own mind. The hard thing about doing this – and then following the rules – is that they aren't *certain to work:* they may be incorrect. This seed of doubt makes it hard to obey them: you, after all, are the one who has made the cogni-tive choice to establish them in the first place – why, then, can't you also make the cognitive choice to ignore them 'in the heat of action'? To obey them, the diamond has to take itself seriously and obey the rules it has set for itself – not an easy task, for the mind is *the* uncontrollable organ.

The following thought will help: one's own mind's stopping rules are fallible, but they're the best it can do – and they're certainly better than the alternative, which is to allow the mind to fall into a closed cir-cle, so that it won't give up a theory or belief that has crumbled when confronted with reality. The history of science tells us this can almost always be accomplished – even with flair and elegance – as shown by the following anecdote from Imre Lakatos:

A physicist of the pre-Einsteinian era takes Newton's mechanics and his law of gravitation (N), the accepted initial conditions (I) and calculates, with their help, the path of a newly discovered small planet, p. But the planet deviates from the calculated path. Does our Newtonian physicist consider that the deviation was forbidden by Newton's theory and there-fore that, once established, it refutes the theory N? No. He suggests that there must be a hitherto unknown planet p' which perturbs the path of p. He calculates the mass, orbit, etc. of this hypothetical planet and then asks the experimental astronomer to test his hypothesis. The planet p' is so small that even the biggest available telescopes cannot possibly observe it: the experimental astronomer applies for a research grant to build yet a bigger one. In three years' time the telescope is ready. Were the unknown planet p' to be discovered, it would be hailed as a new victory for Newtonian science. But it is not. Does our scientist abandon Newton's theory and his idea of the perturbing planet? No. He suggests that a cloud of cosmic dust hides the planet from us. He calculates the location and properties of this cloud and asks for a research grant to send up a research satellite to test his calculations. Were the satellite's instruments (possibly new ones, based on little-tested theory) to record the existence of the conjectural cloud, the result would be hailed as an outstanding victory for Newtonian science. But the cloud is not found. Does our scientist abandon Newton's theory, together with the idea of the perturbing planet and the idea of the cloud which hides it? No. He suggests that there is some magnetic field in that region of the universe which disturbed the instruments of the satellite. A new satellite is sent up. Were the magnetic field to be found, Newtonians would celebrate a sensational victory. But it is not. Is this regarded as a refutation of Newtonian science? No. Either yet another auxiliary hypothesis is proposed or … the whole story is buried in the dusty volumes of periodicals and the story never mentioned again.[16]

How about a contemporary version of this morality tale? Here goes:

A financial engineer of the pre-Black Swan era believes she has found a way to measure the value at risk in a major financial transaction to three times more bits of accuracy than previous or current models. She rests her new algorithm for measuring value at risk on well-tested and well-tried facts, such as these: that returns are normally distributed (so that the algorithm designer's only problem is to measure the parameters of the underlying Gaussian distribution); that other participants in the market are rational (in the sense that their preferences are acyclical, anti-symmetric, and reflexive); and that in general, causes have proportional effects (such that the price system is a quasi-linear evaluator of the new information one feeds into it).

With a $10 million injection from a New Canaan–based venture capital firm, she turns the algorithm into a neat new software package and gets a large Midwestern bank to try it out. The bank uses the package to evaluate its value at risk on several large transactions. The estimates turn out to be wrong by factors an order of magnitude higher than those predicted by her algorithms. The financial engineer is called to account for her brainchild. She is, alas, prepared for that meeting, and brings along a Power-

Point presentation showing how the interface between the program and the real-world data is constrained in such a way that the algorithm cannot apply its full computational prowess. She asks for $2 million of additional funding (non-recurrent engineering costs) to fix the underlying problem. The bankers agree to this.

She returns to work and produces Version 2.0 of the software package … which once again produces estimates that are far off base. The bankers, scandalized, call her back up and ask her – less politely this time – to account for herself. She smiles: 'I have it now. There's an error in the algorithm that systematically overemphasizes "outliers" of frequency distributions, and therefore unduly skews the predictions towards estimates that are unreasonably far from the central tendency one should aim for. But we've developed a patch that, with an additional $5 million of funding, we can harmonize with the rest of the program, to block those stupid false leading indicators of ludicrously unlikely six-sigma events that were distorting our predictions.'

With a sigh, the bankers accede again to the entrepreneur's 'vision,' and $5 million more goes into the start-up's local bank. The next time, a real six-sigma event comes about, rendering most of the predictions of the little machine invalid. The entrepreneur gets a phone call demanding that she show up early the next morning. Does she relent now?

Well, what do you think? If she could get away the first two times with postulating 'machine errors' – or 'flukes' – that came up in her own machine, how much easier will it be now to postulate machine errors in that 'other machine' – you know, the one that begins with an 'M' and is often referred to by economists who have never traded as 'perfectly efficient'?

Like the financial engineer, our Newtonian expert had fallen into the *White Swan illusion*. At no point in his story – a rather expensive one, in public funding dollars and human creative energy – did he *stop and think* about the cognitive choices he was making; as a consequence, he bet on increasingly far-fetched 'fortifying' hypotheses in order to salvage his core theory. By contrast, the diamind would have mapped out a space of cognitive choices that it knew it would have to make, along with stopping rules for ruling out the choices it knew it would not make. In this way, gone would have been his slavish dependence on 'data' or 'theory' in order to figure out the truth about the world: goodbye *certainty*, hello *choice!* The Black Swan hunter's motto is: *gotta choose, or you lose!* The 'price' you pay for following this path – *yes, there is a price!* – is that you have to become a *pragmatist* about your ideas before you can choose among them at will and in ways that heed the expected costs and benefits. *You have to lose your mind in order to gain it.* How do you do *that?* Read on: we're about to tell you.

Hold this state of mind! Yes, the one you're experiencing just now. Notice what it feels like. It is a state in which you expect that a new, surprising, and possibly good answer will emerge – a state in which you're willing to work to understand this *new thing* you're about to see. It is the dominant mood of the diamond: of the Black Swan hunter and the engineer of lollapalooza effects. And once you can hold it, learn to go back to it – to summon it at will by remembering what it felt like. The first step towards a new stance is an open kind of *mood*, a feeling closer to a sensation than to an emotion. If you can recall the way this feeling feels to you, you may be able to go back there during those times when mind and body clamp down, behaviour becomes habit, and habit becomes identity.

There is, from here, still some work to do to uncover your mind's defences against reality – the mechanisms of its addiction to the 'necessary illusions' that veil *what is* – and then to wean your mind from its robust but counterproductive routines. Below are some suggestions.

Explanation and Prediction. Pick a past event that has been precisely recorded (for good example, a significant rise or fall in the price of a stock you know something about). Write down what you believe to be the best *explanation* for that event. How much would you bet on the explanation being *valid*, and why? Next, make a *prediction* based on your explanation (another movement in the stock's value within a certain time window). How much would you *bet* on the prediction being true, and why? Are the two sums equal? *Why* or *why not?*

Interpersonal Explanation and Prediction. If you want to watch yourself think, listen to yourself talk. But not to *anyone*, of course – rather, with a person with whom you feel you can be fairly self-revealing. With this person's permission, record or – even better – videotape a conversation. Then review the tape. Press the pause button as 'randomly' as you can (i.e., without allowing yourself to 'pick the spot'). Make a *precise* prediction about what you or the other person will say *next*, and write down the prediction and the precise reasoning that led you to make it. Continue to play the tape until your prediction has been proved or disproved, then stop. Next, write down an explanation for the event you tried to predict (whether you were right or not), along with the reasons for that explanation. Compare those reasons with the reasons you gave for your predictions.

Watch your language! For a period of three weeks (remember that a habit is something you do for three weeks in a row), replace all *explanations and justifications* in the way you speak to others with *predictions and commitments*. For instance, instead of trying to explain to someone why large-capitalization stocks are making a comeback, make a prediction about their performance in the next three months. Instead of explaining to someone why you think America has lost the battle for moral ascendancy in the world order, make a prediction about a concrete foreign-policy event. Instead of explaining to someone why you were late for a meeting, make a clear commitment for future behaviour or a prediction of your future behaviour. *Delete all explanations systematically and replace them with predictions.* Not just any predictions, of course, but predictions that can be shown to be true or false within a reasonable time span; and not just any commitments, but highly testable ones. For example, 'I will not be more than five minutes late in more than one of the next five of our meetings.' Keep a *journal of your predictions and commitments* for the duration of the three weeks, and keep a record *of correct versus incorrect predictions* and *kept versus broken commitments*. Review. Repeat. Review again.

Distancing: The Thing and the Name of the Thing Are Two Different Things. This is a *relativization* exercise. (Note: This one could be detrimental to your short-term mental well-being but will likely be beneficial to your long-term mental acuity. After all, feeling good and doing well do not always go hand in hand.) The point of it is to wean your mind off the comfortable illusion that words unambiguously refer to the objects and events we take them to refer to, and that sentences or propositions are true independently of their context. How does it work? For a period of three weeks, you will be *relativizing* all of your assertions and definitions, making them explicitly dependent on speaker, circumstance, and language. For instance:

- *Relativize to social practice.* Following the practice of an ancient tribe whose descendants still dwell happily in the Amazon rainforest, stop saying, 'This is a dog.' Instead say, 'We *call* this a dog.' Replace all 'this is X' and 'and X is a Y' statements with 'we call this an X' and 'we call an X a Y.' Make these switches when thinking and – even more important – when *talking*.

- *Relativize to source of the information.* Replace all your context-*independent* declarative sentences – for instance, 'Vitamin C boosts immune system response' – with context-*dependent* ones. For example, 'John Doe [the reporter] writes that Nurit Arpad [the researcher] says that vitamin C intake boosts immune system response.' The idea is to reduce the generality of the claim at hand by being very precise about its source and the circumstances in which you came across it.

- *Relativize to background assumptions.* A lot of information comes in the form of 'facts' – for example, 'consolidation in industry X leads to higher profitability of the business in the industry.' This is not a *raw* fact; it's a *stylized* fact. A stylized fact is a fact that relies on a mechanism or universal law being true in order for the fact to be valid. The universal mechanism here is that industry profitability goes up with concentration because a smaller number of sellers increases the bargaining power of the sellers relative to that of the buyers, and therefore the sellers benefit from a credible threat to undersupply the market, which is the foundation of monopoly power (mechanism 1). Moreover, with a smaller number of firms in the industry, the sellers can more easily collude, because collusion involves coordination and the coordination costs of n firms rise as the square of the number of the firms (because there are $n(n - 1)/2$ possible pairwise connections between n firms, which is approximately equal to n^2). In case you're wondering: antitrust regulation does not make the problem of collusion go away; it only makes the coordination problem more difficult for the firms 'in power' because now they have to coordinate in such a way as to avoid detection by the Federal Trade Commission (in the United States). Thus the validity of a given fact is contingent on the validity of these mechanisms. So – and this is the challenge – *in your everyday speech*, replace as many statements of fact as you can with statements that highlight the dependence of the facts on the underlying theories and mechanisms that must be valid in order for the statement of fact to make sense. For example, 'Monopoly power and coordination cost mechanisms suggest that industry profitability will go up with consolidation.'

Seeing It in (at Least) Two Ways: Don't Just Mind the World, Diamind It! The essence of the diamond is that it can take at least two different views of the same set of 'plain and simple facts' – facts that have radically different implications for how it should act so as to *avoid obsessive states of being* that impede its ability to take action. Remember: the idea is to heighten the vigilance that corresponds to the *bi-stable* mind we described earlier in this chapter. Bi-stable vigilance enables you to experience reality in at least two ways at any one time. To develop this state, you need to fully experience reality first in one state – which means *acting* in a way that corresponds to that way of experiencing reality – and then experience that same reality in the *other* state – which again means *acting* as if that state is most closely connected to 'the truth' – and then, finally, learn to flip back and forth *at will* between the two states. The following two manoeuvres can be powerful:

- *The 'minds and brains' exercise.* Think of the person you're interacting with as *a brain* connected to motor neurons, muscles, viscera, and so on, and interact with her as if she were no more than a brain connected to other equipment. For instance, you could, when she asks you a difficult question, produce soothing oral noises that have nothing to do with the content of the question, but rather are aimed at bringing down the emotional temperature of the situation at hand. Or you could ask simple questions – 'What shall we have for dinner?' or similar – in a tone that indicates that a lot rides on the answer. The point here is to get her to answer more quickly than would otherwise be the case (thereby avoiding the annoying period of dithering that precedes ordering off a menu). Do this for one week with one person. Then *flip*. Now think of yourself as interacting with (i.e., co-reasoning with) her *mind*. Take seriously every question she asks you, following each argument to the very end, however much emotional discomfort this produces in you and in her (*Watch out!* This could threaten the relationship even more than the 'brain' approach to managing the interaction. So pick the woman carefully.) Do *this* for one week also. Repeat until you feel you can actually flip at will between the two states.
- *The under-over-responsible exercise.* Causal responsibility for one's actions is highly ambiguous. You can explain being late for a meeting in terms of things that happened to you (such as a traffic jam) or in terms of choices you made (such as to set the alarm clock earlier, or not). The point of this exercise is to exploit this fundamental ambiguity in order to increase your ability to choose at will among under- and over-responsible states of being. This exercise requires some ingenuity and creative construction of arguments, so you

might want to rehearse some of the moves in advance, with pen and paper. Here, then, is the exercise –

For *one week*, when talking to all other people, account for your own actions *solely* in terms of external factors: things that have happened *to* you, or are about to happen, or are now happening. Ingenuity is required here because you'll trying as hard as you can to *not lie*. Late? Blame it on the traffic (if the traffic was indeed bad), or on the misfiring alarm clock (if that was indeed the case), or on the fact that you *had* to go to sleep later than usual because of an emergency task or assignment (if that was actually true). Now, *flip*. For *one week*, go into *overresponsible* mode, taking responsibility for events that, normally, you would explain or justify in terms of external factors. Does the *other person* get angry with you (as evidenced by thinning lips, blushing, and dilated pupils)? *Actively* take responsibility for his emotional state by *naming* some action of yours that led him to feel angry. Late? Blame it on *your* not having set the clock at the right time, on *your* not having had the foresight to plan your assignments so that you'd be able to get enough sleep. *Keep a journal* of what happens during the two weeks. Repeat until you are able, at any given point in time, to explain your own actions using *either* the over- or the under-responsible strategy.

3 Mental Meliorism, or Stretching the Mind's Eye

The Mind Has a Window ...

Your mind has a window, through which it experiences the world. The edges of this window are hidden in such a way that you can see *through* the window but can't – without some training – see the window *itself*.

Let's try to describe the window by means of a graph. On the horizontal axis, plot *how much* you know: the total number of covarying entities or variables that are *salient* to you and that your mind makes use of *in real time* as it thinks. This axis measures the breadth of your mind: how much you can take into account when thinking, without panicking or losing interest – that is, without becoming too anxious or too bored to keep on thinking. For example, if you can memorize one or more entire phone numbers (including area codes), your mind's memory can hold within it at least seven independent chunks of information while performing a simple task, such as copying that information onto a keypad as you dial. If you play chess at masters' level, you can probably hold in your mind at least seven or eight possible 'scripts' for each move, each script consisting of a sequence of three or four forward moves by each of the two players. (Herbert Simon estimates that a chess grand master stores about fifty thousand different chunks of information in his memory; however, that person will not have to *deploy* all of this knowledge at any one time; so a more realistic estimate of the number of independent information chunks that make up the actually working memory of a chess grand master is much lower.)

Now for the height of the window. On the vertical axis, plot the level of difficulty of the tasks your mind carries out while it thinks: how many operations per unit of knowledge your mind can correctly perform in order to arrive at 'answers.' This measures the *depth* of your mind: the amount of 'pure thinking' you can or are willing to do without panicking or losing interest, given a certain amount of information. For instance, ordering a random list of names according to rank or alphabetical order will take you $n \cdot log_2(n)$ operations to carry out, or $log_2(n)$ operations per name. By contrast, figuring out how to play 'the perfect' chess game – the game that wins against all possible other chess games – will require a very large number of basic steps to solve. Even though this problem can be solved in a finite number of steps, that finite number is so large that it has yet to be calculated.

Now put the two axes together (Figure 3.1). Let's mark the hypothetical points where your mind 'caves in' from too much complexity B^*, D^*. The quadrangle [0,0], [B^*,0], [B^*,D^*], [0,D^*] constitutes your mind's *window* on the world. You 'see' only what is *inside* the window. You can't see what's *outside* your current window – unless you work at enlarging it by making your mind broader or deeper or (ideally) both together.

... the Window Seems to Be Fixed ...

We're now ready to take in some sobering news, courtesy of John Holland and his colleagues: most people (whatever that means) can only keep track of, at most, *three* covarying variables at the same time.

That's rather disappointing: if you're a CEO for a manufacturing corporation whose quarterly profits, market share, and advertising and R&D expenses covary even in simple ways; *and* if you vary your choice of 'generic' strategies ('profit from the core,' 'unrelated diversification,' etc.); *and* if you have to make 'real-time' decisions (as you would during a top-management meeting or a meeting with three or four key investors whose interests you have to balance and co-opt) that affect these variables (and perhaps the ways in which they covary); *and* if you're part of the 'most people' group (a good, modest assumption), then you're up the creek without a paddle: you can likely only make *local* judgements that don't necessarily make sense when put together, then 'hope for the best.' What 'saves' you, of course, is that you don't 'know' you're making these mental choices *while* you're making them – they 'feel' like 'good judgements' or 'common sense' at the time you make them, so you can keep on functioning without panic (or worse). A queer notion of 'saving' yourself, to be sure.

Well, you might retort, what good is thinking about what I *don't think about* if I *can't* think about it in the first place? Sure, it makes one look

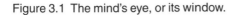

Figure 3.1 The mind's eye, or its window.

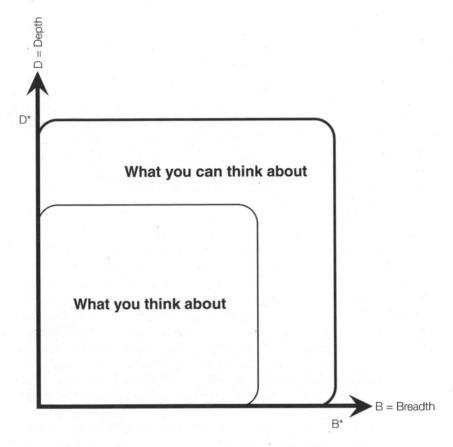

wise to talk about the 'unknown unknowns' of business, but in *practical* terms, what good does it do us if they remain unknown? The assumption on which this question rests, of course, is that they *have to* remain unknown and that you *can't* think about what you (currently) don't think about – which is precisely the kind of pickle that self-confident talk about 'most people's' patterns of reasoning gets us into: we confuse averages with laws of nature, and difficulty with impossibility.

… But It Can Adapt and Change …

Let's map different human ways of thinking onto our mind's window so that they start to look familiar. A logician – such as a software designer, a theoretical physicist, or an economist – typically invests in *deepening* her mind. She truncates the number of variables she concentrates on, and she spends more time trying to figure out the connections among them and their logical implications. She solves 'logically deep' problems: mile-deep, inch-wide ones, such as (supposing she's an economist), 'If all traders in a market were rational and interpreted relevant information in the same way, what is the equilibrium price of a commodity that has just started trading?' The mile-deep mind cuts through the messy complexities of human action and much of 'reality' – for instance, the reality that actual traders may well interpret the same information in radically different ways; that some traders are far more savvy than others (which these *others* know, so that they 'follow the leader' and get into speculative bubbles); that some of these 'leaders' may not trade on religious holidays, which can cause significant disruptions in the market and significant gains for those who are willing to speculate on this behaviour by the appropriate methods; that many traders may lack the intelligence to determine the logical consequences of their beliefs and/or the fortitude to act on those beliefs (or on their consequences, if they *have* figured them out) …

Need we go on? Needless to say, finance theorists have a field day examining models (again, inch-wide and mile-deep) of 'herd behaviour,' 'rational bubbles,' 'irrational bubbles,' and so on. Yet they remain anchored in a *sparse* set of assumptions and look at a *narrow* set of variables that are deemed 'salient': they all try to *explain a lot by a little* – the avowed aim of economic theorists, and perhaps of the scientific mind more generally (Figure 3.2).

Contrast the *mile-deep, inch-wide mind* with the *mile-wide, inch-deep mind* – that of the historian, the journalist, the salesman, the documenter of the particular and the immediate. He will not care a jot about explaining what he observes in terms of the 'invariant laws of human behaviour' – which, again, need to be 'few' in number. (Why so *few*? Well, we'll let you guess at that one right now, though it's a tricky question – one that Albert Einstein could not answer satisfactorily. We'll venture an answer in chapter 4.) The inch-deep, mile-wide mind is all about describing events 'thickly,' using many facts and many different perspectives on the same observations, and possibly making use of a lot of evocative allusions and connotations, rather than explanations and denotations alone.[1]

And, regarding enumerating lots of events: 'There's the sale funnel

Figure 3.2 The window of the mile-deep, inch-wide mind.

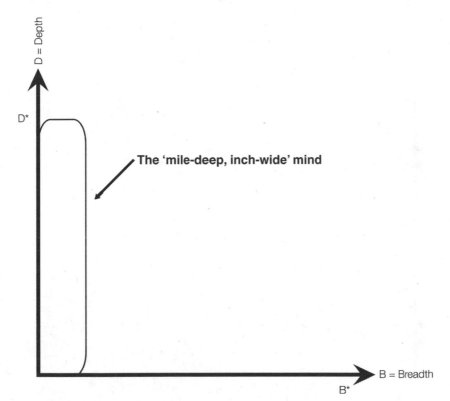

size to consider. And customer *x* does not want the latest upgrade. So, where is R&D going with this? And I don't know how creditworthy the Middle East telcos are, so I cannot hang my quota on them. And …' says the mile-wide, inch-deep mind of the salesman. One feels like stopping the avalanche of 'ands,' bringing the facts together somehow, deepening the logic that holds it all together.

Not that this proclivity is limited to sales and marketing people. The student of managerial action needs to get into *who knew whom*, and *who knows what* (and *how*); he needs to get into (even more important) who knew what *when* – because events happen in real time, not in some ethereal dimension that mile-deep, inch-wide minds love to concoct in . order to make their graphics and models look pretty. Because of this, he will care and pay attention to who went to whose parties, in what

Figure 3.3 The window of the inch-deep, mile-wide mind.

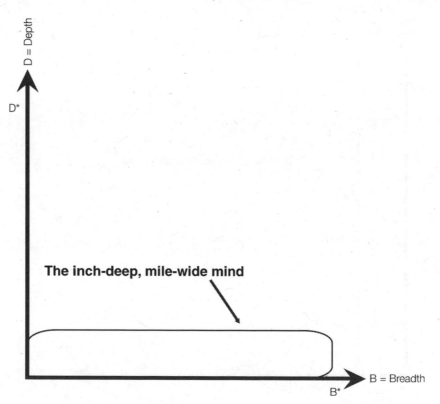

sequence, and to who slept with whose spouse – and why? And he will heed all of the possible ways that all of this can 'fit together' into a collage of images, sounds, text, and sensations that persuade not through the force of deduction but rather through the force of feeling and perceiving. The mile-wide mind does not care about explaining 'a lot by a little': it is perfectly happy to explain 'a lot by a lot' or even 'a little by a lot' (Figure 3.3).

Is there an unbridgeable chasm between these two kinds of minds? Are these two kinds of thinking and ways of being to remain in the splendid isolation they have been in since the minds of empiricists and rationalists started to diverge a few centuries ago? Can we not go back to the time when Plato could talk to Aristotle, even as they evinced profoundly different ways of thinking and being? The tension we have

Figure 3.4 Illustrating the tension between 'deep' and 'broad' thinking patterns.

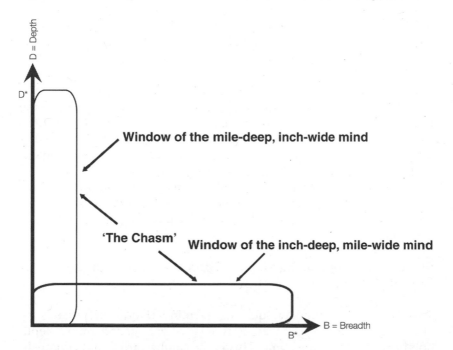

in mind is depicted in Figure 3.4. More often than not we were trained – as students, professionals, and practitioners – to simplify and specialize, but at the same time we're often rewarded, as 'people of action' in the world of business, for being closely connected to 'the facts.' This tension is hard to deal with. One often feels like asking the world, 'Do you want me to know a lot or to think a lot?' The implication being that there is a one-for-one trade-off between the two. But is there?

The question is not as rhetorical as it seems at first sight. After all, why can we not have a division of mental labour in business and society such that mile-deep, inch-wide minds do mile-deep thinking requiring no more than an inch's width of 'data'; while inch-deep, mile-wide minds do no more than an inch's depth of thinking about at least a mile's worth of data? Ponder the question for a while before proceeding further.

The answer: of course you *can* have such a division of labour! Indeed, we see it evolve quite naturally between experimental and theoretical physicists, between game theorists and behavioural game theorists, between engineering and design groups on one hand and marketing and sales and business development groups on the other. But all of these different groups rely on an 'invisible mind' that has designed the basic language, coordination framework, and problem statements they focus on. And this invisible mind is the *diamind*, which can see the advantages of mile-wide *and* mile-deep thinking and which can *design* problems, languages, and interactions that make optimal use of both styles.

Still, you might ask, 'Why is this mind necessary?' Why can't the logicians simply 'get along' with the anecdotists? Answer: *Because they need a medium* through which to communicate, a point of reference that both can accept as valid and that in turn accepts each of *them* as potentially valid. And that medium can only be supplied by this diaminded 'third person,' who understands both while *a priori* favouring neither. So now, to go along with Adam Smith's invisible hand, we have an 'invisible mind' – the diamind. How do we build one, using our 'window' metaphor?

Stretching: Bootstrapping Methods for Achieving Depth and Breadth Together

We can build a diamind by 'squaring the mind' (Figure 3.5) – that is, by stretching it, working our way 'northeast' to enlarge the mind's depth and breadth at the same time. This is the calling card and distinguishing characteristic of the diamind: the willingness to *resist* making the trade-offs between 'generalizability and goodness of fit,' between the ability to *explain a lot by a little* (the hallmark of the mile-deep mind) and the ability to *see and observe a lot,* come what may. The typical stance of the diamind is to add detail and texture when faced with 'deep' theories and to think deeply when faced with a lot of information: to 'go wide' when faced with deep thoughts and to 'go deep' when faced with wide thoughts.

To see how mind stretching works in 'real-time,' consider Richard Feynman's autobiographical account of a seemingly miraculous episode of computational clairvoyance:[2]

> One day at Princeton I was sitting in the lounge and overheard some mathematicians talking about the series for e^x, which is $1 + x + \frac{x^2}{2!} + \frac{x^3}{3!}$. Each term you get by multiplying the preceding term by x and dividing the next number. For example, to get the next term after $\frac{x^2}{4!}$ you multiply that term by x and divide by 5. It's very simple. When I was a kid I was

Figure 3.5 How mind-stretching works, pictorially speaking.

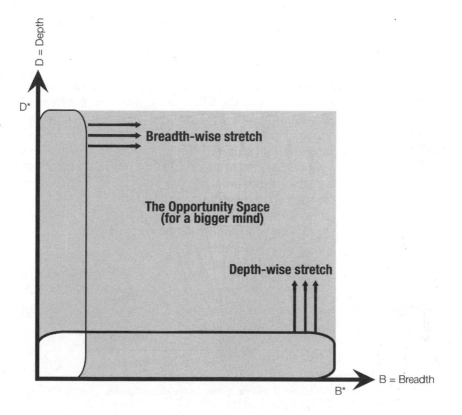

excited by series, and had played with this thing. I had computed e using that series, and had seen how quickly the new terms became very small. I mumbled something about how it was easy to calculate e to any power using that series (you just substitute the power for x).

'Oh, yeah?' they said, 'Well, then, what's e to the 3.3?' said some joker – I think it was Tukey.

I say, 'That's easy. It's 27.11.'

Tukey knows it isn't so easy to compute all that in your head. 'Hey! How'd you do that?'

Another guy says, 'You know Feynman, he's just faking it. It's not really right.'

They go to get a table, and while they're doing that, I put on a few more figures: '27.1126,' I say.

They find the table. 'It's right! But how'd you do it?'

'I just summed the series.'

'Nobody can sum the series that fast. You must just happen to know that one. How about e to the 3?'

Now, Feynman was what one might consider – in the world of business – an 'ultimate' deep thinker: a mile-deep, inch-wide mind of the type one expects to find only in the Chief Technical Officer offices of large technology firms. He was a physicist's physicist, not necessarily because he won the Nobel Prize in his field, but because he was known in particular for bringing deep thinking to bear on any problem – whether he was modelling electrons or figuring out what made the space shuttle *Challenger* blow up in 1986 (while serving on the Presidential Commission appointed to investigate the accident).

He knew that 'e to the 3' was 'hard stuff' – logically speaking – and he knew his interlocutors knew it too. So he bought a little time.[3]

'Look,' I say. 'It's hard work! Only one a day!'

'Hah! It's a fake!' they say happily.

'There's some trick': the mile-deep mind is 'not enough' to pull this off – they say. Or, is it? But, then:

'All right,' I say, 'It's 20.085.'

I say, 'It's hard work, but for you, OK. It's 4.05.'

As they're looking it up, I put on a few more digits and say, 'And that's the last one for the day!' and walk out.

'There's no trick' – they reason now – since no single trick can seemingly account for all of these complicated calculations at lightning speed. Or is there? Back to Feynman for an explanation of the 'advantage play':

What happened was this: I happened to know three numbers – the logarithm of 10 to the base e (needed to convert numbers from base 10 to base e), which is 2.3026 (so I knew that e to the 2.3 is very close to 10), and because of radioactivity (mean-life and half-life), I knew the log of 2 to the base e, which is 0.69315 (so I also knew that e to the 0.7 is nearly equal to 2). I also knew e (to the 1), which is 2.71828.

The first number they gave me was e to the 3.3, which is e to the 2.3 – ten

– times e, or 27.18. While they were sweating about how I was doing it, I was correcting for the extra 0.0026 – 2.3026 is a little high.

I knew I couldn't do another one; that was sheer luck. But then the guy said e to the 3: that's e to the 2.3 times e to the 0.7, or ten times two. So I knew it was 20 point something, and while they were worrying how I did it, I adjusted for the 0.693.[4]

The diamind is *stretchable*, and it uses the following stretching principle: use *calculating* and *remembering* as manoeuvrable building blocks for *thinking*. You can buy more insight by optimally mixing and matching *calculating* and *remembering* to produce the desired outcome. Of course, Feynman was a *real* thinker – that is, a *tinkerer* who tried tirelessly to *figure things out*. He had figured out the basic principle behind the mind-stretching technique by observing another 'stretcher' – Hans Bethe – at work:

> When I was at Los Alamos I found out that Hans Bethe was absolutely topnotch at calculating. For example, one time we're putting some numbers into a formula, and got to 48 squared. I reach for the Marchant calculator, and he says, 'That's 2300.' I began to push the buttons, and he says, 'If you want it exactly, it's 2304.'
>
> The machine says 2304. 'Gee! That's pretty remarkable!' I say.
>
> 'Don't you know how to square numbers near 50?' he says. 'You square 50 – that's 2500 – and subtract 100 times the difference of your number from 50 (in this case it's 2), so you have 2300. If you want the correction, square the difference and add it on. That makes 2304.'[5]

So he had figured out that *someone else* could do it, and he had also figured out how that someone else did it – by following this basic principle: '*thinking = remembering + calculating*.' To figure out a lot very quickly, one has to use memory and computation as building blocks for thinking and thereby *configure one's mind* as an instrument suited to the task at hand.

More pedestrian examples: If you have to calculate 2^6 and you know nothing else, then you have to compute 'from scratch' – $2 \times 2 = 4 \times 2 = 8 \times 2 = 16 \times \dots$ – all the while *counting* the number of times you're multiplying 2 by itself. But if you know *certain* powers of 2, like 2^5 (32), 2^{10} (1,024), and 2^{16} (32,768), then all you need to do to get 2^6 is multiply 32 by 2, to get 2^9 is divide 1,024 by 2, and so forth. Get it? *Get good at the switcheroo!* – that is, at adaptively switching back and forth between *remembering* and *calculating*.

Would you like a more practical example – one that's useful in day-to-day practice? Okay: how long does it take for $1 million to double in value at a compound interest rate of 25 per cent? Finance students will get out their calculators or laptops (preprogrammed, of course), but the 2 minutes and 35 seconds it takes for the laptop to boot is way too long in the midst of a final negotiation for buying 10 per cent of FastFlyer. com. That is *not* what seasoned investment bankers do: they have a simple rule that optimally combines remembering with calculating, as follows: if you want to know how many years it takes for an investment to double in value at a compound rate of Y per cent, just divide 71 by Y. So, 2.8 for a Y of 25. Of course, when you ask any professional what it is that makes her do what she does as well as she does it, she will give you *theories;* then, when you watch her in action, in the real-time tumult of her life, the only thing you will see is a set of *tricks*. And there will be a method to those tricks: they will all be *mind stretchers*. At stake in figuring out how mind stretching works is no less than achieving 'a better mind' – one that can remain connected to 'reality' while retaining the ability to think its way past the immediate pull of various elements of that reality.

For a number of reasons that don't bear detailed treatment here, psychological science is at a loss to describe the workings of the diamind; but literature is not. Want to watch a mile-deep mind stretch itself to cover a hundred miles' worth of new facts? Listen to how the mind of Swiss playwright and novelist Friedrich Durrenmatt unfolds its workings:

> The Caliph Harun al-Rashid and his Grand Vizier were hard pressed by the Christians, in that the Christians, who knew how to whip themselves into a battlefield frenzy by partaking of alcoholic beverages before battle, had a slight advantage over them. The caliph and his Grand Vizier decided to use scientific means to get at the root of the matter, and the holy Imam, a great scholar of the Koran, granted them permission to drink several captured bottles of Châteauneuf-du-Pape for research purposes. After they had drilled themselves thoroughly in Christian battle tactics, having drunk three bottles of Châteauneuf-du-Pape they began – neither knew just why – to speak of women. The grand Vizier owned a beautiful slave girl, whom the Caliph demanded he give him as a present. The Grand Vizier swore by the beard of the Prophet that he would not give his slave girl away. The Caliph declared his readiness to buy the slave girl; the Grand Vizier, strangely stubborn, which was quite out of character for

him, swore by the beard of the prophet that he would not sell her. After two more bottles of Châteauneuf-du-Pape, the Caliph likewise swore by the beard of the Prophet that the slave girl would be his personal property that very night.

No sooner had he uttered his oath, than they both stared at one another in alarm – each had sworn by the beard of the prophet the opposite of what the other had sworn. They summoned the holy Imam, who entered weaving and reeling, for he too had been allowed to take along a few bottles of Châteauneuf-du-Pape for research purposes. The Caliph and the Grand Vizier explained their dilemma to the holy man.

The Imam yawned. 'Great Caliph' – he said – 'the problem is easily solved. The Grand Vizier shall sell you one half of the slave girl and give you the other half, and thus he will not have broken his oath; for what he swore by the beard of the prophet was neither to sell nor give away the entire slave.'

The Imam was rewarded with a hundred pieces of gold and he went home. The Caliph and the Grand Vizier drank another bottle of Châteauneuf-du-Pape, and the slave girl was led in. She was so beautiful that the Caliph swore, unfortunately once again by the beard of the Prophet, that he would sleep with her that very night.

The Grand Vizier turned pale, uncorked another bottle of Châteauneuf-du-Pape, in the name of science, and mumbled thickly, 'O mighty Caliph, you have sworn a new impossible oath by the beard of the Prophet, for the girl is still a virgin; and by the law of the Koran, you may first sleep with her only after rites lasting several days.' The dismayed Caliph summoned the Imam. The holy lawyer, awakened now for the second time, listened to the tale of woe.

'Great Caliph,' he said, 'easy as ABC. Call a male slave.' The slave was called and stood quivering at attention before the Caliph. 'Give the girl to be this slave's wife,' commanded the Imam. The Caliph obeyed. 'Now the slave shall express his desire,' the holy man continued, to be allowed to divorce this girl. You shall perform the divorce, and, according to the law of the Koran, you may sleep with a divorced woman any time you wish.'

But the girl was so beautiful that the slave refused to divorce her. The Caliph offered him money, ten pieces of gold, in vain; the slave remained obstinate.

The great Imam shook his head. 'Great Caliph,' he yawned sadly, 'how meager is your knowledge; nothing can impede the law of the Koran. There are still two possibilities. Hang the slave and bed his widow whenever you please, for the widow of a hanged man is without honor.'

'And the second possibility?' asked the Caliph.

'Free the slave girl,' the Imam calmly commanded.

'She is a free woman,' said the Caliph.

'You see,' the Imam asserted, 'now you can divorce her from the slave against his will, since she is a free woman and he is a slave; and the marriage between a free man and a slave woman or between a slave and a free woman can be dissolved at any time – there is no telling what would become of our social order otherwise. And now I am finally going to get some sleep.'

The great lawyer was paid a thousand pieces of gold; he bade them good night and departed. The Grand Vizier had fallen asleep by now and was borne out of the palace; the slave was hanged anyway; and the Caliph Harun al-Rashid was left alone with his beautiful, freed slave girl and the last bottle of Chateauneuf-du-Pape.[6]

What makes the Imam's a worthwhile mind to model and emulate is the nimbleness with which its model of the situation adapts to the ever-changing landscape of 'immutable facts.' Sure, this mind works according to a 'theory' in which it is well schooled – the law of the Koran. It can quickly and masterfully figure out the *consequences* and implications of these assertions to the situation at hand, by interpreting emerging facts in the light of agreed-upon rules – it is, in this sense, 'mile-deep.' Moreover, it can do so *quickly:* it thinks 'on its feet,' as a recruiter of MBA graduates would say of a successful interviewee, so that it can afford to behold a large number of emerging facts without feeling overwhelmed – and in this sense it is mile-wide. There is something that remains constant in its thinking – the 'rules' – whose entrenchment gives the Imam his authority. Yet his instructions change in real time, closely tracking changes in the situation, without doing any harm to the rules on which they're based.

See? A bigger mind *is* an identifiable and describable way of being – one that *you cannot pay too much for*, because its usefulness shines through in the very ways in which we describe it. One does not really need 'an empirical study' to determine whether the ability to 'think on one's feet' like the Grand Imam of our story is a useful trait – whether or not a mile-wide, mile-deep mind is better than either a mile-deep, inch-wide mind or a mile-wide, inch-deep mind: one can just see that it is.

'Sure, sure,' you might think – all of this proselytizing *on the basis of a fictitious story*. Moreover, you might argue, *identifying* a way of being is not the same as describing the ways in which one achieves it. 'Where's the mechanism?' you could ask.

Touché: you're right! So let us look at some *non*-fictitious examples and try to uncover the design principles underlying mental meliorism.

Angels, Demons, Chequers, and the Power of Inverse Thinking

Here is a typical interview question (slightly adapted) that recruiters of MBAs – especially consultants and investment bankers – use to test the ability of their interviewees to think *on* their feet rather than *with* their feet:

> You find yourself in front of two doors. [Don't worry about *how* and *why* – though it's tempting, is it not?] Behind the first door, there lies Hell. Behind the second door, there is Elysium. In case you're wondering, you want door number 2. The problem is that the two doors are not clearly labelled (or the labels have faded with time). In front of each door stands a nondescript Creature. One of the Creatures is a demon. The other is an angel. One Creature [usually the angel] always tells the truth. The demon, on the other hand, always tells the opposite of the truth [sometimes incorrectly called a 'lie' – 'incorrectly' because 'the opposite of the truth' bears a simple deterministic relationship to the truth and is, in fact, a *pointer* to the truth; a lie is far more devious than 'the opposite of the truth' because it contains no such pointer]. The two Creatures are your only sources of information about which door leads where. Now, you can only ask one question of either one of the two Creatures in order to figure out which door to open. Whom do you ask what – and what do you do after receiving the answer?

The startled interviewee is asked to cogitate on this. (We hope our discussion of this problem will bring its career as a brain-teaser-of-MBAs to an end, and that recruiters will use their imagination to come up with something new – and better.)

Now, what most often matters to the interviewer is not *whether* you know the answer, but *how* you come to know it. Even more important, the interviewer cares whether there is something we can learn in the process of solving this problem that we can usefully apply to other problems. So, take a moment – if you don't already know the answer – and study the question. If you do 'figure it out,' try to write down the steps you went through in order to answer it. If you don't figure it out, identify the point at which you became 'stuck' in your thinking. Focus on that stuckness for a bit instead of trying to escape it by reading on: What does it *feel* like, *why* do you think it feels that way, and what does the mind want to do to try to escape it? Watch your mind: What is it doing?

This problem is typical of the sort in which several variables – door 1, door 2, angel, demon, Hell, Elysium, question to be asked – have to be taken into account together. The path to the answer can be thought of as a function that maps those seven variables onto two variables: the answer to the question, and the 'right door' to go to.

Now, seven is an interesting number: it is exactly what psychologists have found to be the greatest number of independent chunks of information that 'most people' can keep in their short-term memory, and three greater than the number of codependent variables that 'most humans' can keep track of competently. So this problem is a 'stretch' both for both the inch-wide, mile-deep mind and for the mile-wide, inch-deep mind. As a 'mind stretch' problem, it tests whether the interviewee's mind can stretch to the boundaries of what 'most humans' can routinely do … unless, of course, she has read this book, in which case she will know that the category 'most humans' is a highly dubious one and that the stretchability of the mind is not born, but cultivated (and quite easily, at that).

How? Well, imagine that you've just solved the problem and that you now *know* which door to go to. What has to be true in order for you to just *know* that? Well, at the very least, the combination of the question you asked and the answer you were given has to *point* you towards the right door. The question you asked has to have been such that, if you had got a different answer, you would have gone to the other door. So your question has to have had a *binary* answer, such as *true/false* or *door 1/door2*.

You are in a good position to reconstruct the 'search space' of this problem – the space of all possible solutions. You know that the problem has to have a binary answer, so you can just limit your search to the set of questions with yes/no answers (Figure 3.6). You strongly suspect that the question should ask about the position of Hell or Elysium, so you can further constrain the scope of your search to questions about what lies behind the doors. Is there anything else? Well, if you assume that the angel and the demon not only always *tell* the truth but also always *know* the truth, then you might also consider asking one of the Creatures about the beliefs of the *other* Creature, about the beliefs of the *other* Creature about its own beliefs, and so forth.

Figure 3.6 Successive refinements of the problem search space in the angel-demon problem.

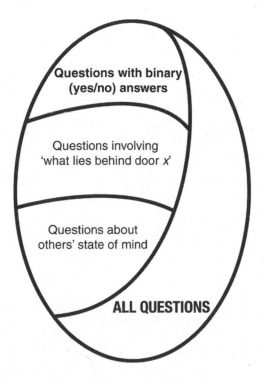

Now, how do you search this space of possible questions? How do you come to know which question to ask and what to do once you get to the answer? Well, you need to write down – and we literally mean *write down* – all of the possible combinations of *Elysium, Hell, door 1, door 2, angel's answer, demon's answer,* and *choice of door* that could result from asking either of the characters in front of the doors this question: 'Is Elysium behind door number 1?' This is in order to generate a constraint space, which here is a list of conditions that any solution within the search space has to satisfy.

What is a solution? It is a *point,* or a set of points, in the problem search space – precisely those that satisfy the problem constraints. How do you find a point in a space? Well, the simplest heuristic is to *eliminate* all of the *other* points in the space so that the only points you're left with are the ones you're looking for. And you do *that* by checking

Figure 3.7 Possible states of the world (constraint space) based on answer of angel or demon (x) to the question: 'Is Elysium behind door number 1?'

X says	X is	Elysium is behind	State of world is...
'Yes'	Demon	D_2	Possible
'Yes'	Angel	D_2	Not possible
'No'	Demon	D_2	Not possible
'No'	Angel	D_2	Possible
'Yes'	Demon	D_1	Not possible
'Yes'	Angel	D_1	Possible
'No'	Demon	D_1	Possible
'No'	Angel	D_1	Not possible

every point in the space against the constraints. Let's try it: start with the most 'obvious' question in the search space, which is, 'Is Elysium behind door number 1?' The constraint space (Figure 3.7) is such that there is no one-to-one relationship between the answer you get and the door you should try to open. If the Creature (X) says 'yes,' then Elysium could still be either behind door number 1 or door number 2, depending on whether X is a demon or an angel. The same goes for the case in which X says 'no.' There is, nevertheless, great security and peace of mind stemming from the fact that no question of the grammatical form 'Is Elysium behind door number ...?' will give you the right answer. Without this assurance, you would find it a lot harder to search for alternatives, because it is always tempting to retrace your steps and search one more time, just to make sure you haven't missed something.

What to do? Well, remember (a) that the diamind is as interested in obtaining a solution to a single problem as in developing a *problem-solving technology* that will allow it to solve many other problems, and (b) that the search space–constraint space technique is precisely such a technology. For now, the diamind has a problem-solving paradigm to work with: pick a solution from the search space, run it through a stress test in the constraint space, discard it if it doesn't pass the test. If you assume that both the angel and the demon are omniscient (i.e., that they know all that might be relevant to the problem – something that many of our recruiter friends don't realize), then you can go deeper into the search space of Figure 3.6 and ask: 'What would the other one say if I asked him whether Elysium is behind door number 1?'

How now? Well, the situation is decisively improved because there is a one-to-one mapping between the answer (yes/no) and the prized door: if X (whoever X turns out to be) answers 'yes,' seek Elysium behind door number 2; if X answers 'no,' seek Elysium behind door number 1 (Figure 3.8). It is the discipline of constructing the search space that has led us to the correct way to search.

What Charlie Munger calls the 'power of inverse thinking' can be understood as the effects of an enhanced ability to construct good search and constraint spaces for our problems – an ability we display when we can look upon the future (the time when we have solved the problem) as if it were the present (the time when we do not yet know anything about the solution to it). Listen:

> Generally I recommend and use in problem solving cut-to-the-quick algorithms, and I find you have to use them both forward and backward. Let me give you an example. I irritate my family by giving them little puzzles, and one of the puzzles that I gave my family not very long ago was when I said: 'There's an activity in America, with one-on-one contests, and a national championship. The same person won the championship on two occasions about 65 years apart. Now, name the activity.' Again, [to the audience] I don't see a lot of light bulbs going on. And in my family, not a lot of light bulbs were flashing. But I have a physicist son who has been trained more in the type of thinking I like. And he immediately got the right answer, and here's the way he reasoned: 'It can't be anything requiring a lot of hand–eye coordination. Nobody eighty-five years of age is going to win a national billiards tournament, much less a national tennis

Figure 3.8 New constraint space, generated by the question: 'What would the other one say if I asked him the question: Is Elysium behind door number 1?'

X says the other one would say	X is	Elysium is behind	State of world is...
'Yes'	Demon	D_2	Possible
'Yes'	Angel	D_2	Possible
'No'	Demon	D_2	Not possible
'No'	Angel	D_2	Possible
'Yes'	Demon	D_1	Not possible
'Yes'	Angel	D_1	Not possible
'No'	Demon	D_1	Possible
'No'	Angel	D_1	Not possible

tournament. It just can't be.' Then he figured it couldn't be chess, which this physicist plays very well, because it's too hard. The complexity of the system, the stamina required, are too great. But that led into checkers. And he thought, 'Ah ha! There's a game where vast experience might guide you to be the best even though you're eighty-five years of age.' And sure enough, that was the right answer. Anyway, I recommend that sort of mental trickery to all of you, flipping one's thinking both backward and forward.[7]

The 'mental trickery' involved here is the 'time reversal' trick. Suppose you've 'almost solved' the problem – in other words, you've already generated a search space that contains the solution. This is typical of problems that require a mile-wide, mile-deep mind to solve. Here, the search space is the catalogue of all possible two-player games that are sufficiently well-known in North America to warrant a national championship. Now search the catalogue. You will need to hold it in mind while doing so. Find reasons for or against a game being the right game, then proceed to the next game, all the while storing in memory all the games you've already considered. Daunting, no?

How can you search a catalogue more efficiently? Two things: First, eliminate as many of its items as possible, instead of keeping them around so that they weigh down your thinking. Second, break the cat-alogue into subcatalogues and pick the 'winner' from each. To *eliminate* possible solutions, you'll need to apply criteria such as these: 'The game can't require a lot of eye–hand coordination [billiards, tennis]'; or, 'The game can't require a lot of stamina [chess].'

The same criteria also provide good *demarcation points* for breaking the list into sublists. These sublists enable you to *configure your mind* to process the uncomfortably large search space more easily. Key to exer-cising such mental prowess is, of course, that first *leap* that allows you to take in the whole search space at a glance, which in turn is based on the human mind's unique ability to engage in time travel – that is, to treat the future as if it were the present.

Did you register that? *Look upon the present as if it were the past.* Then *look back* and – by eliminating all the paths you could *not* have taken – figure out how you must have travelled from the present to the future.

Okay, but what does this have to do with *business*? After all, could it not be the case that Charlie Munger is *self-deceived* about the mental proclivities that are truly useful to business success? After all, we start-ed this enterprise by stating up front that successful business people are not necessarily successful thinkers, and that successful thinkers are not necessarily aware of the foundations of their success. It is time, then, for a 'real' business story about time travel.

Howard Stevenson: 'What Do You Think She Thinks He Thinks I Think about It?'

But first, an anecdote – one that's plausible enough, given the protago-nist, though truth may not be counted among its merits:

A young man with an intelligent face walked up to U.S. Secretary of

State-to-be Henry Kissinger 'out of the blue' and asked if he would help the young man secure a job with a state bank. After exchanging a few words and glances, Kissinger decided to help the young man. He called up the chairman of a large U.S. commercial bank whom he knew to be looking for a new vice-president and mentioned that he knew someone well-suited for the job who also happened to be Rothschild's son-in-law.

The chairman was interested. Kissinger next called Rothschild – whom he had heard to have an unmarried daughter – and mentioned he knew a young man who had made a stellar ascent at a large American commercial bank and also happened to be unmarried. The deal went through – and Henry's credibility thus remained intact, having made his words true, rather than merely spoken true words.[8]

How do you know a diamind when you see one working, without having had the chance to see any results? Well, *audacity* is not a bad place to start. And what *is* audacity, besides a cool-sounding word? It is precisely the proclivity to make the abductive leap that takes one to imagine a desired state of the world that is implausible or even inconceivable right now – to take seriously the notion that this implausible state of the world is real and then work to bring about the conditions that will supply *the best explanation* as to how it came about. *Talk about the future as if it were the past* (sound familiar?)

Here, then, is a slightly longer movie, to take us from the *almost* real to the *really* real: It was the mid-1980s, and Howard Stevenson and his partners found themselves confronting a problem from Hell. They had just purchased the Lincoln Pulp and Paper Company in Lincoln, Maine, from Chapter 11 bankruptcy. 'Stinkin' Lincoln,' locals called the town, not least because of the pollution the paper mill pumped out. The partners had paid $8.5 million, of which they had put up $700,000 of their own money; the rest had come from a $1.3 million loan against receivables and a $6.5 million loan against the company's total assets from the Federal Street Bank in Boston.

They quickly realized that the critical bottleneck in the pulp production process was the capacity of the plant's boiler. Replacing it would increase revenue by $14.6 million per year – a 30 per cent increase in gross margin – because of the better-quality paper the new boiler would make possible. It would also lead to a 95 per cent reduction in the output of pollutants. The new owners estimated the boiler's price at $9 million. Babcock and Wilcox, the general contractor they had selected to build the beast, estimated that construction would take two years. If they could finance the project, they would end up sitting pretty atop a business 30 per cent more profitable and significantly larger than the one they'd originally bought.

If ... For when they went to the bank that had financed the acquisition in the first place, they ran into 'guidelines' that forbade the bank from making loans against more than 50 per cent of a firm's receivables or against more than 80 per cent of inventory. So it was a 'no.' *But* ... The bank did offer a two-year bridge loan, provided that someone was willing to buy out the mortgage at the end of the two years. What to do?

Stretch goes the instinct of the diamond as it expands the search space *along with* the constraint space. And the way to expand a search space is to *ask a new question*, one that's guided by the new set of constraints. Here, the question was, 'Who would go for a loan against future cash flows with an "incentive kicker" to sweeten the pot?' Insurance companies were known to do this occasionally, and Stevenson (now VP Finance) found several that were chomping at the bit, so much so that he got one of them – Hancock – to go for a cut of the profits generated by the new boiler instead of a dilutive equity stake in the paper mill. But there was a catch: 'No boiler, no loan,' said the Hancock execs. They would only make the loan after the boiler was built, or once they were convinced it would be successfully built – which, currently, they were not.

So much for 'stretch,' apparently. The bank had agreed to make a two-year loan provided that someone else agreed to buy it out; and someone else *had* agreed to buy it out, provided that the project the bank's money was supposed to finance would be completed.

How now? *Stretch some more,* goes the inner voice of the diamond. Stevenson learned that the U.S. Economic Development Agency (EDA) was making loans of up to $1.5 million to businesses that could show that the projects thereby financed would create at least thirty new jobs. Such a loan would reduce the bank's concern about the paper mill's leveraged position, provided it could be persuaded to treat the EDA debt as equity. But there was a catch: the EDA's decision to lend the money was contingent on 50 per cent matching funding from a local development agency – and (you've guessed it!) there *was* no such agency. How now?

The solution: *Establish one.* Stevenson and his partners took their case to the Lincoln City Council, before which they argued that the city would benefit significantly if the boiler were built. Jobs would be created, pollution would decrease, *and*, most important, an extra $180,000 per year in incremental property taxes would be generated. 'Sounds good,' the good citizens of Lincoln said in effect, 'but who's to say the boiler will be built and will *work* once it's built? That's what *we* need to know before we buy bonds in the deal.' A technical guarantor was needed, and Babcock and Wilcox were not about to be it. They said they could guarantee their own work but could not be expected to guarantee the results of the work of local subcontractors on the project, of which there would be plenty. How now?

Need we spell it out? The partners could, by this time, glimpse the fruits of their hard labour. They fired Babcock, sweetened the pot, added a kicker, and found a large, bondable contract engineering firm that would be willing to provide an unconditional guarantee that the project would be completed. City Council was pleased, and Hancock's executives were appeased. Municipal bonds provided the matching funding required by the EDA to go forward with the federal loan. This solved the bank's apprehension about the mill's leverage, which allowed it to make the two-year commitment, which in turn was safeguarded by Hancock's agreement to buy out the mortgage after the project was completed.

'QED,' one almost feels like saying – as if this kind of situational engineering is a form of logic. *Which it kind of is* – though it isn't the logic of *modus ponens* and *modus tollens*, but rather a logic of expanded search – of *augmentation,* as Keith Oatley has called it.[9] *And* – so we claim – thinking about the future as if it were the present or the past *helps* with this augmentation process. In the preceding story there's a sort of relentlessness to how Stevenson and his partners expanded the search space. It reminds us of how tenacious children can be when solving complex jigsaw puzzles: they *just know* there's a solution and that to find it they need to pose the problem in just the right way – that is, they need to set up the right search space. But it takes *confidence* to expand the search space. The future, when you try to address it, can look vast, ambiguous, and unknowable – indeed, terrifying – but it can be less of all of those things when you know there *must* be a solution to the problem you're posing it.

'All right,' you might say, 'that's just *one* story. How do you know it isn't a fluke?' Well, we don't *know* it isn't a fluke, though you'll have gathered by now (i.e., from chapter 2) that we believe that *knowing* is a pipe dream: all we can really go on are daring but testable conjectures. Nevertheless, if you'd like to see this again, here's another story – a slightly darker one, more in tune with our times. The protagonist is

Diminba (for 'diaminded investment banker'), a banker with a prominent New York investment house. In 2004, Diminba was retained by the broadband wireless start-up Flarion, Inc., to sell the business to the highest bidder. Flarion has no cash flows to speak of – like many high-tech start-ups, it has been losing millions of dollars a year on sales that barely break $25 million. Which means that any 'normal' discounted cash flow calculation of the enterprise's value will turn up a large negative number. Yet Flarion's technical founders have what technical founders often have, which is *chutzpah:* they have declared that they have the silver bullet for unlocking the broadband mobile wireless bottleneck. They also hold the patent – awarded by the U.S. Patent Office in 2002 – on a new technology called FlashOFDM, an enhanced version of a technology for turning digital bits into analog voltages.

Diminba already knows the 'algorithm' for selling businesses that fail discounted cash flow valuation tests: 'Create a list of potential buyers who want the technology, approach them through the firm's network of relationships, visit the ones that show interest, amplify the fears and hopes that could cause each to make an offer, create a bidding war between at least two of them, and sell to the highest bidder.' Had this been 1999 rather than 2004, the algorithm would have attracted multiple offers within days. But ever since the 2000–1 meltdown in dot. com and telecom stocks, the terrain has been considerably more arid, even in terms of companies that see FlashOFDM as the next-generation alternative to CDMA (for which big, bad Qualcomm has been charging predatory licensing fees amounting to as much as 15 per cent of top-line subscriber revenues). So the search space – which comprises firms sympathetic to the new technology, including Intel – seems to be the size of a handkerchief.

That is, until Dinimba applies the 'expand' operation we have already seen at work: 'What about Qualcomm itself?' he asks himself. He has sniffed out that Qualcomm is in the middle of a father-to-son hand-off of the CEO position. Most likely, this entails the usual anxieties, which raise this specific question: Will the father want to ensure that the upstart OFDM technology won't steal a march on Qualcomm over the next decade? Not that the question would need to be put quite that way. But as it turns out, the question is worth asking, for Qualcomm does indeed show significant interest when approached. One thing leads to another, and the due diligence process culminates in a $200 million bid for Flarion. Not bad for a high-tech company that lost millions in 2004.

But the bid isn't high enough for Diminba, who turns down the offer with a hint of contempt, which is meant to suggest that a larger offer from a competitor is in the making. Who could that be? Well, Intel's broadband wireless division – the guys and gals who brought us RF Home and WiMax – seems like a plausible candidate. Though Intel has shown only passing interest in the deal, Diminba makes a point of meeting every week with the head of that division on an 'informational' basis. Now he uses the information from those meetings to cause the managers of his one and only bidder to believe that a much richer offer from a feared rival is in the works. And he is able to do this without once having to name either the source or the competing bidder. The result is a new, $600 million bid from Qualcomm, exclusive of milestone-based project completion payments. This new bid is viewed as outrageously high even by analysts who are usually starry-eyed about Qualcomm's deep, dark genius for turning IP into cash flows. The 'expand' command has worked its magic once again: a non-existent bidder has become real – because it was real in its effects. The moral of this story: It isn't the validity of a fact that counts when you're trying to make things happen; when you're dealing with that great chasm called 'the future,' the *perception* that a fact is valid (i.e., its plausibility) can often be equally powerful. The *chutzpah* required to act on this is – quite simply – the willingness to reverse-engineer the causal chain that takes us from the humdrum present to the desired future. It involves relentlessly re-architecting the space in which we search for the paths that connect the two, which we call 'solutions.'

Now, for contrast and colour, what would a self-limiting – rather than self-stretching – way of thinking look and feel like? Here is a sketch:

You go to the bank to get a mortgage on the house of your dreams. You aren't quite sure if you're making enough money to qualify, but wishful thinking being what it is, and imagining the prospect of a nicer lawn, a better school for the kids, and a better kennel for the dogs, you say: 'Why not?' After all, you do have 20 per cent of the value of the house stashed in some liquid account, and mortgage rates are at all-time lows – or so you hear. 'And so they are,' confirms your friendly neighbourhood banker (FNB). Much to your surprise, it takes the bank less than a day to approve your application … and more. 'We can give you the loan, sure,' says your FNB. 'But why not take advantage of the all-time low interest rates, and instead of borrowing just 80 per cent of the value of your house, take out a loan on 110 per cent of it? That way, you could keep your down payment and use it to buy another house, which you could use as a rental property, who knows?' The suggestion

is intriguing at the very least. All of a sudden, the slightly shameless af-
fluence of some of your friends who seem to have borrowed rather than
worked their way to a postmodern (i.e., leaner but glitzier) version of
the American Dream seems to make sense.

'But I'm confused,' you reply with the last scraps of your scepticism.
'If you can give me 110 per cent on every property I buy, why would I
ever need to use my savings – or the extra 10 per cent kicker, for that
matter – for anything at all? And while we're at it, how many of these
things can I get from you?' The FNB smiles, a bit condescendingly, and
explains to you that 110 per cent leverage works for owner-occupied
homes – 'We want to feel like we have you, you understand' – but not
for rental properties. 'But of course, we do consider rental income as
income, and since you *can* deduct your mortgage payments here in the
U.S. of A. ...' You complete the thought for him: '... I can triple my
income just by waiving a paycheque and a savings account voucher at
you.' 'And don't forget,' the FNB smiles with incipient jubilation, 'that
real estate appreciates at 7 per cent a year, as the last ten years' figures
show, which means you're net positive year over year if you can get
ten-year money at 5 per cent – like you can do right now. So how exactly can you lose?' *How, indeed?* A no-brainer, that ...

... to go with another no-brainer. For no sooner have you signed the
four mortgage agreements with your FNB than the loan itself is off the
bank's books and into a pool of duration-matched securities that are
freely bought and sold on the market. *'Come and get it!* A $1.577 million
current-dollar thirty- or thirty-five-year stream of monthly payments
with an annualized 0.032 probability of default or cancellation, back-
stopped by the $950,000 current value of the house, which is expected
to grow at an annual inflation-adjusted rate of 3 per cent. Would you
pay 70 per cent of its face value for it to me? 65 per cent? 60 per cent?'
Seems like a bargain, no? Just add the probabilities – they come from
one hundred years of actuarial data on the consumption and living patterns of the American middle class (AMC), so how can you go wrong?
After all, he who has the most data 'wins' – at least in the sense of being
'most right' – no? Another no-brainer ...

... that fits well with the third and last no-brainer. No sooner have
you signed off on your shiny new bundle of AMC mortgages from your
FNB than along comes a Shakespeare-quoting insurance salesman: 'To
be thus is nothing, but to be safely thus' – *Macbeth* sounds eerily comfortable in a Canali suit. Guess what he'll be selling you: a package that
will really take the worry off your mind and really cancel out the effects

of the deadbeats and the bank surfers – you know, those subclasses of the AMC that give the willies to your FNB. And how can you say no to that? Chalk it up to another no-brainer. (This third no-brainer has other versions as well, some involving an investment banker who comes and offers to underwrite a series of put and call options on the value of the securitized debt, which jointly function as an insurance plan – for a fee and a kicker, of course. Same concept. Different suit.)

And of course, the essence of a no-brainer is that you don't need a brain in order to commit to it. It is simple. Linear. You can just hear your inner voice (or maybe it's someone else's) whispering: 'Why make it more complicated?' Notice that there is no patent 'irrationality' here, in any of the simple-minded approaches to the subject peddled by cognitive psychologists or behavioural decision theorists. Every single agent has acted on the basis of the information at hand, having weighed both long- and short-run interests. These interests are not in the same class as the ones involved a decision to try cocaine on a dare, having sampled your first Ecstasy tablet on your third date with someone you want to impress. The affective temperature of these interests is low. There is no immediate visceral reason for the mind not to work. In each case, a mind has thought through *the information at hand* in a suitable way. *The information at hand*, however, is whatever information is placed in your hand by someone else – so it may be better to call it *the information IN hand*.

The results of this concatenation of no-brainers are today well-known: an unprecedented tightening of credit markets in the face of a wave of defaults; and a self-fuelling decrease in home prices, housing starts, and home values; followed by a short-selling frenzy (remember those options?) on the equity of the security holders, the lenders, the insurance companies, and just about everyone else affected by the ensuing economic contraction. So, we have a cool little model for the massive destruction of wealth and value: localized, specialized, optimized problem solving, combined with the relentless pursuit of no-brainers (which does *not* coincide with a decrease in average brain size, coincidentally). Therein lies the essence of the *uni*mind.

'All right,' you might say, 'but would one of your diaminds, thinking the way it does, have done differently? *Better?*' Let's see. If one could have figured out that the base distributions (actuarial tables, etc.) on which the risk classes associated with various mortgages – which then figured into the discount factors affixed to the associated asset-backed securities – were not actually independent of the incentives of the AMC protagonists on whose micromotives and macrodreams the whole scheme turned; that therefore the cash flow generation (from regular and rental income) required to sustain both the growing demand for mortgages and the asset-backed securities based on them was not realistic; that the sensitivity of the value of the securitized debt to any of a large number of combinations of macroeconomic factors was of an order that would justify a massive discount on the prices those securities commanded; and that there were no countervailing incentives to exercise prudence and care in the entire value-linked activity chain … well, then, yes, one could have avoided being hurt – indeed, one could actually have *profited* from others' pain.

But that would have required the kind of stretch of the knowing/ calculating window of the mind that we have seen in our diaminds. It would have required scrutinizing carefully, two years ago, the data on which the FNB's prognostication of home prices growing at 7 per cent per year was based (a ten-year window). It would have required raising one's eyebrows at the fact that while just a handful of firms had achieved a triple-A borrower rating in American corporate history, *65,000* bundles of sliced-and-diced asset-backed securities (sliced-and-diced mortgages) had achieved this rating by mid-2007. It would have required looking at the zero-income earners who had qualified for jumbo mortgages purely on the promise of the continued increase in the equity value of the underlying house, with no 'out' in the event of a downturn. It would have required scrutinizing carefully the idea that dozens of years' worth of actuarial data on the spending, saving, and default patterns of the AMC would reflect their behaviour in a situation that apparently gave them the chance to wiggle out of the earn-and-spend grind of daily life. It would have required wondering at the mental models of traders who had begun to sell short the equity of many banks and insurance companies. These are precisely the sorts of 'stretch' manoeuvres that one expects from the diamind – manoeuvres that broaden simultaneously the information the mind considers at any one time and the depth of calculation one performs on that information – thereby expanding the window of the mind. Thus the fact that Empirica LLC was up over 100 per cent in current value during the crisis, and that the Baupost Group – the private wealth management fund that Stevenson co-founded, was up over 50 per cent – are not Black Swans, but *white* swans. To the diamind, the collapse cannot have been surprising, though predicting its exact timing might have caused a few nervous moments: not surprisingly, NNT speaks of the credit collapse of 2007–8 as a white swan, one that was both *ex ante* predictable and *ex post* explainable. From *that* window, at least.

You Can Do More with Your Mind Than Your Mind Thinks You Can … : Shakespeare, Durrenmatt, and 'Computational Augmentation'

By experiencing the future as the present, we get to use our far superior capabilities to reverse-engineer causal chains – rather than plan them, which we, by many accounts, as a species, 'suck' at. For instance, the following problem swamps many people:[10]

P1. We are all prejudiced against prejudiced people.
P2. Alice is prejudiced against Bob.

Problem: Does it follow from *P1* and *P2* that Chester is prejudiced against David?

Well? Does it? The answer is that it *does* follow from *P1* and *P2* that Chester is prejudiced against David. What is required to *just see* this is an operation called *recursion*, by which we apply an operation or rule repeatedly to objects, events, and even rules themselves ('I believe that I believe …') to get a new result. To wit: If Alice is prejudiced against Bob, then David – being part of 'all people' who are prejudiced against prejudiced people – is prejudiced against Alice, and Chester – by the same rule – will be prejudiced against David. The level of recursion required to get the result (i.e., the number of operations your mind has to perform to get to the result) is 3, a result that could be considered 'embarrassing' for the 'most people' who don't get it, until someone – like Robin Dunbar – points out that the level of recursion that actually *makes* a play like Shakespeare's *Othello* captivating is 5: 'Shakespeare *intended* [1] that his audience *realize* [1] that the eponymous Moor (Othello) *believed* [2] that his servant Iago was being honest when he claimed to *know* [3] that his beloved Desdemona *loved* [4] Cassio.' Or points out the level of recursion that gives life and zest to Friedrich Durrenmatt's *The Judge and His Hangman:* 'Detective knows [1] that the actual killer believes [2] that the detective believes [3] that the "officially" suspected killer knows [4] why the detective wants [5] to have the actual killer [6] pursue the suspected killer'; or to Durrenmatt's *The Physicists:* 'Man-in-asylum believes [1] that the asylum owner believes [2] that he is [3] in fact *not* the mathematician Mobius, although, he in fact [1] *is* Mobius, pretending [2] to be a lunatic in order to [3] catch a physicist who [4] is a patient in the asylum who seems to believe that he [5] is Einstein.'[11]

There is a tension here, if not quite a contradiction. How can complicated recursive relationships actually make narratives and plays *enjoyable* if, the moment we strip them down to their logical structure, they become tedious brain-teasers with no apparent point? Well, *the point* is the answer: the mind's work is *motivated* – thoughts are forms of intentional behaviour, even if that behaviour is not always consciously planned or executed. A narrative provides a structure of meaning that turns complicated recursive structures from pointless brain-teasers into 'point-ful' patterns of mental behaviour. In the process, the mind 'gets deeper': the ability to engage in deep recursive thinking is precisely the hallmark of the mile-deep mind.

... and You Can Store More in Your Mind Than You Think ... : Flaubert, Einstein, and the Turing Machine

But this isn't all that building thick narrative can do for the mind. Keith Oatley and Maja Djikic have recently argued that writing augments the all-important working memory required by thinking.[12] What *is* working memory? It is the memory you use *as you think* – hence the name. It's difficult to mentally multiply two large numbers (1,267 and 9,845, say) because doing so requires the storage of *intermediate* products, which, when summed together, give you the global answer. For instance, you might decompose the multiplication of 1,267 and 9,845 as follows: 1,267 x 9,845 = 1,000 x 9,845 + 200 x 9,845 + 60 x 9,845 + 7 x 9,845. From here, you might store the partial products and then add them to get the total product. Pen and paper help *a lot*, for they allow you to *augment* your working memory to hold the partial products that you will then sum. And the way to sum them efficiently is – as you might have anticipated – to use, recursively, the same approach: form partial sums, store them, then sum them. Boosting that reluctantly narrow working memory can work wonders for how 'intelligent' one's mental behaviour is. (Is it really that shocking that IQ is significantly related to working memory size?)

Oatley and Djikic argue that writing a novel is precisely the kind of mile-wide, mile-deep thinking task that can benefit from significant augmentation of short-term memory. As you write, you have to keep in mind each of your characters: their positions, identities, opinions, and ways of thinking, feeling, and acting – and that is only the start. For then you also have to see each character from the perspective of every other character, as well as the relationships among all of the characters as they evolve – and there are $n(n-1)/2$ possible links among n characters, which means that for a seven-character novella you have to track up to twenty-one possible relationships as they evolve as a function of the actions of each of the characters. Even a shallow, insipid, two-dimensional character (typical of light North American fiction) will likely display one of three possible emotional states, each leading to one of three possible actions, each leading to one of three possible outcomes that change the nature of the twenty-one possible relationships among the seven characters. Clearly, the search space you're facing (even as a budding, 'cheap fiction' North American novelist hoping to get on airport kiosk shelves, and having little care about poetic form, metaphoric content, and the rhythm and musicality of language) has just expanded to an unfathomably large $[(7^{27})(7^{27}-1)/2]$ possible number of possible relationships among the characters. Now *that* is room to play!

So, what do the Flauberts of the world do? Well, because of Oatley and Djikic's research, we can do even better, and ask: 'What did *Flaubert himself* do?' Which helps, because frankly, there aren't that many Flauberts around these days. Their answer: He *wrote in order to think*, rather than the other way around. The master novelist and stylist produced some *thirty thousand* pages of drafts to his novels and novellas, using each draft as a *working memory augmenter*, which made clear to him the problems he would need to resolve in the next draft. In this way every draft supplied him with a ready-to-hand rendition of his new search space, within which he could look for the *mot juste* that he became renowned for obsessively seeking.

Not that this sort of *augmentation* is an operation that we only encounter with novelists. Albert Einstein famously said: 'My pen is smarter than I am.' *Why*? Because his pen allowed him to see the intermediate product of thinking and in that way informed his subsequent thinking. If thinking about a scientific problem – as Herbert Simon urged – can be usefully understood as a recursive search in a space that varies in size as a function of the amount of thinking we have already done, it is clear that a fundamental constraint – in formulating the general theory of relativity as in writing *Madame Bovary* – is the working memory that stores, at any point in time, the search space you're currently facing.

… as Long as You Are Willing to Change the Way You Think about Thinking: Writing as Thinking – and the Strategic Use of Strategic Stories

When we ponder the model of *writing as thinking*, many of the pathologies of modern-day business practice appear as failures of augmentation. In this vein, the damage done by the communicative ethics of PowerPoint presentations – of using 'points' and 'lists' typed up on slides to summarize claims and arguments – to the substance and validity of business thinking is inescapable. Lists are the typical mental structures of the mile-wide, inch-deep mind. They're objects in terms of which such a mind thinks. The relationships among the objects on the list – and there are at least $n(n-1)/2$ possible ones among any n objects – remain hidden; and as a consequence, those all-important inferences that are the nuts and bolts of insight remain inaccessible to both the presenter and the audience.

We say 'at least $n(n-1)/2$' because there are different *kinds* of relationships among any n mental objects. For instance, we could have spatial ('right of,' 'left of') and constitutive ('part of') kinds of relationships that link together any n objects. We could have temporal ('before,' 'during') and causal ('is a cause of') relationships that link together any n events. And, as Aristotle was the first to point out, there are many different *kinds* of causal connections – for instance, *material causes* relate to what we currently think of as mechanical or physical causation, whereas *final* causes relate to what we currently think of as goals or purposes ('I did X for the purpose of getting Y to happen'). We could also have logical relationships between reasons and arguments, and these logical relationships could be of the deductive ('A follows B'), inductive ('A has followed B k times in the past, therefore it will do so in the future'), or abductive ('A is the best available explanation for B') kind. We could have *intentional* relationships ('A likes B,' 'B dislikes A'; 'A believes p,' 'B believes that A believes p'). Stories allow us to simultaneously reveal spatial, intentional, and constitutive relationships; lay bare temporal and causal sequences; and (often implicitly but no less effectively) show the basic logical connections among universal and particular facts – all of this while at the same time conveying, through tone and rhythm, the implicit emotional landscape of what we are trying to say.

A good trick, no? No wonder stories are humans' preferred vehicles for storing knowledge in memory. No wonder the strategic planners at 3M 'tell stories' – and have come to do so in a self-conscious and purposive way, as a means to add knowledge to information (instead of the other way around). As Shaw, Brown, and Bromily write, stories allowed strategic planners at the company to overcome the 'intellectual laziness' associated with the pointwise argumentation typical of the PowerPoint geek, in order to make clear the complexes of relationships that together make *insight* possible.[13]

But there are even subtler arguments in favour of making storytelling your own mental habit (and remember here our panopticon argument: the way you make something into a mental habit is to first make it into a communicative habit: *talking and writing shape thinking!*). What might these arguments be? Well, for one thing, the *grammar* of natural language is more (not less) sophisticated than the grammar of scientific and mathematical discourse.

An example, borrowed from Bertrand Russell: The question 'Is the King of France bald?' is one that few ten-year-old children would have trouble answering: 'There is [currently] no King of France.' But a system that plays purely by the rules of declarative first-order logic – which includes the one that says: 'a proposition has to be either true or false and neither both nor neither' – would have to state that the proposition 'the King of France is bald' is either true or false, which would simply be *inaccurate*. Similarly, such a system would have a great deal of trouble assigning a truth value to a proposition such as 'she *could* be cheating on me right now,' because in standard declarative logic, one only speaks of sentences with definite truth values, and this excludes the all-important class of statements we call modals, which relate to *possibilities* rather than to facts or actualities.

All of which suggests an interesting link back to the central problem with which we've occupied ourselves in this chapter – namely, 'How do you stretch your mind's window on the world?' The link is this: stretching the mind – a cornerstone of the diamind's way of being-in-the-world – is all about the wilful augmentation of the mind's faculties of real-time thinking (the vertical axis of our window) and beholding (the horizontal axis of our window). And augmentation is something we do more naturally when thinking in terms of narratives and trying to explain what already happened than when engaged in the prototypical managerial activity of 'planning.' The diamind constantly 'leaps ahead' of itself and of others. *Constantly* is the important word in the preceding sentence: mental meliorism is all about the mind turning what it currently does into what it may plausibly do – by *stretching*.

Exercises

How to Make Your Mind Bigger, with a Pen (or a Laptop) ...

This exercise asks you to record – with as much detail and precision as possible – your own thinking through a problem. It will help a great deal if the problem is a genuine one – that is, if it involves a genuine discrepancy between the way you perceive things *are* and the way you think you *would like them to be*, rather than some question you already know the answer to (and about which fact you are trying to make yourself feel good). Start from a simple articulation of the problem statement. Write it down. Now write down each of your thoughts as it comes to you. *Do not edit them* before writing them down: you want to have access to the closest rendition of a pure stream of consciousness that you can possibly produce, and also to wean yourself off the mental habit of 'thinking before you write,' which implicitly but misguidedly has been inculcated in socialized humans in the developed world. From time to time – ideally, whenever experiencing a feeling of 'stuckness' – look at the thought record you have produced. Audit your steps. Repeat, until you reach either a satisfactory answer or a conviction that no answer is possible given the information you currently have. *Compare* the problem-solving results you obtain by using writing-as-thinking with those you obtain by thinking without the aid of writing. Maintain the new habit for at least three weeks. *Compare* thinking-by-writing with thinking-without-writing as problem-solving protocols at various points throughout the three weeks.

... and Here's Another Way ...

Pick a difficult personal situation – one that led to an undesired or negative outcome for you. In written sentences, describe the situation in the way that you typically would when talking about it with a friend or family member. Next, figure out – and write down – the basic *causal structure* of the narrative you've written up: what caused what, who had responsibility for what, and why. From this point on, the exercise asks you broaden, widen, deepen, and otherwise 'thicken' your description of the event in order to expand the range of possible causal chains that you believe were at work. The idea is to write down a *microscopically detailed* account of what exactly happened, how you felt, what you thought, what you (or others, if appropriate) said and did, what the reactions of the protagonists to one another were, and so on. To do this, divide up a page so that it will serve as the 'canvas' on which you render your experience. An example follows:

	What I/he/she said	What I/he/she did	What I felt (visceral)	What I felt (emotion)	What I thought
0					
1					
2					
3					
...					

Next, reconstruct the causal chains of events that together made up the experience (in 'this caused that' form). Compare the new causal chains with the causal chains you created to summarize the original narrative. Have any changes to your narrative resulted from this exercise?

... and Here's How to Do It by Using Another Mind ...

Perhaps you've picked up on the fact that a 'deeper, broader mind' will help you 'think on your feet' more successfully. This exercise tries to 'go the other way' – to get you to develop a deeper, broader mind by forcing you to think on your feet in a carefully constructed context. Select a partner and prepare a fifteen- to twenty-minute presentation for her of an idea (argument, theory, or belief). The purpose of the presentation is to persuade her of the idea. A large part of the difficulty of making persuasive presentations is that opportunities for genuine interaction (including agreement, disagreement, clarification, and elaboration) are passed by because (a) the presenter focuses narrowly on the script of his presentation (saving on that working memory again!), which (b) makes the intended target feel ignored or neglected, which often (c) makes the presenter more apprehensive about the presentation, which (d) makes him cling even more closely to his script, which ... (you get the picture: the regress from here on is recursive). The point of the exercise is to force your partner to respond directly and forthrightly to your claims, while at the same time forcing you to respond directly and forthrightly to her reactions to your claims.

But ... getting an associate to give you feedback, especially cutting, negative feedback, is not easy (and the closer she is to you, the harder it is). So *arm* her with a deck of file cards, on each of which is written one of the following in capital letters:

WHY?   FOR WHAT PURPOSE?   BY WHAT MECHANISM?
SO WHAT?   I DISAGREE!   I AGREE!

Now, proceed. The rule is that your associate has to raise a card whenever it represents her reaction to what you say, and you have to stop and address her query, prompt, or disagreement as signalled by the card she has raised, up to the point where either (a) she declares herself satisfied that you have addressed the point, or (b) you both agree to a set of conditions under which either the difficulty would be resolved or the argument would have to be modified.

Carry on with the exercise for long enough to stop feeling any discomfort at being 'interrupted' in mid-presentation by the showing of a card. Then compare the results of your presentation (in terms of persuasiveness, connectedness) after this period with the results beforehand. Also, compare your problem-solving results (see the first exercise) before the training period with your results after the training period.

... or a Whole Bunch of Other Minds ...

To increase the complexity of the previous exercise:

1 Add people to the audience. Adding people with fundamentally different training, education, and so on will likely increase the complexity of your predicament more quickly than adding like-minded people to the audience. Adding people will often confront you with the problem of having to decide which concerns you will address first; this in turn will increase the number of problems you will have to resolve in real time.

2 Add cards (and associated messages). The cards above can be sup-
   plemented by additional cards, such as these:

NOT NECESSARILY!   ELABORATE!   TOO COMPLICATED!
TOO REDUCTIVE!   INACCURATE!   REDUNDANT!

... or a Whole Bunch of Other Thoughts and Feelings ...

In an even more complicated version of the preceding exercise, *affective*
reactions – not just cognitive ones – are signalled by the associate (and
of course, you must respond to those as well). The number of cards
increases yet again to include ones that signal affective responses, such
as these:

BORED!   TIRED!   ANNOYED!   FRUSTRATED!
ANGRY!   IRRITATED!   DISENGAGED!   CONTEMPTUOUS!

   Your task, in responding to 'feeling reports,' is to bring the participant who has signalled a particular emotion back into a state of being
able to follow the presentation (engaged, present, 'with it'). The exercise requires intense and keen concentration for all involved, as the
participants(s) have to take in the presentation you are making *and* pay
close reaction to their own thoughts and feelings (in order to signal
them in a timely and accurate basis). Also, *you* have to respond to often
contradictory reactions and thoughts 'in real time.'
   The 'radar graphs' provided introduce an even broader spectrum
of emotions and instantaneous 'raw feelings,' which participants can
choose from and use to signal their affective or visceral responses during the presentation. The radar graphs rate these presentations according to their 'positive/negative' (blue) and 'active/passive' (red)
characteristics. (The data on which they are based come from an ex-
haustive inventory of how 'most people' feel about each of the emotions depicted, with respect to 'positivity/negativity' and 'activeness/
passiveness'; see Shannon Seitz, Charles Lord, and Cheryl Taylor, 'Beyond Pleasure: Emotion Activity Affects the Relationship between Attitudes and Behaviour,' *Personality and Social Psychology Bulletin* 33, no.
7 [2007]: 933–47). For any given run of the exercise, you can choose a
subset of these emotions as the basic 'signalling alphabet' for the participants (by writing down the emotions you have chosen on cards and
handing them out to the participants beforehand); or you can give the

participants full freedom to choose *any* emotion on the radar graphs below, while you choose to focus only on a certain subset of them (the most 'active/negative' ones, for instance). In either case, the exercise will give you a sense of the 'real-time' emotional landscape of the communicative space you are navigating during your presentation.

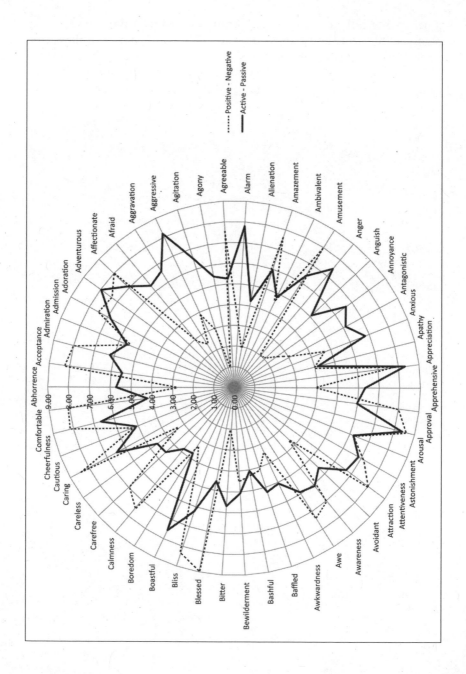

Positive - Negative

Active - Passive

Aggravation
Aggressive
Agitation
Agony
Agreeable
Alarm
Alienation
Amazement
Ambivalent
Amusement
Anger
Anguish
Annoyance
Antagonistic
Anxious
Apathy
Appreciation
Apprehensive
Approval
Arousal
Astonishment
Attentiveness
Attraction
Avoidant
Awareness
Awe
Awkwardness
Baffled
Bashful
Bewilderment
Bitter
Bliss
Blessed
Boastful
Boredom
Calmness
Carefree
Careless
Caring
Cautious
Cheerfulness
Comfortable
Abhorrence
Acceptance
Admiration
Admission
Adoration
Adventurous
Affectionate
Afraid

9.00
8.00
7.00
6.00
5.00
4.00
3.00
2.00
1.00
0.00

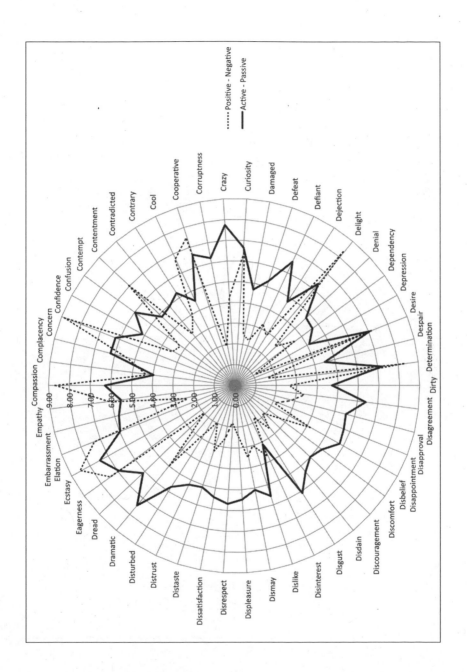

Positive - Negative
Active - Passive

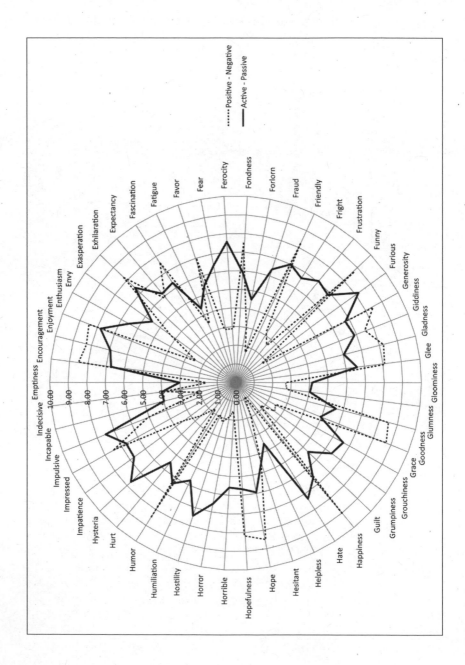

Positive - Negative

Active - Passive

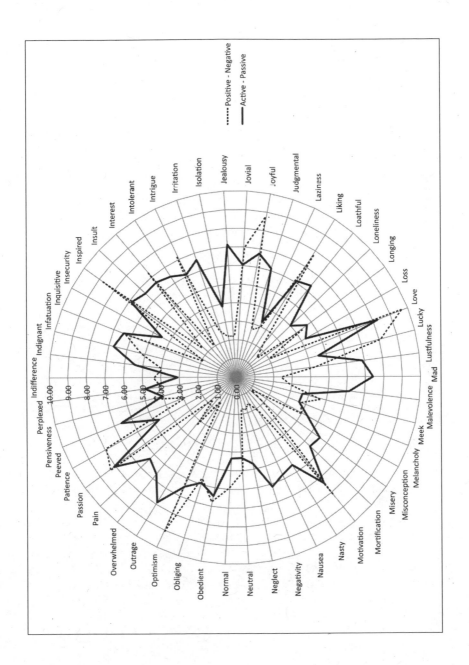

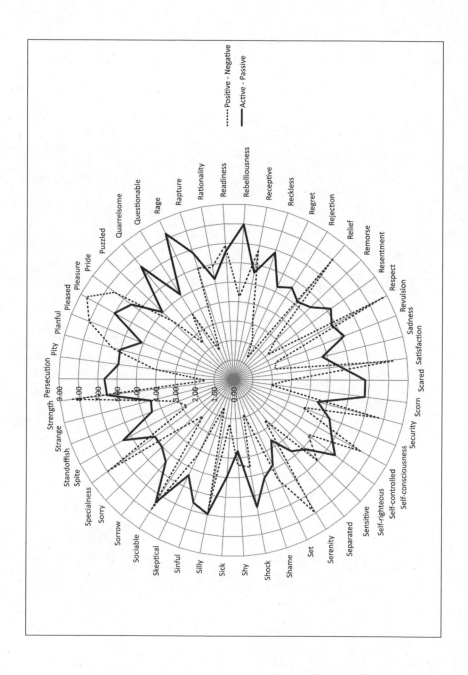

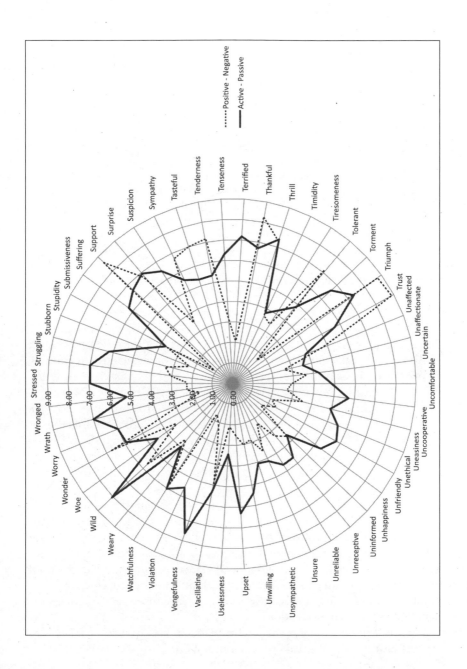

4 The Diamind at Work, in Slow Motion, Part I: A Repertoire of Mental Operators and Operations

> I want to understand everything.
>
> Sir Yehudi Menuhin

> You can [still] understand everything that can be understood.
>
> David Deutsch

A way of being is not yet a tool. It is a set of habits and predispositions to use the mind in various ways. It *uses* tools to actualize itself. This point is consistently missed by chaos, non-linearity, and complexity 'thinkers,' who exhort us to 'realize that the world is actually complex or complicated' without offering up anything in the way of actionable, palpable ways of seeing past the simplicity that the mind doggedly wants to read into 'the world.' Many of these thinkers have seen through the self-therapeutic assumptions that most people make – such as those of linearity, Gaussianity, and rationality – and have declared the world to be 'more complex' than these ways of thinking have allowed one to see it to be – but then *stopped there*. Even a cursory literature search reveals the staggering popularity of words such as 'complexity,' 'paradox,' 'chaos,' and 'non-linearity' in modern business and scholarly management writing, coupled with a pathologically frequent recycling of the word 'beyond,' whose occurrence in a title seems to be a prerequisite for writing a book that sells well. Many of us often try to look 'beyond' various ways of thinking and seem to derive a voyeuristic pleasure from the act – but what do we *see* when we look?

We see *stuff we cannot name* – empty space. We do *not* see a *lens* that would let us peer into this promising beyond; nor do we see a set of tools that would allow us to represent, monitor, and ultimately change the way the mind looks at the world, so that it might become more effective at operating in the realms that lie *beyond* linearity, Gaussianity, and rationality. Armchair philosophers often like to tell us that 'the world is more complex than we previously thought to be the case,' yet *in practice* we revert to Nietzsche's 'necessary illusions' when we have to *interact* with the world.

If we can't be good empiricists, we become *dogmatic ethicists* and declare that others *should* be rational, that they *should* obey certain rules when producing arguments and making plans, that they *should* assume that the world's event spaces are ordered in Gaussian patterns. This sets up a gap – nay, a *chasm* – between knowing and doing.

In this chapter we'll try to bridge this specific 'knowing/doing' gap by breaking down the patterns of thought of diaminds into *mental habits* – kernels of thinking/seeing/doing that allow minds to interact more successfully with this 'too complex' world. But before we start, it's important for us to be precise about how we're to go about mental habit–hunting.

As we've pointed out, mental habits share with Black Swans the characteristic of being very difficult to spot *beforehand* and very difficult to see as new *afterwards*. They're difficult to spot because they're so close to us – so close, in fact, that they *are* us! An age-old question stares us plainly in the face: *How do we see the act of seeing, think through the act of thinking, and know the essence of knowing?* Many people love to raise that question out loud, and to look clever while doing so; but once they have, they *ignore it and just carry on*. The idea here is to quit merely stating it and start thinking about it – *really* thinking about it – in order that we can then *do* something different and useful. So, stop and *think* before reading on: How do you go about seeing your own patterns of looking and seeing? How do you come to be able to think about your own ways of thinking?

The panopticon effect offers a glimpse of an answer: habits of thought turn up in habitual ways of communicating with others. We think in much the same way we speak. A lot can be surmised from the fact that quite often, thinking is 'imposed' on us from the outside; but it's also accurate to say that how we speak reflects how we think! The 'similar to' relation is, thankfully, symmetric: if X is similar to Y, then Y is similar to X.

Here, then, is a first cut at an answer – one we'll be refining as our plot thickens: it's true that you can't 'watch yourself think' easily, reliably, and without disturbing the very process you're trying to observe;

but you can record yourself while you're communicating (on video or audio, perhaps); and if you do so often enough, the self-conscious aspects of 'recording yourself' will no longer shape your thinking. Automatisms of thought – that is to say, mental habits – should then become at the very least *visible* as automatic ways of communicating, as *scripts* you follow.

But not all that's visible is *seen*, because to see, one must first *look*; and in order to look, one must have something to look for. Karl Popper often asked his students to just *observe*, and whenever he did, this question invariably came back: 'What are we observing?' 'That is precisely the point,' Popper would jubilate: to *observe*, you need a *theory* – a mental model of *what* you are observing, in your own language. The *what* is part of the *how*. That's where the 'special languages' developed by students of the human mind – cognitive psychologists, AI researchers, and epistemologists – come in handy. They give us *observation tools*, prisms on the mind that allow us to *watch thinking* in action.

We come, thus, to the second part of our 'mind-design' project: to observe yourself thinking and seeing, you have to develop a language for *representing* thinking and seeing. This representation language is itself a mental model and as such is susceptible to the usual caveats that apply to all mental models: they're *fallible*, and therefore they must be used with care and – in particular – with *vigilance*. This is because one of the mind's chief characteristics is that it's great at *foreclosing* the possibility of error – in particular, the possibility of catastrophic error.

You could, for instance, think of the mind's workings as a set of *computational states* of a machine – states that for their realization do not depend on any particular physical medium. According to this view – at present the most popular one in the mind sciences – the mind is similar to a computer – one, however, that doesn't need any specific hardware in order to run: it can 'run on neurons' as well as it can run on the transistors that make up the latest Pentium processor. But unlike a computer's internal states, the *mind's* internal states do not form *causally closed* loops: new information – including information brought on by moods and emotions – can, as Sartre (following Descartes) pointed out, be thought of as 'senses' for the perception of reality. So the mind-as-computer metaphor is suspect right off the bat: we have good reason to distrust it.

Nevertheless, that metaphor is *the best we've got* right now. And there *is* something magically attractive about the autistic way in which a computer applies the rules of logic to large information sets so that we can

see patterns we didn't know were there and make bold attempts to predict and master the terrifying Future – without becoming sidetracked
by 'moods' and temporary bouts of anxiety and panic. There's something impressive about the integrity with which a computer openly
'fails' and returns an 'error message' when it's run out of memory or
come across an 'infinite loop' it can't escape – instead of producing the
myriad excuses and justifications that humans in a social milieu are so
adept at generating on demand.

Finally, there's something incredibly *precise* about the computer's
ability to represent the world in terms of its own internal states,
and about the ways it can *manipulate* those representations in a truth-
preserving fashion: if the premises of its reasoning are true, then its conclusions cannot be false, because it doesn't make logical errors; if the
object 'table' is to the right of the object 'chair' in its working memory,
then if there are no 'forces' impinging on 'table' or 'chair' at any point
during the computation process, the object 'table' will be to the right of
the object 'chair' when the program stops running. By contrast, humans
who see a table to the right of a chair in a picture and who then are asked
'How far to the left of the chair was the table?' are more often than not
going to give a definite answer rather than correct the questioner.

In many contexts the computer is an ideal reasoner, because it was
built to be an ideal reasoner. 'In many contexts' does not mean 'in all
contexts,' of course: the great embarrassments of AI are with us to
stay and there for us to ponder: we cannot build a computer that has
even the powers of a human baby to navigate the 'complex environment' of a kitchen floor, precisely because the computer cannot use the
'seeing eye' arsenal of feelings and emotions that the baby routinely
commands. Nevertheless, the computer will outsmart the baby at any
well-defined game that has formally articulated rules, from chequers
to chess. And because the world is more like a kitchen floor than like a
chess board, the computer will – likewise – be outperformed by grown-
up babies in *that* world as well.

Clearly, we aren't advocating for the computer as an ideal of human
thought; rather, we're using the precision and integrity of computational models in order to study the hard-to-formalize aspects of successful
intelligence. We *can* and *should* try to learn from machines, and turn
AI – which has forever tried to get machines to learn from humans – on
its head. Not for the purpose of becoming completely like machines, of
course, but for the purpose of appropriating from them what is useful,
while preserving the domains of mental activity they cannot emulate.

So, a basic toolkit for researching your own patterns of thinking and acting is now in place. To make its use most effective, two self-modelling principles will come in very handy:

Principle 1. *To see yourself think, watch yourself communicate.* Really *watch* yourself. *Record* yourself. Create faithful records of your interactions – for example, videos and written, stream-of-consciousness recollections – that you can review later. From those recorded materials, produce screenplay-quality transcripts of your patterns of interaction. And while you're producing those records, remember your *precise* words and gestures during the interaction, not just some narrative reconstruction of your words and gestures. Most important, don't try to explain or justify your behaviour while you're recording it, no matter how unpalatable it looks or sounds.

Principle 2. *Use the mind-as-computer metaphor to build precise models of what you see.* To get precise, ask yourself: 'How do I explain what I'm observing to a computer?' Why a computer? Because it's an observer that can perform very fast calculations and hold lots of information in its memory, but that also has no prior knowledge of anything and (most important) no implicit *understanding* of anything. *That* is the true value of the computational model of the mind: it keeps us disciplined. To a computer, everything must be defined. The shortcuts and sleights of hand we use when talking to others or when thinking have to be made explicit or we'll get the implacable ERROR message. More important, *changes* in your thinking – changes that can arise as a result of changes in your emotional states – have to be signalled so that they can been seen. The neurosurgeon (or trader) who opts for the 'aggressive' approach to a procedure (or a trade) when sitting next to a person who is sexually attractive but for a conservative procedure (or trade) when sitting next to a plain-looking collaborator will have to focus on the *real* difference in environmental conditions when explaining his behaviour to a computer – that is, on the difference that *makes a difference* to outcomes.

Our approach to describing the inner workings of the diamind will follow, then, the inner workings of the software designer, who has to interact with the machine and who therefore takes nothing for granted. We will focus on problems as the organizing schemata for the workings of the mind, and we will introduce language for talking of problems as easy or hard, wicked or tame. We will describe solution-generating processes as searches in the space of possible solutions, and we will focus on kinds of searches – random and not so random – as ways of understanding the ways in which diaminds go about resolving or dissolving problems. By the end of the trip we will be in possession of a mind-tracker, an instrument that can tell us what is going on within our mind and allow us to build a bridge between ourselves and the diaminds.

With these principles in hand, let's start examining some of the building blocks of the analysis. We want to build a representation language for your thinking processes – a language that will allow you to do what we in the first chapter promised you would be able to do: think about thinking *while* thinking, and constantly and intelligently adapt the way your mind works to the ways the world works and to your own goals. Here, then, is that language – a 'mentalese' of sorts.

Problems. It might seem odd that we start with so common a word. But long use has blurred its meaning so much that it's often indistinguishable from 'issue' or 'difficulty' or even 'predicament' or 'situation' (as in, 'We have a situation here …'). So let's clean up the word, by calling a *problem* a difference between a *desired* state of the world and the *actual* state of the world as both are perceived by the problem solver (that would be you). Some examples of problems:

- Computing sums, differences, products, or quotients of numbers ('how to get from a statement of the problem to a state in which the problem solver is certain that the answer has been produced by a valid method').
- Persuading person X to carry out a certain action Y by the use of valid reasons ('how to get X to do Y by reasoning with X').
- Getting a person to carry out an action by whatever means ('how to get X to do Y by whatever means necessary').
- Designing a product or service to a set of feature and cost specifications ('how to get from a current state of knowledge and capability to a state in which external stakeholders are satisfied with the results').
- 'How do I come to lead a better life?' ('How do I get from the current state of … to a state of happiness, satisfaction, etc., subject to currently perceived constraints and conditions?').

Now, the following two 'factoids' might *seem* obvious, but they have extensions that often are not quite obvious.

Factoid 1. 'Minds are always engaged in problem solving process-es.' This echoes Popper's dictum that 'all life is problem solving.' He meant to include all organisms in this, not just humans. It also ech-oes the teachings of the American pragmatist thinkers C.S. Peirce and William James. If you believe this factoid is valid or at least plausible, consider this: Are *you* engaged in solving problems all the time? *All* the time? *Now*, for instance? If so, what problem are you trying to solve *at this moment?*

Factoid 2. 'Most minds are unaware of the problems they're trying to solve at any given moment.' Indeed, the conscious, controlled steps involved in solving problems can prevent you from solving the prob-lem of, say, balancing a trayful of coffee cups above your shoulder.

If these factoids resonate with you – if you believe they're true – then you're likely to agree that *your mind* is perpetually solving problems whose precise statements you often aren't explicitly aware of. *Agreeing* with this is one thing, but can you *feel* it? Can you *feel* that there is prob-lem solving going on in the old 'glucose guzzler' (a.k.a. your brain) and that this problem solving is guided by problem statements that can be only dimly perceived?

What follows is as much an attempt to introduce you to a structured way of formulating and solving problems as an attempt to get you to think about your own thinking *while you are actually engaged in it* – that is, to get you to *feel* what most people only *believe to be true* or think they know. To this end, we'll start with a typology of *problems* – of those enti-ties that guide our thinking all the time – and then examine the mental building blocks we often refer to as 'problem-solving processes.' We'll consider types of problems, types of solutions, and types of solution-generating procedures, and we'll reconstruct ways in which diaminds reconfigure themselves to solve 'the problems of the world' more effec-tively and efficiently than others.

Before we begin our discussion of problem types, a caveat: *all real problems are of infinite complexity.* That's right: infinite! How so? Well, un-like the 'toy' problems found in textbooks and in articles in the *Journal of Irrelevant Research*, real-world problems require that we engage with real objects, real people, and real events and that we map them onto a set of concepts, ideas, definitions, or pictures that are *in our minds*. And this mapping process is hopelessly difficult because it's irretrievably ambiguous. To do away with this ambiguity we would have to solve the all-important 'naming problem' – that is, the problem of attaching a name to an entity in an unambiguous fashion. 'Unambiguous' in the sense that how we attach the name to the object will not vary with context, or the social, cultural, or biological background of the listeners, or the season, temperature, air pressure, and so forth.

Take a simple object such as a hammer. You can hope to 'name it' by pointing to it and uttering the word 'hammer.' But that will not quite get rid of the ambiguity: you could have been pointing to its handle, or to its head. You can try circling the hammer with a gesture in which your finger slices through the air, meant to incorporate the entire tool in your pointing. But again, you could be pointing to the empty volume of space the hammer takes up, or to the slice of space-time the hammer represents. And so on: for every act of pointing, one can come up with possible alternatives.

Not all naming procedures lead to equally plausible results, to be sure. But the big question is this: plausible *to whom*? To successfully perform the act of *naming* – this basic building block of any practical problem-solving activity – we require the complicity of some observer who is willing to forgo an exploration of all the possible alternatives to the link between the act of pointing and the object to which the pointing is supposed to refer. Problems that *really* are of infinite complexity – such as the problem of naming – are *made simple* by this complicity of just the right sort of person to whom we speak. Otherwise, as Willard Quine pointed out, *reference is inscrutable:* you can't know what you 'meant' till you see what others do in response to what they thought you said.[1]

Solving real problems – problems that require us to make the leap from mind to world and its contents – is going to be an infinitely complex task in general, and only finitely complex in the right context. So when we discuss the 'complexity of problems' in order to get a handle on the problems of the world and the special workings of diaminds, we certainly do not mean that problems are simple, hard, or impossible *independent* of the problem solver's mind. Rather, problems are constructs – the best constructs, in fact, that we have come up with to capture the predicament of a mind trying to figure out the world and its place in it. One can always *choose* to consider more or less complex problems, but this choice is not one that all minds will be able to make consciously. It is just that diaminds are especially good at this because they know that believing something is always a matter of choice: they are mentally *choiceful* to begin with.

But if we recognize problems as *constructions*, will we not fail to take them seriously enough to apply ourselves to resolving them? Is not the belief that problems are *given* rather than chosen or – worse – constructed (which kind of sounds like 'construed') one of the 'necessary illusions' of the successful problem solver?

In a word, *no*. There's significant evidence that those who think about alternative ways of thinking about a problem before engaging in solving the problem do better at solving difficult problems than those who do not.[2] Furthermore, as we'll show, there's significant benefit to making mental choices among the types of problems you want to engage with in the first place. To take a painfully relevant example, if you're a CFO trying to raise debt financing in the midst of a credit crunch, how do you define your problem statement? Remember that a problem is defined by two sets of conditions: what *is*, and what you *would like to be* – the *less* desirable present and the *more* desirable future. So, what are your current conditions? Do you take the current management team as a given? The current shareholder base? The employees? What is the desired future state of the world? That the same organization that is in place today survive tomorrow, only with more cash in the bank? That the current directors will be ready to give you a glowing review *no matter what happens* to add to your already well-heeled reputation for dealing with crisis situations? Each of these questions points to an alternative problem statement. The *choice* among these alternatives rests, of course, with only one person – and you just know who that is.

We are all, first and mainly, *problematizers*, or problem framers, consciously or not. We are creators and formulators of our own problem statements. Which leads to this question: Can we say something useful about how to become a better problematizer? You'll learn a lot from our diaminds if you look at them through this lens. Read on.

Types of Problems. The diamind can *flip* at will among problem statements. It can see the world as presenting it with a simple or a hard problem, and thus it can engage the world either in *S*-mode – where predicaments are represented by simple problems – or in *H*-mode, where predicaments are represented by hard problems.

Simple versus Hard Problems. Simple problems are problems whose initial and desired conditions are clearly defined and for which the process whereby one moves from the initial to the desired condition is known and reliable and comprises a small number of steps. You can 'see your way' clearly to the solution. Problems we commonly deem

to be simple include computing sums and differences of numbers –
even large numbers; distributing or broadcasting information to a set
of attendees at a meeting; and producing an Excel spreadsheet for a
well-understood business model made up of products, revenues, costs,
gross margin, and operating profit/loss, having reached agreement on
the facts and figures.

You might think that computing large sums of numbers is not 'simple'
by the common definition of the word. But it is. Consider '1,234,567 +
5,678,910.' Sure, you might need to write it down and actually 'perform'
the addition, which is different from the mental processes that accom-
pany the addition '15 + 3.' But the crucial point here is that *you can just
see your way* to the answer. You know the steps that are required to get
there, and you don't need to go looking for steps that may or may not
exist. Adding in this way is like climbing a long staircase: you can see
the staircase – its starting point (1,234,567) and its end point (5,678,910)
– you know what you need to do to climb each step (add '1' to 1,234,567,
5,678,910 times). You know how to do *that*, so at the end of the day, the
answer is unambiguously 'gettable.' There's no fog in your way up the
staircase of addition.

Similarly, putting together the Excel model of the business once you
have all the requisite numbers of the business model worked out is a
clearly 'mappable' process. Again, you can just see your way to the end
state (i.e., the completed model). Whatever uncertainty exists would
be relegated to matters that lie outside the problem statement, such as:
'Will my laptop have enough battery power for me to finish on time?
Will the final profit–loss be something that someone else (such as an
investor) can live with?' But 'within' the problem you have set for yourself, there is, as before, no fog that blocks the mind's eye from seeing the
way to the answer, even if it does not quite yet *see* the answer.

Matters change considerably when we consider *hard* problems. For
these problems the initial and desired conditions are clear, once again.
You may even have an idea of how to get from the initial condition to
the final condition. *But* you can't 'see your way to the solution' before
actually solving the problem. There may be roadblocks along the way.
There may be missteps. Moreover, the number of steps required to solve
the problem is unknown, or there are too many for you to see past them.

For instance: 'You're managing one of five firms competing with one
another in four product markets, with similar input and operational
costs and facing the usual, downward-sloping demand functions in
each market segment. Each company has manufacturing capacity con-

straints that limit the total amount of product it can deploy in any market segment. What's the equilibrium set of prices in the four contested markets for each of the five competing products? Which firms will enter and which will exit which segment, and why?' Whatever that problem may be, it isn't *simple*. You can 'sort of' see the way to the solution (start by assuming that each firm is maximizing profits, subject to every other firm maximizing profits), but immediately, the problem of thinking about all the ways this could happen seems daunting – your search space is in some sense 'too large' for your mind to behold, and there seems to be no easy way to narrow it down.

Now the 'trick' the diamond pulls is that it can always *flip* between an easy problem and a hard problem as a way of thinking about one and the same particular predicament. *It gives itself a choice.* Faced with the pricing problem above, it may consider it in its full complexity, *or* it may look for a sequence of 'simple problems' whose solutions allow it to cut to an answer quickly.

For instance: 'Five firms and four products is way too large a search space to worry about. So I'll focus on the one or two markets in which I'm one of the two top firms ['simple': just rank the firms' market shares]; figure out the three top reasons why customers come to us rather than the competition [which can be done by polling customers who are "on the cusp," or, more subversively, by interviewing the competition's D and V-level executives]; choose a target of product price/features that "beats" a threshold of desirability or value; then figure out how much product I'll have to build in order to get to the cost of goods sold target.' In this account, there's no joint maximization, no thinking about the competition's best responses to my best response to their best responses to … to my first move, no search space that blows up, exponentially, as soon as the problem statement is understood.

The diamond has tailored its mind's eye according to the pragmatic constraints of the situation. Yet it isn't *stuck* with this particular eye 'shape,' which takes in a few variables and then 'cuts to the quick' with a concatenation of simple problems that essentially 'replace' the hard one. For instance, had that very same diamond been the principal decision maker in a large, unnamed bottled-pop manufacturer locked in a brutal duopolistic battle with a rival maker of a closed substitute, with billions of dollars of revenue, hundreds of millions of dollars of profits, and tens of millions of dollars of bonuses and options at stake in the process, then the 'hard problem' of thinking about what the 'other guy' is thinking you are thinking they are thinking you are thinking …

about the next pricing manoeuvre would have been very much worth formulating and solving, especially if every move down this chain of reasoning would make a few million dollars' worth of difference to the company's bottom line.

Of course, if the diamind can flip between problem types, it can also pick and choose which kind of problem to solve in which situation and then 'mix and match' problem statements. For instance, once it has narrowed the focus of the original problem to one or two markets and a single competitor, it may well become worthwhile for it to engage with the interactive reasoning required to get closer to an equilibrium price more quickly, or to exploit systematic failures of its competitors to figure out the logic of efficient undercutting. And once entrained in the process of thinking as both *ego* and *alter*, the diamind is, as before, not 'stuck in an algorithm' that it has to carry out to the very end ('The very end of *what?*' one often wonders). Rather, it can always 'break off' thinking in strategic terms if this is warranted by new information that might be turned up by that interview with the competitors' directors, and reformulate accordingly.

Tame versus Wicked Problems.   Simple and hard problems, as we experienced them above, are *tame* problems: you know where they begin and where they end. You know the initial conditions, and you know where you want to go. You even have some idea of how to get there: a clear one in the case of simple problems, a foggier one in the case of hard problems. Tame problems have already been *tamed:* they've passed through the sieve of our collective culture and education such that they're recognizable as *solvable* in some way.

Wicked problems, by contrast, are problems whose initial and desired conditions are subject to change as a function of the very process by which you're trying to solve them. 'An example?' you ask. Here's one (which we're willing to bet heavily will ring true with most managers): 'How do you get a certain person to do a certain thing at a certain time?' Note that the problem is not 'How do you *theoretically* get someone to do something?' (the stuff that many bad management and psychology books are written about); nor is it 'What's your *theory* of how to get people to do things?' or even 'How do you get people in general to do things in general?' (the stuff that many useless academic papers are written about). Rather, it's *specific* to a person, a context, and an action.

Now, this problem may strike some people as 'simple' and others as 'hard' – and therefore, in either case, as 'tame.' But it can productively be thought of as 'wicked,' because it asks you to deal with a very special kind of object (another person) with a very special kind of property (it thinks about what you're thinking about and may want to do things you don't want it to do *because* it knows you don't want it to do them, and it knows this because it thinks about what you want and can shape its own wants accordingly). This is not a property usually associated with objects over which we can exert comfortable control (chairs, pens, tables): Murray Gell-Mann once quipped to his colleague Brian Arthur: 'Just imagine how difficult physics would be if electrons would try to figure out what physicists wanted them to do, then decided whether or not they would like to behave in that way.' Well, *imagine* it!

As it turns out, 'how to get X to do Y' is *the* problem that keeps most of the CEOs we've interviewed up at night. Perhaps *that* is the most important argument for viewing it as a wicked problem – it does *wicked* things with the mind of its beholder. It is easy to understand why this must be so, if the definition we've given of a wicked problem is to be followed to the end: 'making it so' in the realm of *human action and behaviour* is completely unlike 'making it so' in the realm of *unconscious objects and animals*, because whatever mental model you deploy to represent the situation, *your subject models you right back*.

You have, to be sure, many options to start with. You could try purely *manipulating* the other into doing something – in other words, try to render her consciousness irrelevant to the outcome. In this case you would look for patterns of automatic behaviour that can be more or less controlled 'from the outside' because the subject is unaware of them, through the use of facial expressions (or the planned absence thereof), or through hidden inducements (i.e., carrots and sticks) carefully embedded in the natural flow of corporatese. You would, of course, have to be on guard against a similar counter-strategy from your target, who just might be watching your moves from behind an either coquettish or imperturbable mask. You could try *co-reasoning* with her mind – a strategy based squarely on the premise that she *does* have a mind – but then you would have to be on guard against being 'out-argued' – a painful and destabilizing experience, especially for a CEO in a public forum, and one that is certainly not conducive to getting your way. You could try *mixed* strategies, wherein you start by co-reasoning but then, as she becomes more comfortable and authentic and reveals the hidden emotional levers of her being (i.e., her identity and core set of narratives), you try using *those* as manipulative levers. But then you would have to be on guard against the very same strategy being pulled against you ...

No matter which 'solution concept' you adopt, it's impossible to write down the full problem search space. This is because the other's reaction will change where you think you are – and may also change where you'd like to be going. For instance, there may be good reasons why getting someone to do X is compatible both with manipulating her into doing X and with getting her to *want* to do X. But having gone down the manipulative path and discovered that X is a highly conscious being, you may change your mind and want to persuade her instead of manipulating her, only to find that it's too late, as your manipulative tactic has breached the trust that authentic persuasion requires.

What does the diamind do when faced with the wicked problem? It *wakes up* and realizes that rapid changes in problem statements are required if progress is to be made. Diaminds recognize that only solvable problems can be solved, that solvable problems are tame problems, and therefore that wicked problems must be tamed before they can be solved – otherwise we will end up with the stuff that obsessions and ruminations are made of: engaging and beautiful under the pen of a Shakespeare, but depleting and damaging when they take the place of sleep. But notably, the diamind does not think that all problems are tame, tamed, or even tameable. Rather, tameness is *always* in question: it's something to be ascertained, discovered, and if possible created.

The diamind's relation to the world's problems is, then, best characterized by what Douglas Hofstadter called 'the *I*-mode' – the intelligent mode of the mind – which he distinguished from the *M*-mode, that is, the mechanical mode.[3] The *M*-mode is what the mind is 'in' when it does routine problem solving of the type that is – counterproductively – often ingrained in young minds through years of schooling. In the *M*-mode the mind behaves just as it does when it frantically tries to multiply 1,234 and 5,678 together on a time-constrained multiple choice test: without thinking *about* thinking, but, rather, by mechanically – and as quickly as possible – running through the operation.

When the freshly minted MBA dives right into 'running the numbers' on a business (with a boost from mindlessness facilitators such as Microsoft Excel and PowerPoint), or when she applies financial formulae mechanically to the cash flows of the business without careful understanding of the source, scale, and scope of possible and likely errors, omissions, and distortions, she is playing out a mode of being – the *M*-mode – that has been well rehearsed from grade school onwards.

In *I*-mode, by contrast, the mind is aware of the wickedness of most of the 'real' problems it poses for itself, and of the difficulty of taming

Figure 4.1 Difficulty-based, tree-structured decomposition of problem types.

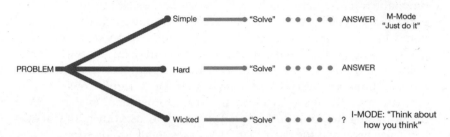

those problems by turning them into simple or hard ones. It can step outside itself and ask: 'What am I doing with my mind? What problem am I working on? What *kind* of problem am I working on? Is this problem worth my time and mental energy? How much will it cost me to drive to an answer? Will I get there in the amount of time I can afford to spend on it?' In other words, it can quickly try out a large number of alternative problem statements in a situation in order to successfully intervene in its world. In the *I*-mode, it behaves as if a 'tree search structure' for thinking about problems is embedded in its workings (Figure 4.1) – and as if it's always 'searching' that tree. And all the while, it keeps the null hypothesis ('this is an irreducibly wicked problem') forcibly before its eye. Indeed, the diamind *is* that search. It becomes one with it. And in so doing, it makes thinking about thinking an integral part of thinking.

Types of Solutions. Enough of problems. Let's go on to more pleasurable topics, such as *solutions*. A solution – remember? – is what your mind searches *for* when it tries to solve a problem. You search for 45,267 when you try to solve the problem of adding 32,156 and 13,111. You search for the least expensive cost structure of your product when you try to figure out the most efficient combination of components that can be used to build it. You search for the causal triggers of someone's behaviour when you search for the (manipulative) solution to 'how do I get *X* to do *Y*?'

Solutions are the stopping points of search processes and the end points of problem-solving activities. Once you've found the solution, you can 'go on to something else' – to another problem, that is, since after all, all of life *is* problem solving. Alas, not all solutions are created equal, and it helps to know what kind of solution you're searching for *while* you're carrying out that search.

General versus local solutions. When adding two numbers, you're searching for the answer: 45,267, say. That's the *local* solution to your problem. It's the solution to the specific problem you're engaged with there and then. But you may also be looking for a *general-purpose* algorithm for adding any two numbers – or for an algorithm that facilitates the addition of large numbers – so that you don't have to invent addition or come up with new shortcuts every time you solve a new problem of this type. When you do this, you're searching for *a general solution* – one that's valid or useful in all possible states of the world. General solutions are optimal 'no matter what.' By contrast, *local* solutions are solutions that are valid under certain conditions – in *these* conditions but not in others.

You search for *local* solutions when you simply look for an answer to the problem at hand. You search for *general* solutions when you look for a solution that is optimal for solving all problems of a particular type, such as the problem of quickly adding up large numbers. A heuristic – a rule of thumb, a solution concept – may be good enough when you search for a *local* solution. On the other hand, searching for a *general* solution requires looking for an *algorithm* – a fail-safe method or recipe for getting to an answer in situations of a particular kind.

Take a product design problem. You're looking for the list of features, components, and manufacturing techniques that will take you to a particular set of attributes and a particular cost of goods sold. It's a lot like 'solving' a jigsaw puzzle: the components need to fit together in particular ways, which are more or less determined by their features, which include size, shape, and interfaces.

You can frame your problem in (at least) two ways: (1) try to minimize costs, subject to satisfying a set of product features; *or* (2) try to maximize the number and quality of the product features, subject to a particular cost limit. Either way, the problem is a hard one as we've defined 'hard': you can't just *see* your way to the answer or to the process for reaching it. You have to 'fumble' and iterate. You have to feel your way towards it, sometimes by groping in the dark.

To see how hard this problem is, compare it with that of optimally packing a knapsack for a three-day trek through the woods. You know you'll need water, matches, dry foods, toiletries, changes of socks and underwear, a knife, and so on – those are akin to your product features.

You also know that the space available in your knapsack imposes a hard constraint. That is your cost constraint. You now have a reasonable mental model for the product design problem: How are you to pack a knapsack for a trip for maximum utility, given a fixed size?

To reach a local solution to the knapsack problem, you just start 'packing stuff in' – food, water, changes of clothes – until you realize you can't fit in something essential, like your toiletries. Knowing this, you unload your knapsack and start again, hoping to find a different arrangement: perhaps you get rid of some clothes, hoping to use the space this frees up to fit the toiletries.

So, *you do it.* Now suddenly you find that you can't fit your cutlery … So, back to unpacking you go, and start all over again. And so on, till you've found a 'solution' – a local one, one that allows you to pack as much as you think you'll really need, given the space constraints.

You can use the same approach when you design a product: you can 'just try it' and go through several possible 'prototypes' in order to figure out the locally optimal set of components that will fit the cost constraints and give you the maximally desired list of features. *Locally* optimal because you can't *really* hope to search through *all* possible combinations of components. Assuming that your product has M components and that there are, on average, n possibilities available from your suppliers for filling out each component with an actual part, then you'd have to consider M to the power of n combinations by building M to the power of n prototypes – which would surely occupy your R&D group for years. And *that* is what you would need to do in order to make your solution a *general* one.

Now the trick, of course, is to *not* do all the work for getting to the globally optimal solution, in such as way as to end up in a *better place* than the locally optimal solution. Otherwise, there would be no more to the diamind than the capacity to think *more quickly* than its counterparts: not a bad trait to have, but not the one we're focused on. So, what is different about the *diamind*ed approach to everyday or business problems?

Well, for one thing, the diamind almost *always* searches for the general solution to any problem and for ways to get there. And it is *always* aware that any problem that is simple is one that has been *simplified*, by someone for some purpose. Because we don't see the process by which the simplification has taken place, we're often fooled into taking the simple problems we try to solve for the problems the world 'serves us.'

As Hilary Putnam put it, the mind and the world work together to make up the mind and the world.[4] By working in both *I*-mode and *M*-mode – by thinking *about* thinking *while* thinking – the diamind engages in problem solving in a dual manner. At one level, it aims at getting to the solution, just like a mind in *M*-mode does. At another level, in the I-mode, it works at figuring out ways of moving to the global optimum, by going back and forth between looking and calculating, between asking 'What problem am I solving here?' and trying to just solve it.

Because of this bifocal approach, the diamind can *transfer* learning between the problems it has solved in different domains. It *learns* how to optimize a new product – how to search a large solution space for a hard problem – from its experiences with packing its knapsack. It learns how to pack its knapsack more efficiently from the exercise of planning a busy morning – where the 'time' available for tasks and meetings is like the 'space' available in the knapsack and the 'cost' available in the product. Because it sees planning a morning, packing a knapsack, and designing a product as basically similar, it can *transfer* its learning from one problem domain to another; thus it has a far shorter 'learning runway' than the mind that works in pure *M*-mode.

Because it has sufficiently distanced *itself* from *its self*, the diamind can develop its own 'problem-solving technology,' one that allows it to learn *across* domains of experience. For instance, once you see planning a busy morning, designing a multicomponent product, and packing a knapsack as instances of the same problem, you can group solution search strategies into various classes ('daring/conservative,' 'quick/slow,' 'convergent/divergent') to learn how strategies from various classes fare against 'the world.' You will then find that with a little work, 'daring strategies' – which require you to leap out and make a guess that's far from your first guess or initial 'gut feeling' about the solution, then search locally around the place in which you've made your guess – will systematically pay off handsomely in problems with large numbers of variables (large knapsacks, complicated products, diabolical mornings).

Brendan Calder: Getting It Done by Thinking It Through

It's time for a story that highlights the *I*-mode of the diamind when it comes to tackling hard problems. It comes from the life world of a Canadian entrepreneur who presidented and CEOed his way to four successful companies in the mortgage business in Canada between 1980 and 2000. In the 1970s, armed with only a bachelor's degree in mathematics ('the first ever awarded') from that would-be MIT of the North, the University of Waterloo, he saw an opportunity to break into the white-shoe Toronto financial establishment by applying the optimal-portfolio-pricing theories of an 'unknown' named Markowitz. Those theories suggested that it was possible to offer efficient portfolio pricing to returns-hungry institutional and private investors. Then in the 1980s, buoyed by the newly engineered possibility of securitizing mortgage debt, he exploited the emerging mortgage market to build one of Canada's premier mortgage lenders, a low-fixed-cost business that paid origination fees to strictly performance-based and -compensated mortgage brokers and that provided duration matching between the underlying loans and the associated securities.

Now, Calder did not *invent* either the securitization of debt or the efficient pricing of equities. He did not *create* the capital asset pricing model or duration-matched mortgage securitization. What makes this diamind remarkable is not a *conceptual* innovation. It is, rather, the special *savoir faire* involved in taking an idea and applying it to an opportunity in order to create a business – indeed, a new market.

If you want to see just how hard a problem this is, try the following: take NNT's (remember him?) *Black Swan* and the more technical analyses of option pricing he has generously written and disseminated, and turn *that* knowledge into an investment or investment advisory or trading business. At the very least, success should be gauged by your ability (a) to *raise a fund* in which the limited partners' 'buy' decisions are based on your explicit investment philosophy, or 'algorithm,' and (b) to register three- or five-year returns that clear the cost of capital. Think about it … and try it …

The 'hard' part of the problem Calder 'solved' was not *understanding* the new idea – the capital asset pricing model has a neat, linear structure, and the securitization of mortgages is a simple enough idea, given a deep enough market. It was, rather, *embodying* the idea in the real world: getting real people to give him real money so that he could make irreversible decisions with it – decisions that could result in his clients losing it forever. *That* required solving a very special type of problem, one that no writer on entrepreneurship has so far fully articulated. Could that be because so few of them have actually *done* it?

The problem you have to solve when bringing a new idea to an established market is this: how to change the operations of a very large machine comprised of the habitual and seemingly hard-wired activity sets of all of the people who make up that industry. To change those, you have to overcome the *behemoth* problem: changing one part of the behemoth requires you to change other parts as well if the behemoth is to keep working. Thus, if you want to implement a new and enlightened compensation system on the factory floor of Volkswagen in Mexico, for instance, you'll need to change a lot more than just how employee performance reviews are carried out, and how year-end compensation is computed. You may need to change the very *definition* of what it means for one to work on that floor, the structure of the human tasks that get measured ... and this may mean that you'll no longer be building Golfs, but Foxes ...

Similarly, selling new investment vehicles in the 1970s to Toronto's Rosedale clique – whose members were used to making buy decisions according to the who-went-with-whom-to-school rule – involved changing an entire pattern of making and validating decisions using norms that had by then become so entrenched that everyone knew that everyone knew them and no one knew why they were valid, let alone questioned them. So, the problem that Calder's mind had to face was that of runaway complexity: How was he to behold the entire behemoth while making changes to the parts? It was the problem of dealing with hard problems.

What makes Calder's mind a diamind is a feature that he himself scarcely notices when he talks about his business life. That feature is the *I*-mode of thinking about problems, an approach informed by a deep understanding of the complexities of various problems. His mind instantaneously *chunks* and *parses* wicked problems into hard problems and hard problems into simple subproblems.

Take a problem that's characteristic of the work executives do: How can a CEO optimally distribute her mental energy among the various claims on her attention that come in the form of e-mails and telephone messages? This problem is at the core of many CEO failures and 'errors.' Yet it has scarcely been acknowledged, because it isn't 'sexy' or 'deep' – it just doesn't sound like a 'CEO problem.' But in fact, it may be *the* CEO problem, because CEOs, as über-generalists and master integrators, come to rely on the information and expertise of people they trust for just about all decisions that affect the business. So this CEO needs some sort of algorithm here, not only for coping with the demands on her time, attention, and psychic energy, but also for *coping with the process of coping* with these demands.

Responding to messages is a potentially hard or 'wicked' problem. So is figuring out *which* e-mails to respond to and in what order. So is fig-

Figure 4.2 Calder's classifier for e-mail messages.

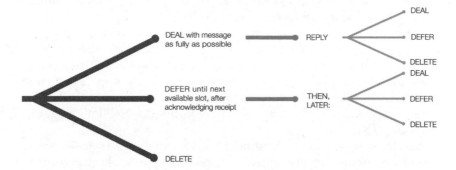

uring out the *depth* to which to handle an e-mail request: Is a complete answer needed? Should the implicit meanings in the message be taken into account? If not, how 'blunt' or 'opaque' should the answer be? How much work should be devoted to figuring out how much work should be devoted to a problem reply? (Try *that* as a hard problem the next time you think your managerial work is 'routine.')

Calder recognizes this as a potentially wicked problem that is central to his activities as a CEO. And he has arrived at a complexity-savvy algorithm for dealing with it: a – you guessed it – recursive tree structure neatly summarized by the '3D algorithm': Deal with it, Delete it, or Defer It. 'Dealing' entails a full and careful response that addresses the manifest *and* latent content of the message – both what the speaker overtly says *and* what the hearer understands the speaker to *mean:* it attempts to fully 'solve the problem' raised by the e-mail. 'Delete' is self-explanatory: it closely reflects the overinformationalization of organizations, as well as the fact that the abundance of bandwidth has been matched by an overabundance of irrelevant acts of self-expression. 'Defer' is a 'catch-all' term that makes the tree structure 'complete': it allows Calder to review the message at hand at a later time, in another mood, with more information available, using, again, the '3D' approach, which makes the tree recursively applicable.

Now, the 3D approach to message parsing seems trivial: Why, you might ask, did we choose this as the first feature of this diamind? What is so special about a tree-structured decision algorithm for dealing with e-mails? Three things: first, the decision 'tree' the approach is based on is highly adaptive to the complexities of both the problems raised in the e-mails and to the 'loading' of the diamind with other activities. It

Figure 4.3 Applying the classifier *within* a message.

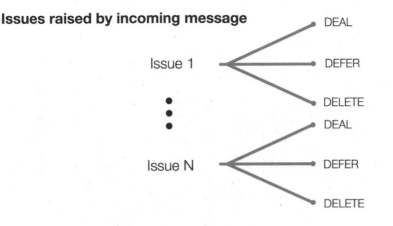

Issues raised by incoming message

Issue 1

Issue N

DEAL

DEFER

DELETE

DEAL

DEFER

DELETE

is 'complexity-adaptive' in that it is a simple algorithm for dealing with hard problems, and one that includes a 'complexity buffer' ('Defer') that takes up the excess difficulty. Second, it can be recursively applied: the structure is applicable to the 'Defer' bucket, so that deferred messages can once again de deleted, deferred, or dealt with; and furthermore, it can be applied to the way in which one *deals* with each message. If a message is treated either as a set of problem statements or as a prompt to a series of problem statements (the most obvious being: 'How do I put together a reply that provides a satisfactory answer to the sender?'), then the 'Deal–Defer–Delete' taxonomy can also be applied *within* an e-mail message (Figure 4.3), and that is precisely how Calder uses the contraption: issues raised in e-mails are dealt with, explicitly deferred, or bypassed either implicitly or explicitly. Once again, the tree provides complexity relief and significant economies of psychic energy, because it is easily applicable to both sequences of e-mails and to the bodies of the e-mails themselves. Third, the approach is remarkable because it is an *I*-mode prompt: it says 'wake up' to consciousness, which all too often is on autopilot when dealing with something as routine as 'doing e-mail.' It brings thoughtfulness to an activity that is often 'thoughtless.'

The same awareness of complexity is visible in Calder's approach to setting organizational objectives. As you might guess, it involves trees to help sift through complexity, as well as recursivity and 'rhythm' to help buffer runaway complexity. As follows: goals are fine, he says, they're the stuff of life – at least, of *some* lives: those that are, according

Figure 4.4 Calder's double-loop objective-setting procedure.

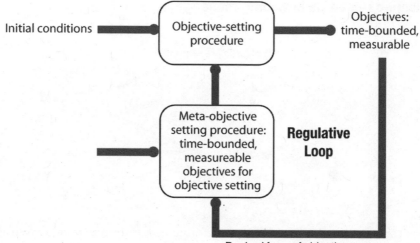

to him, worth living. But to turn goals into something real, to bring them into the realm of action and achievement, you have to turn them into objectives. And what might those be? Well, they're goals that have been made time bounded, measurable, and controllable. The first two are obvious; the third less so, even to Calder, who only explicitly talks about the first two but behaves as if he aims at all three. 'Controllable' means that the objective setter is in a position to do something about achieving the objective. Again, this sounds commonsensical, but in a world full of 'if only the world were otherwise I would achieve great things'-sayers, and the proviso mongering routinely churned out in academe, it is indeed *rare*.

Once again the power of the three-pronged tool makes itself felt, by enabling us to parse hard problems into manageable ones (Figure 4.4). Here is how Calder expresses it: coming up with objectives that are time bounded, measurable, and controllable is itself an objective, one that furthermore must be time bounded, controllable, and measurable. And coming up with a set of milestones for coming up with a time bounded and measurable and controllable set of objectives is itself an objective that has to be made time bounded, measurable, and controllable.

You will ask: 'Doesn't this set up an infinite regress? Doesn't this itera- tive approach *create* more complexity than it helps resolve, by creating

Figure 4.5 The classical decision-making approach to deciding (whether or not) to decide.

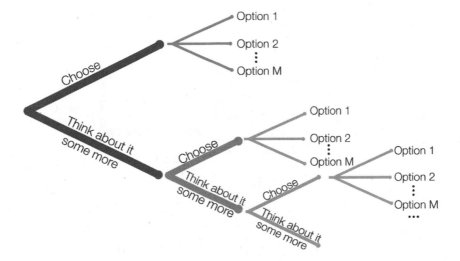

loop-to-loops of thinking about thinking about …?' Well, *no*. That's 'the Calder trick': he only uses two iterations of the objective-definition loop. The *first* loop sets up the first-order problem. It asks for a set of objectives in time bounded, measurable, and controllable form. The *second* loop asks for the along-the-way milestones for arriving at time-bounded, measurable, and controllable objectives. And that's it: armchair theorists who point out with self-satisfied superiority that the problem of thinking about thinking must lead to an infinite regress are left sucking their thumbs, because that is all he needs: to think (which will take him to the objectives) and – if the problem is a hard one – to think about thinking (which will take him to the meta-objectives). Calder cuts through the age-old problem of 'how much to think about how much to think about how much to think … about what to do' (Figure 4.5) by taking his mind to as far as intuition will authentically carry him: You can think about thinking, but do you *really* think about thinking about thinking?

We now have the workings of something powerful: a self-terminating loop for slicing problems into subproblems, for making plans (and metaplans), and for embedding the costs of generating solutions into problem statements. Because this process is self-terminating, it cuts through the 'ruminator's problem' (Figure 4.6) – which, may it be said, will be experienced with disastrous results by any pure theorist faced

Figure 4.6 The algorithmic structure of rumination (in the classical model).

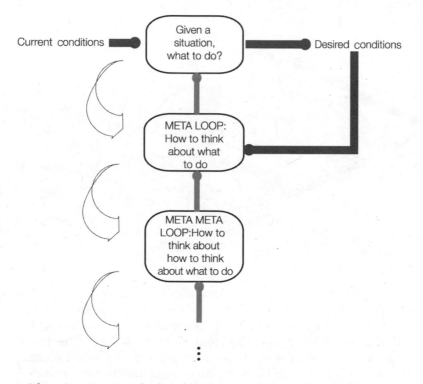

with a situation in which solutions must be acted on and the resulting actions have consequences.

It does so, moreover, by working at two intuitive levels, iteratively: that of thinking about the world, and that of thinking about thinking about the world (Figure 4.7). The first level regulates action; the second regulates the first and disciplines thinking about action.

If you think like the classical economist believes you *should* think – and if you're a bit reflective – you'll end up in the ruminative space of Figure 4.6 and try really hard to figure out when you should choose to stop thinking and when you should choose to think further about whether or not to stop thinking. If you think like Calder, you'll know you have two loops to work with (Figure 4.7), and you'll know that each loop has a distinct problem to solve. Instead of 'making decisions,' you'll be 'solving problems,' with the time constraints already wired into the problem statement. The problem statement will be specified at

Figure 4.7 How double-loop thinking cuts through the ruminator's problem.

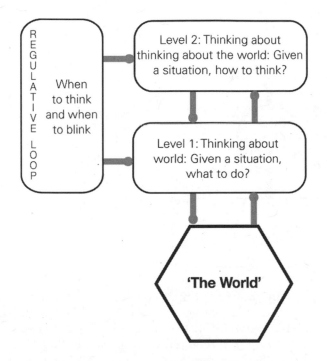

each level by objectives and by the objectives for setting the objectives; and the criterion for the solution will be 'the most accurate ordering of objectives I can come up with, given the constraints of the problem statements at the two levels.'

Now, there's something unique about how Calder picks his objectives: they're *recursively refinable*, and that's why they're complexity-adaptive. Okay, this is going to require some explanation. If my goal is to try to get to the best possible ordering of four core values – say, *truth*, *beauty*, *justice*, and *efficiency* – that I will be using to make CEO-type decisions in my business, I might start by considering different types of arguments for why beauty should trump efficiency in some cases, why justice may be more important than truth in others, and so on. If my 'time is up' and I have to just write out whatever is in my mind at the instant my thinking time has expired, I may have no ordering at all – just a set of arguments (incomplete) and possibly a set of reasons for preferring one value over another.

Figure 4.8 Double-loop, iterative, self-checking procedure.

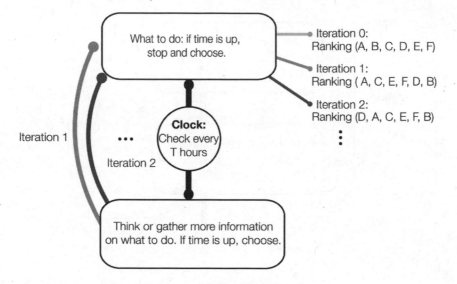

The diamind – which thinks *about* thinking *while* thinking (and doing) – thinks as if it intuitively knows this. So it starts out with an ordering that it just 'blinks' about instead of thinking about (say, *beauty > truth > efficiency > justice*). It then refines or improves that ordering with each additional thinking step. So no matter what 'the time is' – no matter how much time the diamind has left in its thinking process – it has an answer, which is, literally, the best answer it can come up with. This 'recursive refinement' process (Figure 4.8) is one of the more useful 'thinking tricks' that Calder uses to discipline his thinking.

You're now armed with a problem-solving technology that's dangerously effective because it can generate recursively refinable answers to very difficult questions. Does this remind you of someone we've encountered before? Listen:

> … what's *e* to the 3.3?' said some joker – I think it was Tukey.
> I say, 'That's easy. It's 27.11.'
> 'Nobody can sum the series that fast. You must just happen to know that one. How about *e* to the 3?'

The diamind knows, deep down, that it's *doing really complicated stuff*. It knows that in truth, all *real* problems are of infinite complexity. So it has no problem making leaps in the space of possible solutions and then performing searches in the neighbourhood where it's just landed. Calder has no problem doing local searches around the blinked-on first ranking of objectives that comes to mind. That's one of the most important mental habits of a *thinking doer* like Calder. Unsurprisingly, it's also one of the mental habits of a *doing thinker* like Feynman.

And it is unlike a search conducted by a 'standard economist' (Figure 4.6) for an Archimedean point that may always lie beyond the next branch of his decision tree. Instead, the leap-and-look search is *a priori* bounded. This problem-solving process *has* to converge: the diamind has *constrained* it to do that by arranging for it to stop once it's run out of time, wherever that point happens to be. That is how Calder can embed the market's metronome – that is, the promises he's made to would-be backers and financiers, and the expectations they've developed – into his thinking process. No wonder he feels there's something 'easy' about turning new ideas into organizational activities.

There's one more trick of this diamind – one thing still missing from the delineation of the problem – and that is a time constant for the two loops: 'time bounded' … remember? But 'time bounded' signifies nothing without a specific time bound. And that is precisely what we see: 'One year is a good time for a set of personal objectives, three years for a set of organizational objectives,' says Calder, without feeling the slightest need to justify his answer. Then he adds: 'With weekly and quarterly milestones along the way, of course.' And one of those milestones will be the milestone of specifying the objectives in such a way that they are time bounded, measurable, and controllable.

Note that when you time-bound problem-solving activities, you're also complexity-bounding the problems you set for yourself. It's an automated complexity-savvy adaptation mechanism. Think of it this way: as an entrepreneur, you're at the root or source of a large number of potentially high-impact events that interact with one another. And with others. And with you again. When you set up – with rigour and precision – a sequence of 'checkpoints' along the way of your sequence of activities, you're doing two things: first, you're *sampling* or *measuring* the reality you've created periodically, thereby giving yourself a better chance to respond to new conditions; and second and no less important, you're *disciplining* the minds and bodies of the *others* – you know, the ones on whom you depend for getting things done – so that they'll maintain the problems *they* have to solve at a manageable level of complexity.

Figure 4.9 How a steady beat helps rein in runaway complexity.

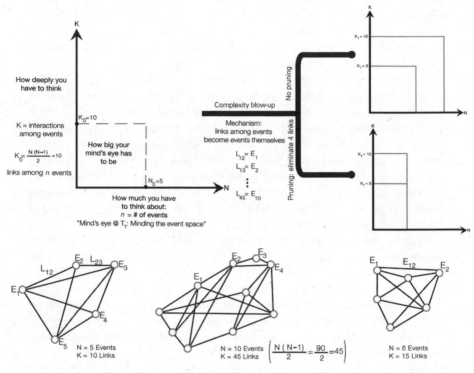

Events (E) and relationships (L) among them at T_1

To understand how this works, go back to the 'mind's window' metaphor of chapter 2. The number of possible interactions (K) among n events during a period of time T is proportional to the square of the number of events – that is, it's equal to $n(n-1)/2$. If all of the $n(n-1)/2$ new events interact with one another again, this means that after $2T$, one has $[n(n-1)/2][n(n-1)/2-1)/2]$ events to think about, and at the end of $3T$ one has $[n(n-1)/2\ n(n-1)/2-1)/2][(n(n-1)/2\ (n(n-1)/2-1)/2-1)/2]$ events to think about, and so forth. Awareness and 'thinking' can come to quickly lag planning and action. So Calder's obsessively metronomic timekeeping and milestone setting serve a crucial purpose in his thinking strategy: complexity – that part of life that tends to run away with itself and from you – is kept in check, and the event space that must be managed is kept within the span of the diamind's mental 'eye.'

If a metronome with the precise period T is obsessively maintained, the mind can hope to 'prune' the event space that interactions have created, in order to end up only with the 'differences that make a difference' – the events that matter. And how do you 'prune' an event space? By using the 'Deal–Defer–Delete' sorting rule, which is as useful for sifting through the crushing mountain of e-mail messages that accumulate in the executive's in-box as it is for filtering an overwhelming number of events down to a manageable set – one that fits inside your 'mind's eye.'

At the proverbial end of the day, Calder's diamond has created not just a set of local solutions to a problem, but a solution to a general problem as well – one that he calls the problem of 'getting it done.' Yet he doesn't realize that this problem is as much a problem of *doing* as it is a problem of *thinking through* the complexity of doing while continuing to think and do. It's as much a problem of *getting it done* as of *thinking it through*. His tree-structured hierarchical decompositions of goals and subgoals, his stopping rules and their associated convergent subroutines, and his timekeeping and variable pruning techniques aren't random tools from a toolkit – they're a coherent technology for thinking through the complexities of business life.

John McEnroe versus Howard Stevenson: Wicked Wicked-Problem Solving

The essence of the wicked problem is its ineffability – the fact that the problem changes even as you plough through a solution-generating procedure for it so that you can't ever feel like you have your 'mind's finger' on it. Sometimes it changes *under your very mind's eye* as you try to *think* your way to a solution, without really trying to *do* anything.

Let's take a patently 'non-cognitive' example: John McEnroe's 'point architecture.' The winner of seventeen singles and doubles Grand Slam championships improvised and 'composed' his points – both on serve and on return of serve – so masterfully that his opponent's moves and countermoves seemed choreographed – by McEnroe, to be sure. Examples can be seen in many YouTube™ streamings of McEnroe's classic encounters with Borg, Lendl, Connors, and Wilander. Come to think of it, winning a tennis point against a player of equal ability is a *prototypical* wicked problem: there are too many possibilities to think through in terms of where to place the ball, how hard to hit it, and the opponent's likely response. You can't suspend the action and think your way through all the possibilities. Anything you try to do changes the problem statement. And in the heat of the moment and at the pace of modern graphite technology, anything you *think* about will probably reflect itself in something you *do*, which means your opponent may come to know what you think before you do (but then, so will you about his thinking, if that helps any). How, then, does one end up *composing a point* in these circumstances? It seems that understanding *that* could provide a glimpse into a technology for solving wicked problems – no?

McEnroe's point architecture was remarkable in that it emphasized adaptivity over closure until the very end of the point – which, most often, was a McEnroe volley into the open court. Forget the slash-and-bang approach of post-1990 serve-and-volley players like Becker, Stich, or Edberg – who needed only come in behind their monstrous serves to tap away an easy volley. These players set up *easy* problems for themselves at net. Once the first serve went in, the point took care of itself – at least, about three-quarters of the time, which was what they needed to win in order to hold serve comfortably. McEnroe, by contrast, almost always faced a *hard* problem, and very often a wicked one. We have already seen how well he handled the hard problem of figuring out the best placement for his first serve, which would require a game theorist to solve for a mixed strategy Nash equilibrium – a scary thought for most tennis players. (McEnroe did not need to, because his intelligence seems to have been embodied rather than purely cognitive.)

Now, McEnroe had a big and uncomfortable serve – he was a lefty – but it wasn't a *monster* serve. It wasn't even close to the Sampras or Ivanisevic class in terms of speed. He had a very good return of serve, but it wasn't of the Connors or Agassi calibre. What was lethal about McEnroe's game was the sheer *speed* with which he could make intelligent decisions in the midst of a point, which allowed him to 'craft' his points the same way a master choreographer crafts a dance or a master manipulator prearranges the outcome of a discussion without seeming to have done so – at least not to any of those involved. Because he lacked a 'killer shot,' McEnroe often found himself solving a wicked problem when crafting a point. The problem was wicked because the opponent's response to his manoeuvre was often potent enough to change the problem statement altogether: a Connors backhand return off a serve in the ad court could force McEnroe to dig the ball from his socks; a Borg forehand return down the line off a deuce court serve could force him to stretch so wide to his forehand that he left the whole court open for a passing shot. McEnroe's 'solution concept' was a classic case of real-time adaptation: instead of going for the kill on either serve or first volley, he would dump the first volley in an uncomfortable, counter-intuitive place on the court, then *watch* intently for the few hundred milliseconds it took to figure out whether his opponent was hurt or rattled – in which case he would move in closer to the net and cut the angle for a passing shot, and usually ended the point with a volley into open court. As on serve, so on return of serve.

McEnroe's was one of the very first tennis strategies based primarily on reflexes and speed of foot. It's well known that return of serve is what 'wins' Wimbledon for many players. What seems to have won it for McEnroe was a particular philosophy of the return: he used it as a probe, a test, rather than as a point-ending shot. It was a shot that posed a dilemma for the server: attempt a passing shot (McEnroe usually attacked both first and second serves) and risk missing or getting out of position; *or* attempt a safer shot and risk a McEnroe volley into the open court. And – here's the catch – McEnroe allowed himself time to figure out what his opponent had committed himself to. It's as if he'd studied matters carefully and decided it would take most of his opponents 900 milliseconds between the time they made a commitment to a shot and the time they executed. And since he had an extra 400 milliseconds on any of them, he could just take his time, watch, and then respond with lightning speed with the optimal riposte.

Wicked problems would seem, then, to require some wicked, abnormal capability on the part of their solvers. Can a general problem-solving *wisdom* substitute for it? Consider the predicament that faced Howard Stevenson in the mid-1980s when he returned to Harvard Business School at the invitation of its new dean, John McArthur, to launch the school's Entrepreneurship Group. Piled up against Stevenson were a formidable pedagogical and intellectual landscape and strong institutional forces of inertia. Entrepreneurship was a phenomenon, to be sure, but at the time it wasn't really viewed as worthy of serious scholarly study and pedagogical investment. *Could* it be taught? *Should* it be taught? What *was* it, anyhow? Such questions were almost always behind the vaguely ironic grins of faculty members and scholars.

What was Stevenson to do? If he took a hard-line approach to defining entrepreneurship along the lines of Schumpeter or Hayek – that is, as disruptive or 'creatively destructive' economic activity that rearranges the rent-generation process or the information transmission process in a market, via the price system – he risked alienating a lot of economic theorists in the school's other faculties (and in an academic institution, getting buy-in is the *only* way to get things done). Falling back on more conventional definitions of entrepreneurship – from neo-classical or transaction-cost economics – would raise the question of why a new area was needed in the first place. And *that* question had no good answer. One could also, of course, leave 'entrepreneurship' undefined – like many an economist had done with concepts such as 'choice,' 'preference,' 'utility,' and 'belief' – and allow a mysterious new discipline to develop around the word. But what was possible for Walras, Malthus, Edgeworth, and others was no longer possible in the post-modern high-capitalist landscape of HBS in the 1980s.

So again, what to do? Stevenson's approach was in some ways very similar to McEnroe's. Just as McEnroe *posed a question* with his returns and his volleys, watched for the opponent's answers, then quickly chose his riposte, Stevenson *questioned* others' motives and beliefs vis-à-vis entrepreneurship by floating a definition that was vague but in highly precise ways: 'the pursuit of opportunity beyond resources currently controlled.' That definition has since become famous, for even though it seems to define something *inclusively* (i.e., in terms of what it is), in fact it defines something *exclusively* (i.e., in terms of what it is *not*). One could argue that most human action is a *pursuit of opportunity*, so that in itself can't be thought of as a positive definition. *Beyond resources currently controlled* is a disclaimer, of course; but however intuitive it may be, it isn't any more of a definition than *the pursuit of opportunity* is. For what counts as 'resources not under control'? Clearly, one's body can't go there, yet most entrepreneurial opportunities involve the entrepreneur's body (and how!) in many different ways. And while we're at it, what are the 'resources' in question? The word brings up images of financial, intellectual, and social capital, but how much of this capital is currently *under the control of the entrepreneur?* The cleverness of Stevenson's definition is that, stretched one way, it would include all human action (it is noteworthy that von Mises's book on economics, which is the foundation of much Austrian School theorizing on entrepreneurship, is called *Human Action*). Stretched the other way, the definition can't specify any domain of human action or behaviour at all. Stevenson had crafted for himself a masterful approach shot, a probe into a frenzied and wicked intellectual and institutional landscape.

Then he *waited*, because he knew he would be able to react quickly enough to whatever the field brought his way. 'It is too much work trying to change people,' he would explain. 'You have to hire the ones that will do, enthusiastically, without coercion, what they like doing best.'

Which is exactly what happened. Within a decade the Entrepreneurship group would be able to boast that it had enrolled 45 per cent of the second-year students at HBS. This was because Stevenson had nimbly adapted the group's strategy and hiring practices to accommodate and further the research and teaching interests of a large number of intellects – psychologists, economists, engineers, sociologists – who were attracted both to the school's prodigious research reach and resources and to the freedom that Stevenson's 'strategic definitional vagueness' had created. Like the best of wicked problem solvers, Stevenson had embraced the ambiguity and tension of the problem statement. His 'solution' – the broad but attractive definition – was not, in fact a 'solution' but rather a turning of the problem back on itself, a restatement that made it possible for others to 'bring' solutions that Stevenson could nimbly weave together into a real solution.

Stochastic versus Adaptive Solutions

Back to our discussion of *solutions:* we aren't through. We've seen how general solutions differ from local ones. Next we want to consider a different distinction: the one between stochastic solutions and adaptive ones. Stochastic solutions are valid under *most* conditions you deem relevant. They work well *on average*. They're the solutions of the sort your mutual fund manager develops when betting with or against 'the field' when investing your money for you. By contrast, *adaptive* solutions can be adapted to changes in local conditions.

An example will set the stage. John Maynard Keynes wanted to develop a model of what happens when a new equity is floated on the market. He asked himself: 'How much should one be willing to pay for it, under different conditions?' So he concocted a game in which 100 people in a room all submitted a number to a central clearing house. The number had to lie between 0 and 100, inclusive of the end points. The winner of the game would be the person whose guess came closest to a fraction (say, 2/3) of everyone else's guesses.

In what way, you might ask, does this game model the pricing of an equity? Well, because when pricing an asset, you're essentially *guessing* at something – in this case, the number. But it isn't just the intrinsic value of the asset that should count (the present value of the free cash flows of the business, say); others' estimates of that number should also matter, because the value of the equity is what the market says it is, not what you think it *should* be, given some formulae or algorithms you use to value the asset. So you should try to figure out what others should on average be willing to pay, and your willingness to pay should be *under* that average. So you should, essentially, be willing to pay a little less for the equity than the average of all the other traders' estimates.

- *Question 1.* What would you bid when playing this game? Think about it for a while before reading on.
- *Question 2.* What would happen to your answer if everyone thought exactly as you did in answering question 1? Think about *that,* too, before reading on.
- *Question 3.* What would happen to your answer if everyone thought the way you just did in answering question 2? Think about *that* for a while, as well.

Needless to say, the questions can go on. But will they stop at some satisfactory point? Will you 'get ahead' by asking and answering them? Is there an Archimedean point at which thinking about what others think about what you think about ... will stop?

Well, there *is* such a point in this game – the number 0. The perfectly reasonable guess in this 'beauty contest' game is, in fact, 0. Why? Because 0 is the average of all the guesses of the participants, if each participant submits a guess of 0. Furthermore, 2/3 of 0 is 0. So, it doesn't benefit anyone to unilaterally deviate from 0 as their guess. See?

So here goes question 4: is 0 the only such number? Or are there others?

Well, let's try some: how about 10? Well, if everyone submits 10 as his or her guess, then the overall average will be 10, and 2/3 of 10 is 6.66666 ... So if you *know* that everyone will be guessing 10, you should submit a number *less than* 10 (such as 9, or 8, or 6.66666 ...). Then you'll 'win' ... Except if someone else anticipates this; and if *everyone* anticipates this, then *everyone* will submit 6.66666 ... as his or her guess, and 2/3 of *that* is no longer 6.66666 ..., but rather 4.44444 ... And if everyone thinks *that* through, the number is no longer 4.44444 ... but rather 2/3 of *that*. And so forth. So it really *does* seem that 0 is the only – and somewhat paradoxical – 'right' answer. Is it not?

'Not so fast,' you might say. You're assuming that everyone will think about what everyone else thinks everyone else thinks about ... all the way to the equilibrium point. Is *that* a realistic assumption? Suppose they don't. Then if you guessed 0, you'd be right but you'd lose. And what good is being right when being right is doing badly – at least in a market?

One approach – the *stochastic solution* – is to try to figure out through experiment what others typically guess. Keynes's game has been around for a while, and there is this thing called the Internet that holds all kinds of answers to all kinds of questions, so why not this one? So you check. When you do, you find that indeed, the experiment has been run many, many times with all kinds of different groups in different countries in different contexts. So the stochastic approach would say *just use the average:* figure out what most people do when playing the game, take the average of all that, then take 2/3 of that average, and that is your best guess *against the field.*

Not a bad idea when the stakes are relatively low and the average winning answer is relatively uniform across all groups. So if you find that the answers most people give do not stray far from 30 or 36, then guessing 20 or 24 isn't such a bad idea. But if you have a lot of money at stake and only one shot at the game, you may want to examine that assumption more carefully: 'Does the winning answer vary a lot from group to group?'

It does. CalTech undergrads submit guesses that average about 24. So the 'winning' answer at that school is the one closest to 2/3(24), or 16. On the other hand, members of the University of California Board of Regents submit answers that average 31. So the winning answer there is the one closest to 20.6666 … What about game theorists? Remember, these guys think about what others think they think others think … *for a living.* The answer *there* has got to be 0. No?

No. Why? Well, because *one* of the bunch that are playing the game always either has a sense of humour that compels her to submit an 'irrational' answer (like 70), or she makes some kind of 'input error' – perhaps pressing the 70 button rather than the 0 button – which, when factored into the average, makes the average greater than 0 (makes it 0.7, in this case). *Then* the winning guess will be something close to 0.1, or 2/3(0.7). So even with game theorists, *it depends.*

And that is how – and when – *adaptive* can trump *stochastic* when solutions are being sought. The adaptive mode of thinking looks for cues in the environment (e.g., in the structure of the game and the nature of the other players) that help the mind identify the strategy best suited to the problem at hand – and *not* the best strategy against a mixed basket of all possible player types and game structures. To think this through for yourself, imagine playing the beauty contest game against the following: your family members, your peers or colleagues, a bunch of hotshot economists, a group of financial traders, a randomly selected handful of professional investors, a randomly selected sample of all professional and non-professional 'market traders' ... What changes? What do you focus on in order to make your decisions?

More often than not, what changes is the amount of logical depth, of computational intelligence, that you're willing to attribute to the typical player from the group that's playing the game. And it's this 'typical player' against whom you imagine yourself to be playing, no? Because after all, when we talk of 'averages,' we make them useful by a mental trick that turns the average of the individuals into an average individual, who has a set of properties that is the average of the values of the properties in the group or sample. A highly dangerous feature of the mind, that! Which is why it is essential to be highly precise about the nature and distribution of the various properties in the group you're playing the game against.

So, is there some 'adaptive mental model' of the beauty contest game that you can use to adjust your expectations quickly to the cues and clues that you have regarding the group of players you're matched against? Here's one suggestion – not the greatest one, but a start – courtesy of Colin Camerer and Teck-Hua Ho, two behavioural game theorists.[5] Divide the group of players into several different types, as follows:

- Type 0 players don't think at all about what the other players will think. So they may just be thinking that, since 50 is the average of a set of numbers from 0 to 100 and 33.333 ... is 2/3 of 50, then 33.3333 ... is the optimal guess.
- Type I players think about what other players think and also think that the group is made up of a combination of type 0 and type I players.
- Type II players think about what other players think, think about what other players think they think, and think that the group of players is made up of a combination of type 0, type I and type II players.
- Type III players think ...

You get the picture? Now, the question is this: What should you assume about the distributions of various player types in the group? If you're a type I player, what's the relative proportion of type 0 and type I players you should assume? Or if you're a type II player, how many type 0, type I, and type II players should you assume are in the group? Well? Ponder this for a moment before reading on.

It turns out that mathematically speaking, and all things being equal – the standard clause in social science, which often vitiates its findings, as all things are rarely equal – it's better to be a player of a higher type and to assume that the distribution of player types is Poisson-type – with some parameters you have to estimate, of course. Get it? So try it! Think through playing the game against the various hypothetical groups you considered above, model them as Poisson mixtures of various player types, and calculate your best move …

The difficulty, of course, is that we've replaced a hard problem – figuring out the equilibrium of 0 for the entire game – with another hard problem, which is breaking the players into classes, estimating the parameters of the Poisson distribution that describes how many players are in each class, and then calculating the optimal strategy, given our estimate of the parameters of that distribution. And this is a hard problem for the same reason why most hard problems are hard: you can't 'see your way' to the answer from the problem statement because the answer lies outside your mind's eye.

The moral of the story is that if you want a solution to be truly adaptive, you have to make it adaptive not only to the structure of 'the world,' but also to the constraints your mind faces when perceiving and thinking. A practical adaptive solution, then, is to draw up a little 'look-up table' in your mind, which comprises the results of various experiments reporting the ways that players from different professional fields, backgrounds, ages, and so on play the beauty contest game (what is the 'average guess'?) and then figure out which class of players the group you're playing against best fits into.

If you're playing the game against undergraduates from any field other than economics, an average guess in the 20s wouldn't be too bad. (The CalTech result was noted earlier.) Against economics majors? Well, if they've taken game theory, trying guessing something close to 0, as many of your opponents will be aiming to display their newly acquired knowledge by putting forth the Nash equilibrium of 0 (though one or two may go astray). Against elderly respectable retired professionals? Use the University of California Board of Regents results as your guesstimate. And so forth. (If you're in a mixed group, it's a lot easier to calculate the average of the estimates than to estimate the Poisson-weighted average.)

Want to see how this works in a more lifelike environment? In *The Black Swan*, NNT arranges a hypothetical encounter between two acquaintances who likely would never meet in reality: Dr John, a neat, predictable PhD in electrical engineering from the University of Texas at Austin, who builds and runs computer programs for a large financial institution and who is fastidious and methodical in his speech and thought; and 'Fat Tony,' an overflowing (in many ways) Brooklynite who apparently makes money where money is to be made. NNT asks them: 'I have a fair coin. I flip it 100 times. It comes up heads 99 times. What are the odds of heads on the next toss?' Dr John, with 'self-evident' look on his face, replies that since the coin is fair, the probability of heads on the next toss is 50 per cent. Fat Tony demurs, signalling that he's ready to bet on odds on heads that are much closer to 1 per cent than to 50 per cent. To NNT's question regarding the 'correctness' of Dr John's response, Fat Tony 'winkingly' replies that 'these guys' are easily suckered in situations where they're tempted to fall back on their own pet theories. 'What's the chance,' Fat Tony seems to be asking, 'that you're actually telling the truth that the coin is fair?' Of course, NNT's problem statement did *not* contain any self-delimiting information, any hint about the validity of *the problem statement itself*. But that is precisely what growing up 'on the street' – Wall Street, in this case – teaches those who would listen and learn. To echo Gilles Deleuze: 'To the answer embedded in every question, answer with a different question, one that sheds further light on the question at hand.'

... which suggests that Fat Tony might not have given this answer on a PhD qualifying exam, for he would have realized that the stuff of such exams is not the real world but an ersatz one concocted by academics, wherein the payoff accrues to those who play by the rules, not those who would win in the real-life contests that the academic-language game purports to represent. He would likely have adapted – which is more than we can likely expect from Dr John, for all the depth of reasoning of which he is obviously capable. What's special about the diamind is that it can flip among approaches that seek general solutions, approaches that seek local solutions, approaches that seek good-enough-on-average solutions, and adaptive solutions, depending on the situation. This fundamental resourcefulness in matters of the mind is what singles the diamind out.

Types of Solution-Generating Procedures

Talking about solutions (i.e., that which your mind searches for when trying to solve a problem) can of course be quite useful, but by itself it isn't enough. After all, knowing *what* to look for is not necessarily

Figure 4.10 How to tinker with your thinker, efficiently.

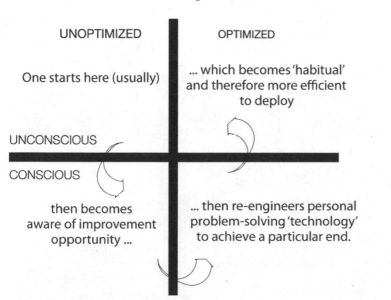

Problem-Solving Process

UNOPTIMIZED

OPTIMIZED

One starts here (usually)

... which becomes 'habitual' and therefore more efficient to deploy

UNCONSCIOUS

CONSCIOUS

then becomes aware of improvement opportunity ...

... then re-engineers personal problem-solving 'technology' to achieve a particular end.

knowing *how* to look. At the same time, knowing *how* to look – or knowing how you *do* look – at any one point in time is a lot harder than figuring out *what* you're looking for, because *looking* is something you *do* – usually unconsciously or at least without full awareness – whereas what you're looking for is something you know or *behold* in your mind's eye and are, therefore, more likely to be conscious of. Unlike the substantive knowledge exemplified by a solution or a solution type, the procedural knowledge embodied in search procedures is more often known *implicitly*. We'll soon see that it's useful to make even the most entrenched and 'basic' solution search procedures *explicit* in order to ascertain their utility in various settings and to improve on them – even if the new, improved solution search procedures that emerge as a result of the process of mental design engineering and tinkering later become unconscious – and thereby more efficient (Figure 4.10).

To see the difference between a solution type and a solution search procedure, consider how you would search for your lost cellphone in the Blue Room of the White House (Figure 4.11). Where would you start?

Figure 4.11 A picture of the hypothetical room where you have just lost your hypothetical cellphone. What is your search 'algorithm'?

Source: The White House Historical Association

The problem statement says 'your' cellphone, so it would make sense to start with places in the room that you had visited. Perhaps the armchair. Perhaps the table. But you did not *actually* lose your cellphone, so of course you can't *remember* where you've been inside the room, because there's nothing to remember. Nevertheless, pretend. Where next? The 'next place over' in the room? The next most likely place you might have been, had you really been in the room? And how do you search *within* these smaller neighbourhoods? If the question strikes you as trivial or bizarre, consider that humans often stare straight at objects, people, or places of interest without really noticing them. So, what procedure do you use to search *inside* the mind that is conducting the search? How do you search your own mind for traces of the impressions that the lost cellphone will have produced on your visual cortex, working visual memory, and long-term visual memory? You could, for instance, say out loud – while searching – the names of all the objects you see and thereby simultaneously search with the use of your visual memory ('something that looks like a cellphone') and with the use of your auditory memory ('a word sequence that sounds like "sel foun"').

Consider, also, how you'd search for your lost, stolen, or misplaced cellphone or Blackberry in these locations:

- A crowded nightclub in Karachi.
- The entire length of the Rock'n'Roll Marathon in San Diego (26.2 miles along the Pacific Coast).
- A Muslim gathering in Kabul.
- A group of your close friends (supposedly, anyways), who are trying to keep you from using it to call your spouse or some other person.

Does your search procedure change in any way across these scenarios? Are you more *aware* of your search procedure in one situation than in another? On what does your search procedure depend? The geographic location of the incident? The size of the space to be searched? The relative neutrality or friendliness of the relevant others? What changes? What stays the same? Can you say how and why? And by the way, what was your search procedure for the answers to the above questions?

There's something contrived about asking you for your search procedure in this case. A *procedure* is reliability oriented: it's something you carry out consistently because it's effective in a reliable way. There may well not be a procedure that you follow systematically when searching for your lost cellphone; and even if there is, it's possible (likely, even) that you aren't fully aware of it. It may simply 'not be worth it' for you to design or introspect the search process accurately, because losing relatively small objects of relatively small value in relatively large but still manageable spaces is not quite among the really important problems you face in your life. (Even so, depending on how often you lose your keys, phone, wallet, and so on, you might want to reconsider. A better search process could save time, anguish, and who knows what else?)

Your stake in having a search procedure – or in *knowing* that search procedure, given that it's already been designed in the subconscious darkness – will likely be a lot greater when the object to be found is of significant or critical value. If it is, you'll likely come up with a more extensive list of procedures. How would you go about the following searches?

- For a specialist to treat a usually chronic, reputedly terminal, and imminently debilitating illness with which you've just been diagnosed.
- For a specialist to treat a usually chronic, reputedly terminal, and imminently debilitating illness with which your child has just been diagnosed.
- For the quickest and most advantageous social route to a person of influence (POI) whose acquaintance you want to make.
- For a life partner or soulmate in your hometown.
- For a fun, brief, safe, and anonymous sexual encounter in your hometown.
- For a competent new financial adviser.
- For a solution to one of the 'hot' problems in your professional field (this could entail searching for such a problem to begin with).
- For a solution to the social problem (childhood famine, illiteracy, the intellectual bankruptcy of higher education) that you care most about.
- For the activity or pastime that is most meaningful to you, that confers meaning on your life, and that you'd pursue independently of its ulterior payoffs.

The question to consider is: Are there general characteristics of your search processes that you can identify and hold up to scrutiny? Map out the search as a problem-solving process of the type we've considered above, wherein the actual condition is your current state of ignorance or unknowingness and the desired condition is a state in which you feel confident enough to take action on the basis of your answer. What kind of searcher – or discoverer – are you? And why are you this kind of a searcher?

Deterministic versus Probabilistic Procedures

The following distinctions among search processes are highly relevant to diaminds:

With *deterministic* procedures, the input to each step of the problem-solving process depends solely on the output of the previous step and the overall problem statement. Can you picture this? In other words, your next step depends solely on what you're trying to find and where you currently are in that search. For instance (Figure 4.12), suppose you're searching – using a flashlight that provides you with a 5 metre

Figure 4.12 Search procedures for looking for your car keys inside a dark football stadium, with a flashlight that gives you 5 m visibility radius.

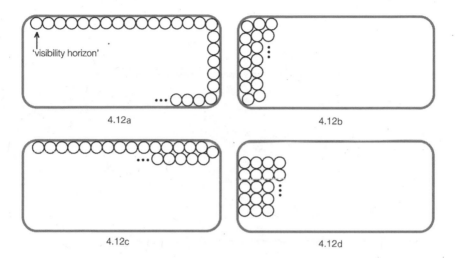

4.12a   4.12b

4.12c   4.12d

radius of visibility – for your car keys, which you've lost on a football field that is completely dark. Deterministic search procedures (Figure 4.12) proceed by steps that are both logically and causally linked to one another. You might search the stadium in concentric ellipses (4.12a), vertical hashes (4.12b), horizontal hashes (4.12c), or squares (4.12d), to name a few options. In all cases, you know at each step what to do next.

By contrast, *probabilistic* procedures do *not* depend entirely on the problem statement and the output of the previous step. They contain a random element that *you yourself have introduced,* even if unwittingly. You could, for instance, search the stadium using the following procedure: start in just the place you find yourself and walk in the direction you feel the wind is blowing. If there's no wind, walk in the direction you're currently facing. While walking, search only directly ahead of you. When you come to a wall, follow it up to the point where it starts to change curvature, in a direction determined by the toss of a coin: heads means go right, tails means go left. When you feel the wall starting to curve or straighten out, toss the coin again and choose the next direction of your search according to this rule: heads – keep following the wall; tails – walk right across the field. Got it? Okay, let's plot a characteristic path followed by a searcher who uses this procedure, across our hypothetical field:

Figure 4.13 Search path of someone looking for car keys in unlit stadium using the probabilistic algorithm described.

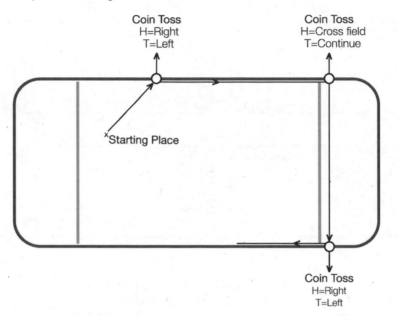

Right off the bat, you see a difficulty (or *it* eyes *you*): the procedure guarantees that you'll *never* search some large portion of the stadium, for your search path is constrained so that it lies along the stadium's edges. So if that isn't where your keys happen to be, you're stuck: you'll never find them.

Why, then, would you even *want* to consider a non-deterministic search procedure? Well, because the costs of actually performing the steps in the search would be far lower than if you had set out methodically to follow your own design (Figure 4.12). In the latter case, you'd have to wonder: Am I turning in the right place (4.12d) with the right curvature (4.12b)? Am I taking the right step size? All these things would add significant along-the-way anxiety to your overall search – not to mention the fact that having to think about implementing your strategy would slow down the process by which you implemented it. So if you can come up with a 'random' search algorithm that allows you to cover – in time – the entire surface of the field, you'll have something special: an 'automatic' search procedure that saves you the costs of obsessing over whether you're 'doing the right thing' at each step

Figure 4.14 Bouncing billiard balls on round and rectangular billiard tables trace out closed orbits. The 'bouncing ball' search algorithm, if implemented in a round or rectangular stadium, would leave a large part of the stadium 'unsearched.'

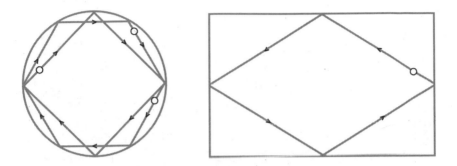

and that is guaranteed to cover the entire surface of the stadium. Well? Can you think of an algorithm like that? Take a moment to ponder that question ...

The answer comes from an esoteric branch of physics called 'quantum chaos' – specifically from such pioneers in the field as George Zaslavsky.[6] Briefly, quantum chaos is meant to sound like a non sequitur: quantum mechanics is a linear theory, and chaotic dynamics – sensitive dependence to initial conditions – only arise in the context of *non*-linear systems. A paradigmatic model for the periodic solutions that characterize linear systems is the billiard table: particles in a quantum well (so the story goes) behave in some spaces much like billiard balls on a round or square table. Because the table is closed, they exhibit *closed trajectories* (Figure 4.14), with each closed trajectory corresponding to a state of the system, which could represent (for instance) an electron bouncing around in the 'quantum well' surrounding a hydrogen nucleus. Both square billiard tables and round billiard tables will exhibit such closed trajectories.

Zaslavsky and his co-workers asked this trick question: What happens when you take two linear systems and add them together in a particular way – for example, putting together a circle and a rectangle to form the realistic shape of a billiard table (or a football field)? Well, *intuitively* you should get another linear system – another set of closed trajectories. But you *don't*. What you *do* get is what's known as *ergodic* behaviour: the ball will traverse every region of the billiard table – no matter how small – after a large enough period of time (Figure 4.15).

Figure 4.15 The stadium billiard: Using the 'bouncing ball' algorithm for searching the stadium indeed covers – after a sufficient amount of time – all of the stadium's area.

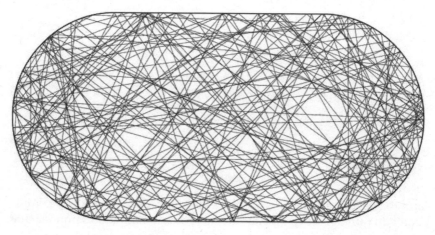

So, there's your algorithm: *make like a ball*, and *bounce off the walls as if they were perfectly elastic* (i.e., so that the angle of incidence equals the angle of reflection). In this way you'll have co-opted the world into supplying you with the randomness you require to make your search process complete – and also quite efficient, in that you've saved on the along-the-way costs associated with more 'intelligent' deterministic procedures.

Of course, your probabilistic algorithm will have to change if you find yourself looking for your keys in a large, dark, empty swimming pool (rectangle), or on the darkened stage of the Hollywood Bowl (round). This highlights the strong dependence of your choice of algorithm on the problem you're trying to solve. So it isn't the principle of the 'stadium billiard' that's worth remembering here – though that's kind of cool, too – but rather the power of a random search procedure, the fact that non all random searches are created equal, and the fact that the success of random searches depends on how intelligently you design them.

With a probabilistic (i.e., random) search procedure, you're trying to add *variety* to your search process. And for that variety you're counting on something that comes *from outside your own mind*. That's where 'randomness' comes in – indeed, it's the basis of the 'little miracle' of genetic algorithms. Such algorithms have come of age in the era of hypercomplexity – among other things, they're being used to optimize chess strategies against grand masters, watering paths for depriving forest fires of fuel, travelling routes for large airlines and railways, and distribution paths for tasks on machine floors. And they work better than 'master planner' approaches because of this one trick: they 'contain' more information than the master planner can possibly synthesize, because they rely on the outside world – sometimes in the form of a random number generator – to supply the 'requisite diversity' required to solve hard problems.

A question, though: Why do we *need* the outside world to supply this inner diversity? Why can't we just mentally flip a coin? Well, *try it*. Can you ever truly surprise yourself with the answer? That's the test of how successfully you'll have done it. The problem, as always, is the countless mental *automatisms* – remember those? – that we rely on to just get by. *And just getting by* gets in the way of true originality, because just-getting-by algorithms have been designed for *just getting by*. We, on the other hand, are students of *extreme performance* and want what Charlie Munger has called lollapalooza effects. That's why we need to look the unknown in the face and have the audacity to interrogate it – along with our ways of thinking about it – head on, like our next guest did.

Rob McEwen and GoldCorp

It's time to meet another diamind. Rob McEwen is the founder and past CEO of GoldCorp, Inc., a Canadian gold mining company that operates what today is the world's richest gold mine. Scroll back to the early 1990s. GoldCorp's key asset was a large tract of land in northern Ontario and a unionized prospecting and mining operation. It wasn't clear at the time whether there was any gold at all under the barren landscape. Now, gold is a fickle asset: it costs a lot to mine, and its selling price can vary widely with market conditions, which themselves depend on a large number of macroeconomic variables. All code for 'a hard prediction problem.' But Rob's real problem was of a different order and much more pressing: Was there gold here? If so, how much? And if there was enough to warrant the start-up costs, what would the best development plan be?

Simple, you might say. Kind of like the silly oil-prospecting problems that HBS professors in the 1970s and 1980s used for drawing decision trees, to show they knew something about business and to teach their students something about decision trees: just assign a range of payoffs to the different outcomes, and a probability to each possible payoff, and remember to take start-up costs into account; then use standard expected utility theory to multiply probabilities by payoffs, discount by the cost of capital in the appropriate way, and figure out the option (here, 'explore' or 'don't explore') with the greatest net present value. Well?

Well, is this how you'd choose a life partner or decide whether to dissolve a sometimes painful and sometimes exhilarating marriage? The entrepreneur's relationship to his life's work is not all that different from these scenarios: the 'standard' approach works well in the classroom but not in many places of real consequence.

So, what do you do? The problem is not dissimilar to that of finding your keys on a darkened football field, except that here, each step costs you a few thousand dollars, and every time you choose a new approach you're incurring a few hundred thousand dollars of expenses.

Oh yes, there's one more thing: Rob had *shareholders* to answer to. You've heard of them, right? They're the people who give you their money to do with as you please, but who also have the terrible habit of coming back later to ask how you've spent it and why their shares haven't risen in value in the meantime. GoldCorp's shareholders weren't going to keep financing Rob without the promise of future cash flows – the stuff that NPVs are actually built on.

'I think I have ADHD,' McEwen said when asked about his problem-solving style. He doesn't smile when he says this. 'I come at things in many different ways, sometimes in ways that are unrelated to one another.' In other words, his solutions are often considered 'weird' by those around him. For instance: An open, mountaintop pit in South Dakota inside the perimeter of one of his mining operations was overflowing and bleaching the surrounding area with chemicals. 'It was a "hundred-year event,"' McEwen recounted. Then he added: 'There are many hundred-year events in the span of five years.' The requisite board meetings produced a plethora of disastrously expensive solutions, such as building additional containment ponds at a cost far exceeding operational cost projections. Then at some point during the deliberations, McEwen fixed his gaze on a neighbouring ski hill. Ski hills have snow on them. Even when it doesn't snow. That's because they have snow machines, which turn water – sometimes runoff water – into snow. What was interesting in the ensuing dialogue – which you can easily imagine – was the reaction of the board members to Rob's seemingly self-evident suggestion: '*How* can we do *that*?' (And *do that* they did, successfully.) Keep this reaction of stupefied bewilderment in mind, for it encapsulates the common – nay, *standard* – *ex ante* response to the diamind's solutions.

Let's go back to GoldCorp's Red Lake mine in northern Ontario. To orient yourself: Canada in the early 1990s. Conservative investors, large start-up costs, large operating costs, large marginal costs of exploration, dwindling cash, prickly shareholders, and tens of thousands of inaccessible acres to look at real hard … with daunting-looking topographical maps around which any prospecting strategy would have to be 'optimized.' Hard, no? And not your typical 'hard problem,' either – rather, one that entails costs for every minute you *think* about the answer, as well as for every step you take to *implement* what you believe the right answer to be. Call this a really hard problem.

Rob's solution was of the 'you can*not* be serious' type. But it was also, *provably,* the optimal solution – though he didn't know how to prove this. His insight can be captured by a surprising little theorem, proved by Lu Hong and Scott Page, which states that *diversity beats ability.* Here's the logic. You have a hard problem to solve. The problem is hard because there are many 'locally optimal' solutions but only one globally optimal one. There are many 'all right' exploration paths around a topographical map, but there's only one 'best path' (or at most, a small handful of them). You want those 'best' ones. The chances that you'll get stuck in either a big trough or a small peak are high – very high. And the costs to finding the small peaks are also quite high, and after incurring them, the temptation to 'just settle' for what you have may be overwhelming. Now, a prospecting strategy is a sequence of 'moves' that can be assembled in many different ways, kind of like the many different components of a product that can be assembled in many different ways, or like the many events that matter to your life that can interact in many different ways. And each combination you come up with will take you to a peak, a trough, or something in between (Figure 4.16).

We can now take in the full impact of the Hong–Page theorem, which talks about the superiority of using many different problem solvers to solve a hard problem over the strategy of using just one master planner: *if* the problem is so difficult that no individual problem solver can always locate the global maximum (the best of the best, or, the *bestest*); *if* the solutions arrived at by each of the different problem solvers can be written down and ranked according to how good they are; *if* there are always at least some problem solvers who can improve on the solutions of other problem solvers up to the global optimum; and *if* there

Figure 4.16 Payoff function for a complex search procedure.

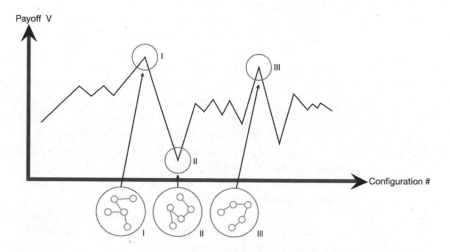

are a multitude of heterogenous problem solvers for you to draw from, *then diversity will trump ability* –that is, a collection of heterogeneous problem solvers will always beat out a single, expert problem solver, provided the expert himself acknowledges that the problem is 'hard' and that he can't 'just get' the solution.

And that is the insight McEwen had (we say insight, because like other of our diamonds, it is doubtful that he understood the mechanics of the Hong–Page theorem). He opened up the maps of the mine to outside proposals for prospecting plans. He placed them on the Internet. He invited proposals from experts all over the world. He asked Bob Mason – a professor of geophysics at Queen's University and an acknowledged expert in the field – for help ranking the various plans that were submitted. (Mason was so excited by McEwen's solution procedure that he couldn't sleep the night after getting the call.) He reached out to the world for the requisite diversity in the solution search process, by combining randomness (any graduate student in geophysics could enter freely) with intelligence (only those of requisite training could input solutions, because one had to know how to read a topo map and how to input the right solution).

One can just *see* the faces of McEwen's management team. 'You want to *give* away the maps? When Placer Dome [a competitor] has its drilling fields right next to us?' *You cannot be serious* was, of course, a response that McEwen had become used to by this point in his career. In his judgement, the net benefit to making the diversity-trumps-ability theorem work for him significantly and comfortably outweighed the risk that a competitor might get a 'better view' of the Red Lake project.

But there's more – much more, perhaps. McEwen's use of the diversity-trumps-ability insight – his 'Wikification' of the prospecting process (a decade ahead of Wikinomics, Wikipedia, and other Wikies you might care to name) – was complemented by another insight, one that helped him solve the problem-within-the-problem that GoldCorp was facing.

The problem-within-the-problem is something that faces all men and women of action – and certainly all responsible managers. It goes as follows: You have a hard problem to solve. You don't see yourself solving it by the usual approach. Moreover, on your desk at your elbow an hourglass is slowly emptying out. The 'sand' in the glass, however, is made of dollars, not grains. That sand is the cash you have in the bank. The hourglass marks the time available to you to solve the hard problem. It marks it in cash. Solving the hard problem is not – and cannot be – something you can do 'offline' (which is how most economics textbooks assume that thinking is done). Problem solving is done 'online.' You can't remove yourself from the *system* in order to solve a problem that has something to do with that system. You're inextricably part of it, and so is your thinking. So the problem of figuring out the best way to solve the hard problem you're facing (itself a hard problem) is also one you have to solve. You and no one else.

McEwen understood this, not just intellectually (though he was an abstract enough thinker to grasp it) but 'in his bones.' And amazingly, it seems that he also understood and acted on the following insight, from deep inside the theory of computational complexity: *Not all problems are created equal!* Some are hard, and some are easy, and furthermore, the distinction between hard and easy can be made with precision.

With *high* precision, in fact. Hard problems require a lot of operations to take you to an answer. 'How many?' you might ask. A better question might be: 'How many operations will be required per salient variable?' In this regard, hard problems require a raw number of operations that is a *greater than any polynomial* function of the number of salient variables. Like an exponential – 2, or e, or 10 – to the power of the number of variables. Which means that the complexity of these problems grows really, really quickly as a function of the number of salient variables in the problem. Which means that you can't 'see your way past your own thinking' about the problem, because the operations you need to go

Figure 4.17 Graphical description for the complexity veil effect: the mind's eye cannot see past the number of operations required for carrying out a complex optimization problem.

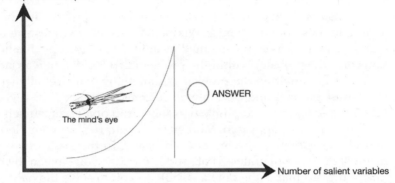

through to see your way to the solution block the gaze of your mind's eye (Figure 4.17).

Simple problems are 'simple' because this computational wall is less prohibitive. The number of operations – basic atoms of 'thinking' – that you require to solve them grows more slowly, as a function of the number of variables in the problem – that is, no more quickly than a polynomial.

And here's the curious thing: humans seem to apply themselves mainly to simple problems. In fact, most of the problems that managers 'solve' are polynomial-time-hard problems, or 'P-hard problems.' They're so good at solving problems like those that quite often they refuse to even try to solve *other* kinds of problems – you know: the kinds that confront your mind's eye with the 'complexity wall.'

And here's another curious thing: many common P-hard problems can be represented as *tree searches* (Figure 4.18a). Remember those? Those powerful little devices for simplifying stuff? A tree search is a prototypical simple problem, one you can attempt to solve quickly in the reasonable hope of achieving an answer. By contrast, the *other* kinds of problems – we'll give them a name shortly – tend to live on *graphs* (Figure 4.18b). Graphs are curious creatures: they have the property that, when you 'search' them, you almost always have to solve a hard problem.

Figure 4.18a Typical 'tree search' (P-hard) problem. Complexity of the search process is at most log (*n*), where *n* is the number of possible end states of the tree. In this case the problem is to find the natural-language five-letter word that starts with 'r,' ends in'd,' and has middle letters drawn from the set (O, U, N).

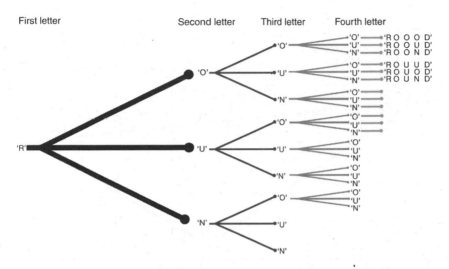

The typical example of a graph search is the warhorse of computational complexity theorists: the Travelling Salesman Problem. In it, a saleswoman has to figure out the shortest route that will take her to visit a number of cities that are home to various clients. To figure *that* out, she has to generate *all* the possible routes through *all* the cities, calculate the total length of each route, and select the circuit with the shortest length. Even if she 'sees' how this might be done, getting to the answer still entails 'doing' it – and that's what takes all the time. Indeed, 90 per cent of the labour in this problem involves *generating* all the possible paths. The part that has to do with ranking the paths according to their relative lengths is the easy part, and one we've seen before: it involves a tree search.

The Travelling Salesman Problem is one of a large class of problems that have been known to designers of computer programs for at least thirty-five years. These problems are called 'non-deterministic polynomial time hard,' or *NP*-hard. They can't be solved in polynomial time or by using a number of operations that is (you've guessed it!) at most a polynomial function of the number of salient problem variables. At

Figure 4.18b Typical 'graph search' (NP-hard) problem. The task is to find the shortest route that connects all of the vertices in a graph. The complexity of a systematic search through all of the routes is exponential in *n* where *n* (in this case 6) is the number of vertices in the graph.

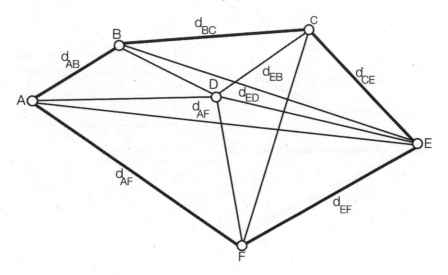

this point you might ask, 'Why are they called "non-*deterministic* polynomial time hard" instead of just "non-polynomial time hard"?' Well, because they *can* be solved using a number of operations that is at most a polynomial function of the number of salient variables. Only, however, by a non-deterministic machine – that is, by a machine that makes at least some probabilistic steps. Ah, the value of a little randomness.

For instance, in the Travelling Salesman Problem, you could assign the subproblem of generating all possible alternative paths that connect the cities to several parallel, automated problem solvers, which will decide at random which path to generate next. And of course, the likelihood of achieving the answer in polynomial time increases with the number of parallel 'machines' – or problem solvers – that are working on the subproblems. Then, when you have all (or as close as possible to all) of the possible paths, you need only sum the distances along each path (an easy problem) and rank the results according to the distances (another easy problem).

This is no small coincidence: Rob McEwen's (dia)mind acted as if it *just knew* this little result from computational complexity theory. He saw the hard problem ('come up with the optimal drilling plan'); saw the hard problem that solving the hard problem in a finite amount of time entailed; and saw that he needed to 'parallelize' the hard part of the hard problem while (a) maintaining control of the parts that had to do with verifying that all the entered solutions were 'bona fide' (which was Bob Mason's job), and (b) establishing the relative ranking of these solutions. The thousands of solutions that poured in – many from graduate students and hackers with time on their hands – provided the fodder for this awesome contraption that found gold.

You might ask: 'Why couldn't a machine *also* do the hard part of the problem as well, and just generate and then rank the "paths"?' Well, because the optimal prospecting strategy is not *quite* like the Travelling Salesman Problem. Instead of having n well defined cities to deal with, along with $n(n-1)/2$ well-defined distances between any pair of cities, you have a continuous area of many thousands of hectares, with hills, valleys, drainage areas, ground cover, and so forth. There's no single way to parse this scene into a finite number of discrete points or loci, nor is there a single algorithm or method for teaching a machine to do the parsing. And *that*'s the sort of machine you'd need in order to turn the Optimal Prospecting Problem into the Travelling Salesman Problem. When there's no such algorithm – or specific and fail-safe method for generating one piece of information from another – you have to rely on the non-algorithmic, often implicit, and frequently heuristic byways of expert intuition. And of course, Rob seemed to know *that* as well, for he did not (and he could have) call up Charlie Leiserson or Ron Rivest at MIT and ask them to design an algorithm to deal with this problem. Instead he called up Bob Mason at Queen's and asked him to oversee the solution validation process. Not bad!

So, why do we need scientists (and science) at all when practitioners can do so much without them (and it)? One reason stands out: to facilitate the *transfer of skill* from one extremely successful practitioner to another. For now, we can place in context Rob's quip – 'I think I have ADHD' – though perhaps he should have said, 'I think I have what most people would call ADHD if they did not understand me.' For if they did understand him, they would see his methods as highly successful and adaptive ways of dealing with very hard problems by quickly and in seeming unrelated ways switching perspectives, models, and solution procedures. For diversity can be achieved not only by cultivating connections with a lot of different minds, but also by learning to be comfortable with radically different *intra*personal ways of thinking and being.

Exercises: DI-ing Your Mind

Thinking about Thinking about Problems while Solving Them

Try to solve the problems that follow this preamble. Keep a record of your thinking process as you go through the steps of trying to solve them. If you find it hard to write down everything you think about at the speed at which you think, record yourself and transcribe the output in order to produce a replica of your thinking. If you find that your mind starts to think 'in images' rather than merely words, try to capture the images in question as part of the transcript. Think about the problem until you reach an 'Archimedean point' – that is, either a point at which you feel like giving up, or a point at which you feel you have arrived at 'the answer' or 'your best answer' for the problem you're considering. When you've finished, go through the transcript you've produced and 'encode it' using the coding language (mentalese) we have developed in this chapter. Your coded system should include the following simplified typology:

- The problem complexity class (easy/hard).
- The solution search process you used (deterministic/probabilistic).
- The type of solution your mind is searching for (global/local/adaptive).
- Your perceived *distance* from the answer to the problem at several points in the problem-solving process.

  'Liars, liars all ...' You find yourself in a strange land called 'Amerika.' You're informed, by a reliable source whom you implicitly trust, that 90 per cent of Amerikans lie 90 per cent of the time. You come across an Amerikan and start a dialogue. At a certain point in that dialogue, she says: 'I'm now telling you a lie.' Within five minutes, you have to decide whether she's lying or telling the truth. Remember that the five-minute time limit *is part of the problem statement*, not something extraneous to it. An answer will only count as an answer if you produce it within five minutes.

  'Bourbon, with water ...' (*after Tom Schelling*). You have two glasses. One is full of whisky. The other is full of water. You take a tablespoon from the glass containing whisky and place it in the glass of water. You stir the mixture. Then you take a tablespoon of the mixture and add it to the glass containing whisky. Is there more water in the original whisky glass or more whisky in the original water glass?

'Complete the sentence ...' *(after Douglas Hofstadter).* You change the sequence 'a b c' to the sequence 'a b d' using a rule. Using that same rule, how do you change the sequence 'm r r j j j'?

Pablo's Challenge. While on a trek through the Amazon rainforest with three of your friends a few years from now, you're caught by the bloody villain Pablo Escobar III and his band. He wants to kill you all, but an aesthetic sense of fair play bids him give you some semblance of a chance. He takes all four of you to a fence. On one side of the fence, he buries three of you up to the neck, facing the same way. He buries the fourth of you on the other side of the fence. On each of your heads, he places a hat, either black or white. He tells all of you that (a) there are exactly two white hats and two black hats, and (b) the one who correctly states the colour of his hat will be spared. Who do you think will call out first? Second? Third? Who is most likely to live? Who is least likely to live? (If you *do* end up in this situation on a future trek, this book may save your life.)

Hoftstadter's Challenge. You have the following symbols to work with – *M, I, U* – and one string of symbols – *MI* – along with the following four rules:

- You can replace *xI* with *xIU* wherever *xI* occurs, where *x* can stand for any symbol.
- You can replace *Mx* with *Mxx*.
- You can replace *III* with *U*.
- You can drop out *UU*.

Here, then, are two questions:

1 In ten minutes or less, through a series of transformations of *MI* allowed by the rules, can you generate the string *MU*?
2 In twenty minutes or less, can you prove that the path you've generated from *MI* to *MU* is the *shortest possible one*?

Russell's Challenge. There is a village in which the barber shaves all and only those who do not shave themselves. Take no more than twenty minutes to answer this questions: Who shaves the barber?

Thinking about Thinking while Thinking about Something That Matters

This last exercise is a highly personal one. In it, you're guided through a process of reconstituting how you think through and about problems, holding your working mind up for scrutiny, analysing it using the language system for speaking 'mentalese' that we've introduced, and then re-engineering it to inject as much of the diamind effect as possible into your own library of mental routines. The exercise has two steps:

Step 1. Representation–Analysis. In this part of the exercise you're invited to record your own stream of consciousness as you think through a problem that is facing you. The only requirement for the problem is that it be meaningful to you. Thus 'how to solve for a set of unknowns in a system of linear or non-linear algebraic equations' will not, in most cases, qualify. On the other hand, 'existential' problems that we normally shy from in everyday conversation ('and why?' we wonder), such as 'What does it mean for a creature like me to be conscious?' or 'If life were no more than a set of physical processes, why abide by any moral laws if I can get away with not?' are *in*. And of course, problems such as 'How do I price this leading-edge pharmaceutical product in a down market, given this competitive landscape?' and 'How do I increase personal accountability in my organization/ team/group/collaboration network?' are also in. The 'representation–analysis' part of the exercise will be easier to follow if you record it on an 11-by-17 sheet of paper (or even larger: remember that you want a 'big window' on your own mind), configured this way:

Stream-of-consciousness rendition of your thoughts	*Codification of your thinking in mentalese*
Problem statement:	

In the left-hand column, then, record the stream of consciousness that comes to you as you apply yourself to your problem. Edit *nothing*, even if you believe you've strayed from the original problem statement. Make no effort, either, to clean up or increase the coherence of your thoughts as you set them down on paper. If you have trouble writing as quickly as you think, then record and transcribe yourself (or use transcription software to produce a record of your thinking). Oh, yes: don't forget to stop – and also to record carefully the place where you *have* stopped. Ideally, you should stop at an Archimedean point in your problem-solving process – some place that's either clearly a 'peak' (an answer, or *the* answer, as far as you can tell) or a trough ('I've identified several non-answers but see a way forward'), a depression ('I've identified several non-answers and don't see a way forward) or a chasm ('I'm lost altogether' or 'I'm working on the wrong problem').

In the right-hand column, use the description language introduced earlier in this chapter to encode your stream-of-consciousness record on the left-hand side. Use the following coding system:

Problem. What's the problem statement in terms of current conditions and desired conditions? What would constitute a satisfactory point of conclusion or convergence in your thinking? Note that the problem can change as you travel down the stream of consciousness triggered by its statement. If it does, signal those changes in the left-hand column. Note also that the problem can break down into subproblems as you think through it. Specify each subproblem. Example: 'How to get X to do Y?' – a (perhaps *the*) prototypical managerial problem – will sometimes lead to 'How to persuade X, using reasons, to carry out action Y?' Which in turn will lead to 'Find the reasons I think X would find plausible for doing Y and figure out whether I can authentically put them forward, as well as the reasons X would find plausible for not doing Y, and see if I can refute or undermine them.' And so forth.

Problem difficulty class. Is the problem *easy* – that is, can you see your way to the solution, or a see how you would get to the solution, having written down the problem statement? Alternatively, is it *hard* – that is, do you see 'fog' when you try to scrutinize your way to a solution? Encode each problem and each subproblem in terms of its perceived difficulty.

Type of solution. What is the type of solution you're searching for, for each of the problem and subproblem statements that have arisen? Here, two distinctions are important:

- *Global versus local.* Are you looking for a solution that will help you deal with a *whole class* of situations (global) or with one particular situation alone (local)?
- *Stochastic versus adaptive.* Are you looking for a solution that will work, *on average*, in a large class of situations (stochastic), or for a solution that you can *adapt* from one situation to another (adaptive)?

Solution-generating procedures. For the purpose of making this distinction, think of each of your thoughts in the 'stream of consciousness' column as a step in the process of solving the problem. Yes, we know: some thoughts just seem random and unconnected to anything. But they just may be useful: perhaps you've subconsciously generated that thought for a purpose, even though you don't see that purpose immediately. Now, what solution-generating procedure does your mind seem to be following? Is it deterministic (i.e., every thought is connected to the output of the previous thought), or is it probabilistic (i.e., some thoughts just seem random relative to the whole enterprise)? What happens to the random thoughts in the stream-of-consciousness transcript? Do they lead anywhere? Do they get overridden or shut down?

Step 2. Reconfiguration-Synthesis. Next, working with the elements of your stream of consciousness as you've identified them in the right-hand column, *reconfigure* your thinking by making point changes in your thinking processes (the reconfiguration step) and then working those changes back into a 'modified stream of consciousness' (the synthesis step). To this end, it might be useful to configure another 11-by-17 sheet of paper in the following manner:

Speculative rearrangement of patterns of thought	Re-engineered twists and turns of thought relative to the original thought record

Now, remembering that analysis works forward and top-down and that synthesis works backwards and bottom-up, we'll *work backwards:* from solution-generating processes to solution searches to problem types:

Solutions and solution-generating procedures. The purpose here is to build up 'mental choicefulness' in the problem-solving process by *switching* between different kinds of searches, such as these:

- *Global versus local.* If you previously searched for a global solution, flip to a local search. If you previously searched for a local solution, flip to a global search.
- *Stochastic versus adaptive.* If you previously searched for a stochasti-cally optimal solution (a solution that works 'on average'), flip to an adaptively optimal solution search (one that optimally adapts to each particular situation), and vice versa.
- *Deterministic versus probabilistic.* If you previously searched in a deter-ministic fashion, introduce randomness to your search. This is tricky. Randomness is something that humans do poorly with, because it's precisely what they try to avoid as they engage in mental behaviour. One simple way to introduce randomness is to carefully isolate a few decision points in your search process and then flip a coin to decide which branch of the decision tree to take. A simple decision point is the one between 'thinking' and 'blinking' (you know, Gladwell-style). At any point in your thinking process you can decide to think further and more deeply, or you can 'just blink' and go with a result you've eyeballed, or estimated by dead reckoning. Another decision point is the one between thinking further and *asking* someone else (and yes, that someone else can be Wikipedia, or one of Google's search engines). And obviously, there's also a choice to be made between blinking and asking. This is a simple 'randomization' algorithm for introducing uncertainty to your problem solving and turning that process from a deterministic one into a probabilistic one.
- *Iterate.* Flip back and forth between the different solution searches and solution search procedures, and examine the effects of each flip on your original problem statement. As usual, ask: Does the problem type change from easy to hard, or vice versa? Does a new problem statement arise that I 'like better' than the original problem statement? Why or why not?

Stop, at least for the time being. Record your observations. The temptation here will be to search for a natural end point to the process. *There is no natural end point.* The process is as much about generating new solutions as about generating new problem statements and new solution search procedures.

5 The Diamind at Work, in Slow Motion, Part II: A Repertoire of Mental Objects

Seems, Madam? Nay, it *is*. I know not seems.

William Shakespeare, *Hamlet*

Problems are everywhere. Talk to humans about decisions and choices and they'll snarl, pout, make small talk, and avert their gaze. Problems, on the other hand, are the stuff that life is made of, which is why it's so easy for us to get ourselves and others in a nodding frame of mind when we talk about them. It's also why the 'problem solving' approach to talking about business is so instantly popular. 'We *do* solve problems,' says the executive. 'We're problems solvers to the world,' says the consultant.

But for a problem to be a problem it must be *about* something. It must have *content*. It must have *meaning*. It can't just be bare structure and empty syntax. 'How do you invert this 2x2 matrix?' *is* at some level equivalent to 'Who will do the dishes tonight, given our chore-sharing agreement from yesterday, which allocates chores to spouses based on marginal value to the spouse and marginal cost to each?' But it's equivalent only *at some level*. Solving the matrix inversion problem does not always solve the chore allocation problem, and in the miraculous few instances when it *does* solve it, *something else* is doing a lot of work.

That something else is a usually a *mental object* – some kind of image, rule, injunction, statement, what have you, that we can agree on and that allows us to *reduce* the problem of chore allocation to the problem of matrix inversion. That mental object, which we have to share if we're to solve the 'same problem,' is a curious entity – one that's *about* some other entity.

'Flower' – the noun – is about a flower, some flower, flowers, and so on. '*This* flower' – the phrase – seems to be about 'this flower' – that is, the part of the plant, unless of course it's being used metaphorically to denote the radiation pattern of an antenna or a beautiful young human creature. A 'credit default swap' also seems to be *about* something – namely, a set of contingent contractual agreements that pay the contractors various amounts of money, positive or negative, based on certain states of the world; but here the situation is messier because the 'plot' that links the words to what they're supposed to refer to is 'thicker,' so to speak. It seems that to understand the proper application of the term 'credit default swap,' you have to be part of some larger game, some community that has started using these words together in sentences in certain ways. Similarly, to understand diaminds' use of mental objects, you have to build a 'decoder' for a whole bunch of mental objects; that's why we'll be extending, momentarily, our incipient 'mentalese' to the realm of mental objects such as statements, models, and theories. Diaminds *think*, to be sure. They think, like all of us, in words, pictures, sentences, theories, equations, and even in verse. But, we find, they make different *uses* of mental objects than most humans do, and they *tinker* with mental objects in ways that are different from what most humans would consider reasonable or 'safe.'

So we will extend our modelling language to cover the objects in terms of which minds do their minding. If language (usually) refers to 'the world,' then the mentalese we shall describe refers to the ways in which we refer to the world. We shall focus on statements, models, theories, and logics and build up intuitions about different kinds and uses thereof, in order to show how diaminds think differently and how this difference makes a difference.

Types of Statements

Let's continue with our 'mind-prospecting project' and focus on the stuff of thought. This will mean drilling down to the level of the basic building blocks of our thinking – at least, of that part of our thinking that's based on language, which is the part we can audit best – to perhaps the smallest unit of thought, or at least the smallest unit of thought that can function as a truth bearer, which is a statement. Now, everyday language and everyday thought are populated with all kinds of statements. Some are grand ('the world is like a fire') and some are not so grand ('the cat is on the mat'); some are troubling ('I believe she's cheating on me') and some are mundane ('there's a quarter in my pocket'); some are straightforward ('the leaf is green') and some allow multiple interpretations ('I can smoke while I pray'). Such statements, taken together, form a *fabric* of thought that can be audited, analysed, and decomposed into constituent parts, which can then be used to further understand how diaminds work, especially when we combine this project with some understanding of the *glue* we use to assemble statements into theories, models, scripts, stories, what have you – which we're about to supply as well.

Universal, Particular, True, False, Possible, Probable, Meaningful, and Meaningless: A Typology of Statements

Not all statements have the same level of generality. At one end of the spectrum we have statements that are *universal* in that they hold in practically all imaginable scenarios, possible worlds, or states of our world: 'water is H_2O,' '1=1,' '1+1=2,' 'all traders act to maximize per trade profit.' Some may be *false*, mind you: traders may trade to maximize profit up to a threshold determined by their pay-for-performance contract with the principal whose money they are trading with, for instance; or water may not be H_2O on some other planet or in some other parallel universe. Generality does not guarantee truth. That being said, universal statements are for *most minds* what a building's foundations are for a general contractor: they're what you build *on*, not what you start tinkering *with*. What one most often *does* tinker with are *particular* statements ('this trader has embezzled $12 million,' 'this water sample is impure,' 'this Q's typeface is 12 point Garamond') – statements that refer to your immediate space-time neighbourhood and that you can readily test and find to be true or false. Particular statements turn immediate sense impressions into assertions; in that way, they're crucial to communicating about the palpable, sensible world.

It's natural to think of sentences – universal or particular – as being either true or false: 'the gravitational force field points away from the Earth' and 'Boston is in Louisiana' are intelligible but false statements. 'I'm now reading *Diaminds*' – uttered by *you*, now – is (hopefully) an unambiguous, true, and intelligible statement.

The 'true/false' dichotomy seems a useful way to parse sentences of all kinds, no? No. For instance, how would you use this dichotomy to parse sentences about *the future* – you know, that indecipherable fog that lurks just ahead? Is a statement like 'the Fed's overnight lending rate will drop by a full percentage point by tomorrow morning' true or false? Or is it something in between?

The sentence is intelligible enough, and it will, without doubt, *become* true or false with the passage of time. But what is it *now*? Surely, it describes a state of the world that's *possible* – one can just picture a world in which the Fed's rate drops by the full percentage point, which is required to make the sentence true. In such a case, however, it makes more sense to speak of the *degree* of truth and falsity of the statement – its *likelihood* or probability – than to speak of its truth or falsity pure and simple. A statement's *degree* of credibility is especially important in a world in which we have to make *bets*, that is, lay down stakes on the truth of sentences that we don't currently know to be either true or false … which is precisely *our world*, and in particular the world in which NNT – like so many others – works, lives, breathes, and plays.

A statement's *probability* is, then, a measure of the confidence you have that it's true. So it makes sense to assign a number to it and to let this number range between two extremes, which represent falsity (probability = 0) and truth (probability = 1). It also makes sense to exclude one of the end points, the one that corresponds to 'truth.' There are many statements that, for all intents and purposes, we consider false for the purposes of our everyday planning ('there will be an airborne terrorist attack on the Sears Tower in Chicago tomorrow at eleven a.m. that will level the building and kill all its inhabitants'). So it makes sense to include those in the calculus of belief we have going, so that we can *update* them in case any evidence comes forward that they aren't as far-fetched as they seem (a new Bin Laden tape released by Al Jazeera, say). However, including statements we consider true in our calculus of uncertainty and ignorance seems like a lot of work for nothing: 'the sun will rise tomorrow' is one statement we'd attach probability 1 to; another is 'Newton's third law will continue to be in operation tomorrow'; another is 'Planck's constant will not change tomorrow,' and so forth. So we exclude those from the calculus of ignorance and make them part of the background assumptions, the assumptions that need to hold in order for the beliefs that support our bets to continue to have a chance of holding.

So we've isolated a range – [0, 1) – to our measure of 'degrees of truth.' But we don't yet know how to calculate it. In fact, there are several ways. Note: not *one*, but *several* – which is something the diamind seems to know in its entrails, and something the *other* kind of mind seems to do its best to forget.

The first way comes to us from the Marquis de Laplace and is of eighteenth-century vintage. It's the concept of mathematical probability: if you have *n possibilities*, then the probability of any one of them is $1/n$. By this measure the probability of heads coming up on a coin toss is always 0.5, because there are two sides to the coin. Not a bad first cut, but there's a bug: by this measure, the probability of the sun rising tomorrow is also, at most, 0.5, because there are two possibilities: 'the sun rises,' and 'the sun does not rise.' This jives poorly with intuition, which demands that our probability measures incorporate all the relevant information we have about the yet unknown sentence whose truth value we're trying to estimate.

So, enter a second definition of probability, this one from Ludwig von Mises, based on the frequency with which a possibility has become an actuality in the past. This measure is the limit – as the number of observations approaches infinity – of the frequency with which the proposition turned out to be true in the past. This measure seems to appease intuition insofar as the sun's having risen a few thousand billion times in the past without fail would make the probability of its rising tomorrow very close to 1 – that is, 'a few thousand billion,' divided by 'a few thousand billion plus 1,' which is approximately 1.

Of course, this measure comes with a caveat, one that many 'applied' statisticians and most social scientists ignore and that relates to the limit of the frequency *as the number of observations tends to infinity*. Therein lies a bit of a rub. Many people approximate *that* by a *very large* number of observations, thinking that a very large number is somehow closer to infinity than is a very small number. *But it isn't.* The difference between a very large number and infinity is equal to that between a very small number and infinity, and it is … infinity. There are, to be sure, situations where the 'large number estimate' is close and constantly converging with the 'infinite' estimate of the probability. *Those* cases, however, seem to be rather *less frequent* than is commonly surmised.

The effects of this bug were expressed neatly by Bertrand Russell: A chicken wakes up every morning of its life to find the farmer bringing it its food. On any particular morning, therefore, the probability it rationally should assign to the proposition 'The farmer is coming to feed me' is very close to 1. One Thanksgiving morning, however, the farmer arrives and chops off its head … which makes the chicken kind of like the myriad traders on Black Monday, Black Friday, and the many other Black Days over the past twenty years, who expected 'just another day at the office,' given the number of 'successful' days at the office they had checked off to date.

Around the same time that the frequentist conception of probabilities was being articulated and refined, another conception of probabilities was put forward, this one by a young British mathematician and philosopher named Frank Ramsey. He said, essentially: 'It would be useful to have a mechanism by which one could extract the degrees of credence that a human assigns to a belief without asking him the question in so many words or "telling" him how to calculate a probability – especially since probability definitions seem to be plagued with all kinds of problems.' Thus the *betting odds* conception of probability was born: if you believe that, with probability 0.5, the NASDAQ will drop by at least 25 per cent of its current value by the end of trading tomorrow, then on this view you will be willing to accept even odds (1:1, or bet $1 to win $1) that the proposition will turn out to be true tomorrow at five p.m. This conception of probability has launched the entire 'behavioural' study of probabilistic reasoning, by allowing laboratory psychologists and decision theorists to 'extract' subjects' degrees of belief from observations of their behaviour when they're compelled to choose among lotteries, given various pieces of information.

Of course, social scientists when they speak and write often 'muddle up' the three definitions of probability: they stipulate that betting odds *should* reflect frequencies, that mathematical probabilities *should* reflect 'uninformed priors,' and so on. They attempt to 'unify' but in so doing they gloss over the little details (where – need we remind you? – God resides, as Ludwig Mies van der Rohe once said). And that, dear reader, constitutes the entire difference between the diamind and the *other* minds: the ability to keep in mind the overwhelming difficulty of saying anything precise about the world, coupled with the willingness to keep trying.

One more distinction is to be made – one that's crucial to the workings of the diamind. Not all statements are *meaningful,* and this applies to both universal and particular statements. 'All red sentences are round,' 'this is a red sentence,' 'therefore this sentence is round' is a perfectly legitimate concatenation of meaningless universal and particular statements. What, then, makes the difference? Donald Davidson ventured a solution that seems both sensible and attractive: meaningful sentences are sentences for which we can state conditions under which they are true (or false). We can state conditions under which 'this book has less than three hundred pages' is true, but we can't state conditions under

Figure 5.1 Tree structure for parsing statements. Try it (on bosses, teachers, experts, spouses, and yourself).

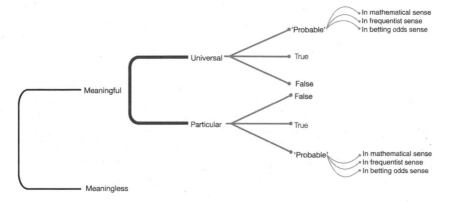

which 'this problem is pink' is true. Thus, 'this book has three hundred pages' is a meaningful sentence even if it is false, whereas 'this problem is pink' is meaningless even if we seem able to 'understand' every word.

There is, of course, a 'grey space' – a middle ground – between meaningful and meaningless, and that's where the diamind treads. How about a sentence like 'the volatility-adjusted risk premium for this equity should be ...' Well? Meaningful or meaningless? *That* would seem to depend on the precise way in which we define 'volatility,' no? Nevertheless, such sentences fill up many pages of textbooks and research journals, with nary a thought to the underlying 'meaningfulness' of the terms they're based on.

We've arrived at a palette with which we can paint a picture of the 'tree of knowledge.' Not surprisingly, it *does* have a tree structure (Figure 5.1), even though it's far more about 'belief' than about 'knowledge.'

Armed with such a tree, you can pass any statement across its branching decision points and end up at a place that represents your state of knowledge about it. Try it with a few different statements, remembering that only grammatically well-formed sentences can be 'in play': single words or parts of sentences are not allowed, simply because they can't be bearers of meaning, truth, falsity, or probability. While doing this, watch closely for 'difficult cases' – that is, for sentences that are hard to categorize as meaningful/meaningless or true/false or possible/impossible. Do you detect a pattern?

Types of Inference: Deductive, Inductive, Abductive

Now that we have the building blocks of knowledge and belief, we can go for the edifice. This is where we study how the mind builds declarative knowledge from propositions – universal, particular, known, probable, and so forth. This is also where we search for how the mind 'knows what it knows' and 'believes what it believes.'

How about this as a metaphor? Think of propositions as the *bricks* in the edifices of knowledge: models, theories, schemata, world views, whatever you like, are built from these bricks. All we need now is some *mortar* to hold the bricks in place. This mortar is supplied by different kinds of logic, which safeguard the links between the bricks – that is, the ways we make inferences from currently knowns to yet unknowns, presumably so that the yet unknowns become more known or at least more or less probable.

Here, also, are choices to be made and options to consider. There are *different kinds of mortar*. (Yes, it doesn't get any easier if you seek rules rather than choices to guide your thinking by. There are options everywhere, which is precisely why one of the most important characteristics of the diamind is mental choicefulness, which in turn rests on the ability to *see* various options among which to exercise 'decision muscle.')

The most common type of logic taught in undergraduate and graduate classes is deductive logic – you know, rules of the following type: 'a proposition is equivalent to itself'; 'a proposition is either true or false and cannot be both or neither'; 'if "if A then B is true" and A is true, then B is true'; and 'if "if A then B is true" and B is false, then A is false.' Simple. Elegant. *Impressive.* Using statements as elementary building blocks and deductive logic as the mortar that holds them together, we can build up large, elaborate chains of reasoning that pass, in most classrooms, for 'knowledge' pure and simple. We can assemble a representation of the 'edifice of knowledge' as it looked to our ancestors *circa* AD 1600. (By the way, that edifice still looks this way to some individuals closeted up in universities around the world, who have missed Hume, Carnap, and Popper and are not subscribing to *Erkenntnis* or *Mind*).

Here's how the edifice works (Figure 5.2). Start with some statements that are both certain and universal – you know, the stuff that you're absolutely certain about, that you're absolutely sure cannot be false or whose falsity you cannot conceive. Now build upwards so that every new statement you add to the edifice of knowledge can be proved

Figure 5.2 The deductive edifice of knowledge: The branches are logical consequences of the roots and therefore can contain no new information.

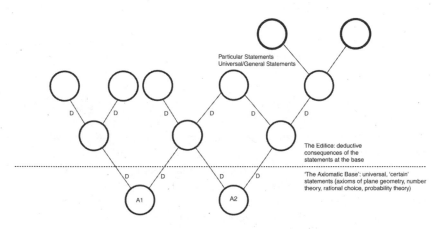

Particular Statements
Universal/General Statements

The Edifice: deductive
consequences of the
statements at the base

'The Axiomatic Base': universal, 'certain'
statements (axioms of plane geometry, number
theory, rational choice, probability theory)

A1

A2

from the statements already in the edifice using the famous rules. Build as high as you can, because in this game the tallest building 'gets the prize.' Of course, it isn't always clear what the prize is before the race begins, but 'up is good and down is bad' is not a bad mental tick for establishing goals, so run with it! Off to work, then, and Godspeed. By the end, you'll have yourself a mountain of knowledge.

Now, where is this going? We're going from more general statements to more particular ones by adding statements about which we're totally certain (we call these 'data' to make them sound more objective – Latin terms are a reliable method for doing that) as well as statements we can deduce from the statements we already know. This sounds like a great scheme for 'building something out of nothing' – you're building new knowledge from already existing knowledge, using just a few operators or rules that you apply to what you already know.

You can also apply the schema 'backwards' – that is, start with a statement you aren't sure about ('121,151 is a prime number'). From there, you use the definition of a prime number ('a number divisible only by 1 and itself') and a few trusty rules (such as the one that says you can always search the natural numbers by starting at 1 and adding 1, successively, to form ever greater numbers; or the one that says a non-prime number is the product of its divisors) to 'figure out' whether it's a prime number: if you 'find' a number greater than 1 and less than 60,575 that divides it, then 121,151 isn't prime; otherwise, it is. Got it?

Try it. When you're done, you can add '121,151 is prime' either to the list of statements that are true or to the list of statements that are false. Done! Complete! *Hasta la vista!* – in just a few easy steps. And – just think – you can do this for *any* number and build your very own library of primes. Highly useful if you're a cryptographer who specializes in unfactorable or hard-to-factor numbers, or a number theorist trying to develop test cases to disprove long-standing conjectures. But not most other times.

Lest you should think it: the 'deductive edifice' is *not* a purely fictitious contraption. Pure mathematics 'works' as an entity by building up more and more complex logical consequences of a very small set of general statements (the 'axioms'). Much of theoretical microeconomics works by building up the logical consequences of a very narrow set of statements (the axioms of 'rational choice' and 'rational belief'). It's strictly forbidden, of course, to mess with the axioms. Not only is it bad form, but you'll come across as 'poorly educated' in important circles. You'll even raise the possibility, in those same circles, that you're a threat to their culture, thereby branding yourself in ways that can't be erased for a period of time equal to the collective institutional memory of the field in which the circle members see themselves as 'belonging' (which right now is probably about five years, estimated by dead reckoning).

So if you're a pure deducer and are faced with a pricing decision in an industry in which two competitors are selling an undifferentiated product to a large number of buyers, whose demand for the product varies in inverse proportion to the price of the product, you make the standard assumptions: 1. 'It costs me and my competitor the same amount to make a unit of product'; 2. 'We're both profit maximizers'; 3. 'We're both rational and know how to carry out the maximization exercise required to figure out the quantity of product to be built that will maximize our individual profits'; and 4. 'Each of us knows points 1 to 3 and knows the other knows it.' And *presto!* You have *the answer*. No shuck, no jive, just results, and millions in the bank! Perhaps.

Want to price a five-year European call option on a standard equity issue? Simple as *bonjour!* Just figure out the expected volatility of the equity ('certain' data point 1), find the right discount rate ('certain' data point 2), and make the usual assumption relating to the Gaussian distribution of underlying returns ('certain' general statement). You already know the time horizon from the problem statement ('certain' data point 3). Next, look up the Black–Scholes option-pricing formula (or – why not? – derive it yourself from the assumptions that Fisher Black and Myron Scholes made in 1973) ('certain' general statement 2). *Eureka!* Once again you're off to the races! You have yourself a nice, shiny new call option, *priced right* – no less – and can charge the standard fee for doing this work – plus a $250,000 (USD, no less) kicker for a 'fairness opinion' on the issue of the options – which is required 'by law.' Not bad! Not bad at all! Now you can look upon the knowledge edifice that deduction has helped you build and exclaim: 'How simple! How elegant! How efficient!'

And how incomplete! Especially when you're dealing with the world as it *actually* unfolds, as opposed to the world as the reductionist mind-set *wishes* it would unfold. The rationalist leaves *that* part of the puzzle to others – to those better able to use other kinds of logic in order to make valid inferences about the world.

And who might those others be? They're the *inductivists*, who make inferences from particular statements to universal ones. Two examples: 1. 'Stock prices have gone down at the end of every second week in January in the past, and *this* is the second week in January; therefore we expect stock prices to go down this week (so we will short the S&P 500)'; and 2. 'Stock prices have gone down by at least Y per cent 99 of the last 100 times they have traded during the second week in January; therefore the probability that they will go down by at least Y per cent this week is 99 per cent.' See? Simple, transparent, to the point: *simple induction*, they call it.

There's nothing simple about it, by the way. Naive, perhaps, but not *simple*. Induction *hides* as much as it reveals. What it hides is *complexity*. Complexities, sometimes. Suppose that the 'January effect' is the artefact of some trading system that's currently being replaced. Then the 'rule' should read: 'The January effect will be in effect only when such and such trading system is in place.' Or suppose that *a lot of traders* come to know and speculate the January effect. Then put options on equity indices will become so expensive as to cancel out any trading gains. And so forth.

The basic 'metarule' is this: 'You can never tell whether a regularity is a *law*.' It may instead be a spurious artefact of a particular situation. *The general depends on the particular* in ways previously not envisioned by the generality pedlar. Of course, many social scientists call such potentially spurious associations *theories. Stylized* facts. *Rules*. Whatever. This move – and it *is* a move, in a language game that has been played by academics over the centuries – seems to have no greater purpose than

Figure 5.3 The inductive enterprise.

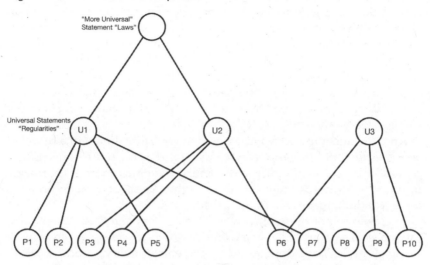

The Empirical Base: Particular statements, or 'data' to be 'explained' by 'higher level' universal statements.

to cloak the social sciences in the respectability of the natural sciences. It arises from the 'fact' – as surmised by social scientists – that natural scientists have discovered the 'laws' that make nature tick. Alas, there is a great difference between 'ticking' and 'clicking': discovering how something *ticks* – what the basic micromechanisms of its operations are at a particular time, as arrived at through *analysis* – is very different from discovering how something *clicks* – how those mechanisms come together and 'click into place' to produce an effect. The latter is the task of design and synthesis, which are the realms of design, tinkering, and engineering. And we need many more 'clicking' insights than 'ticking' insights in the field of human interaction, where 'it only ticks if it clicks.'

Seen through the inductive lens, the edifice of knowledge looks kind of, sort of, like Figure 5.3. There's a whole bunch of basic 'facts' – particular statements – at the bottom of the edifice. Above them is a layer of 'general associations' or laws that are (inductively) supported by the facts at the bottom. And yes, there may even be 'higher-order laws' that explain and are in turn supported by the lower-level laws.

Of course, from any set of particular facts, you can 'induce' many possible rules, laws, and associations. 'Human creatures think at most three moves ahead in chess.' True or false? Well, let's see: let's *run some studies* and check how a lot of humans think in a lot of chess games.

If we find that *no one* thinks more than three moves ahead in any one game, then we can assume that the 'rule' is valid, or highly probable. Some exceptions turn up. How now? Well, we can always appeal to the old 'noise term' in order to justify almost any anomaly. If the exceptions aren't too frequent (and what exceptions *are* frequent, really?), we can 'explain them away' as noise, in a sufficiently confident tone to 'get a publication out of it.' To increase the respectability of the findings, we can even come up with a 'higher-level law' that says human cognitive capacities (computation plus the short-term memory required to memorize a chess position) are bounded. Now we can ask for funding for running experiments that aim more carefully at unpacking memory limitations from the computational limitations of human minds, perhaps by having humans play 'minichess,' Nintendo, or Prisoner's Dilemma games.

Fair enough. But the 'data' base – especially if you include the *noise* terms – also supports a 'law' that says human creatures make *maximizing* decisions on how much to think and when to blink, as a function of each individual's payoffs and marginal costs of thinking and blinking. If we take this route, we're likely to go and ask for funding to design a new set of experiments that involve humans drawn from different categories (poets, politicians, physicists, physicians) playing chess under different payoff conditions.

Remember Lakatos's example of the arch-Newtonian physicists? Inductive edifices are sensitively predicated on the contents of 'the eye of the beholder.' They seem so 'objective' because of the 'feel good' feeling that comes from *simplifying* large, messy sets of data points into single 'laws' or handfuls of laws. Alas, there's a big difference – and a tension – between feeling good and doing well.

NNT's Sally against the Deductinductivists

And that's what NNT's diamind seems to understand intimately. *Intimately* does not mean just 'cognitively'; it also means 'in its innards.' Consider the Dr John–Fat Tony episode provided earlier. Dr John is a more or less pure 'deductive inductivist.' He 'knows' the independence axiom of probability theory, which states that the probability of heads for an unbiased coin is 0.5, whatever the results of the 99 previous tosses. Full stop. And why do the axioms hold in this case, John? Well, presumably because they've worked a million trillion zillion times in the past – so he might venture. End of discussion. He applies them to the *next* case, the 100th toss. He gets the 'right answer' – that is, for the final exam of a course in probability theory.

Not so with Fat Tony, who by NNT's description is 'sloppy.' But that doesn't mean he's a sloppy thinker. Not at all. More like, he's sloppy in the sense of 'more connected with the world.' The world being sloppy on occasion, Tony's interface with it – his body – mirrors that sloppiness. Being more connected with the world, he *looks at the particulars* of each case. And the particulars of this case are not 'this is a fair coin that has come up heads on the last 99 tosses' and 'the independence axiom states that the probability of the next toss should be independent of the history of tosses,' but rather 'NNT *says* this is a fair coin,' 'the coin has come up heads on the 99 previous tosses,' and (of course) the independence axiom. *What is salient here?*

By no means does this question have a clear answer. For NNT may be *wrong*. He may be wrong because he's trying to amuse himself at Tony's expense, or he may be wrong because he really doesn't *know* anything about the coin. (By the way, how *can* you tell whether a real-world coin – as opposed to the theoretical coin of statistics textbooks – is 'fair'? Where in this case is a fair test of fairness?) *Staying close* to the empirics of the case reveals complexity.

Complexi*ties*, that is. Now, there's an *epistemic choice* to be made, at least for Fat Tony. *A choice between interpretations of the sense data at hand* – that's what an 'epistemic choice' means. *A choice between beliefs that can't be resolved by the application of rules* – that's what an epistemic choice amounts to. And this choice isn't at all a 'no-brainer.' It only becomes one in the sanitized world of the *deductinductivist* – who does not, therefore, really *need* a brain. Not Fat Tony, though, who realizes there's an epistemic choice to be made, and who makes it:

> Well, what are the chances of the coin being fair, given that it's come up heads 99 consecutive times? Quick check: the probability of the sequence (heads, heads, heads … 99 times over), given that I accept the belief it's a fair coin, is $(0.5)^{99}$, or 1.57×10^{-30}, or roughly the probability of finding any one particular atom in the universe using dead reckoning. Slim odds – but *against what*? Well, how about against the 'coin is fair' belief? This doesn't seem an unreasonable choice, for *what's the probability that NNT has really gone through the process of determining whether or not it's fair*? Slim odds, that one. And *what's the probability that NNT's test would pass my own test as a fair test of fairness?* Slim odds again. Too many slim odds for the 'coin is fair' belief – as opposed to the 'NNT says the coin is fair' belief, which is really

all I can reasonably go on in the situation at hand. *Really,* that is, if I'm epistemically *modest.'*

And that modesty is a key feature of NNT's Black Swan hunting 'protocol.'

What the deductinductivist *misses* – forever misses, because she can't do otherwise – is that intimate connectedness to the *situation at hand,* which can only come from a radically empirical orientation of perception, thought, and action. An *empirical* orientation – as NNT, the founder of Empirica, LLC tirelessly admonishes. What does this mean? How does it work? What is it about the diamind that allows it to be *more empirical* than other minds?

The *radical empiricist* – to be distinguished from his garden-variety counterpart, who carries deductinductivist credentials and spouts endless generalities that are 'supported' by 'data' – is a species of *abductive* thinker. Abductive not as in *Abduction from the Seraglio,* but rather as in the ab-duction of the best explanation that is consistent with the data, from among a host of competing explanations that may be radically different. The term can be traced back to the American pragmatist philosopher (and *doer,* some forget) C.S. Peirce, who coined the term to explain the pattern of inference that characterizes the process of scientific discovery. The abductive 'leap,' so to speak, is one that goes from a set of data that seem disconnected to an explanation that connects them in the most satisfying possible way. 'Most satisfying' does not mean 'simplest,' by any simple-minded definition of 'simple.' And no, we're not going to define 'most satisfactory' just yet.

An example, to bring us back to everydayness: One fine morning, while camping in the Adirondacks, you see bear tracks in the snow outside your tent. You know there may be bears around, for it's still too early in the winter for them to be hibernating. You infer that a bear must have made the tracks. Follow your mind as it makes each step in the inferential process. The first step is to seek an answer to this question: 'What would have to be true in order for the statement "there are bear tracks in the snow" to be true?' That is where the 'there are bears around' possibility comes up. The second step is to seek *any other* alternative explanation for why there are bear tracks in the snow. You find none. So you pick 'the best' and only explanation consistent with the facts – in this case, there are bear tracks in the snow because a bear has made them.

Now for a variation, to show how the abductive game works: Suppose you know that your campmate is of a playful mind and has brought along a set of bear claws. That is another empirical fact, one that supplies a second possible explanation, which would come up in step 2. You now have two explanations to choose from, and too few facts. So you go and look for other facts that will help you discriminate between the two. How? Well, by using the *subjunctive* manoeuvre of step 1, which entails asking this question: 'What would have to be true if my friend really had played her trick on me?' Here you might check to see if the claws she has brought along are wet; or you might study her face carefully while you're telling her about your discovery, letting your own mirror neurons and facial muscles act as 'anomaly detectors' as you search for a smile, a snicker, or an unduly unruffled response from her.

Think of the abductive game as a *bootstrapping* procedure. One side of the boot is represented by the facts you're trying to make sense of. The other side is the set of explanations you're considering, which could help you make sense of the facts. The 'laces' are the subjunctive manoeuvres: 'What would have to be true if …?' The knot is the abductive leap, the inference to the best explanation, given all the facts you've had time to collect.

Note, also, why the diamind has a distinctive advantage in the abductive game: the 'better' abductivist is the abductivist who can entertain more and more different explanations *at the same time* in his so-called mind, while retaining the ability go on thinking and running tests. The bear example is not all that bad: radically different 'action plans' are entailed by the two explanations ('bear made tracks,' 'friend joking around'). You don't want to pull stakes if your friend was just joking around. You don't want to just carry on with your day if there's a bear lurking around. Your mind is taking you in two different directions at once, and instead of discounting one explanation (because it's low in likelihood) or deleting a fact altogether as 'noise' (in good old deductinductivist style), you try to stay close to the facts (by seeking to conduct a *crucial test* that helps you tell the two hypotheses apart) and to the problem (by doing this test quickly and efficiently, as opposed to thinking about how you might possibly do it if the sun, the moon, and the stars all aligned).

No less important, the *crucial test* is based on a *prediction*, not an explanation. In effect you're saying: 'Her face *will* betray something if she perpetrated the trick,' not 'Her face *showed* …' The basic motto of the radical empiricist is 'explanation is cheap, prediction is golden.' True to the old wisdom of risk and reward, explanation is easy whereas prediction is hard. (Nothing will convince you of this more quickly than a set of experiments in which you test, really *test*, your ability to predict, with strong accuracy, events that you know yourself able to easily explain. Try it. Try it now, before reading further.)

What does all of this have to do with NNT's Black Swan hunting and avoidance protocols? Let's go back to his story of Fat Tony and Dr John. Fat Tony is a bootstrapper. He's a 'first-rate noticer' of the facts of the situation. Being such a first-rate noticer, he aims for the most precise and complete and unpresumptive characterization of those facts possible. That's why he encodes the business about the fair coin as 'NNT says it's a fair coin' and not as 'it's a fair coin,' which is how Dr John encodes it. *That*, really, is all one can say about this. Now, that the coin is fair is *not* a fact. It may, though, be a 'best explanation' for the collection of facts – 'NNT says it's a fair coin,' 'NNT has reason to know this,' 'NNT has reason to tell me the truth' – as well as for the additional generalization 'NNT does what he has reason to do.' If any one of these facts or pseudo-facts is false, the 'bestness' of the inference is radically undermined.

What Fat Tony has – and what NNT also seems to have – is a built-in 'belief acceptance testing protocol' – a BAT protocol, for short. A BAT protocol compensates for the rather poorly developed human capacity to suspend belief and deploy doubt at will. The radical empiricist uses a BAT protocol to get out of the ZOO, that is, the *zone of oblivion*, which is where Dr John – who 'obviates' the complexity entailed in the passage from 'NNT says X is true' to 'X is true' – lives and breathes.

A BAT is a razor-sharp instrument. Like all sharp instruments, it cuts deeply in whatever direction you apply force to it. Apply it in the wrong direction and you'll quickly doubt whether you're still alive and reading this sentence (as opposed to, say, *dreaming*, or *a brain in a vat*, wired up in just the right way by a team of bioengineers). *That*'s the way of the sceptic, who gets his jollies by wreaking havoc and mayhem on dogmatic friends, acquaintances, and colleagues, but who's quite useless when it comes to pricing options in ambiguous predicaments. The *problem* you're trying to solve should guide your BAT – which is why we started our quest to speak mentalese with *problems* rather than with statements, decisions, or solutions.

The diamind's BAT protocol, then, is one by which 'facts' are recognized as BEPSPs – that is, as 'best explanations for patterns of sense perceptions.' They're 'theory-laden,' as some philosophers of science somewhat pompously put it. This means they've got theories embedded in them, which give them meaning and intelligibility in exchange for incorrigible bias. And cleaning up facts from the theories that clothe them is the hallmark of the radical empiricist, a.k.a. the Black Swan hunter.

Example: 'Fact: profits go up with market share.' *Fact*? Well, let's see. Some studies have shown a positive correlation between the two, and a logic of value appropriation under asymmetries of demand and supply has been advanced as explaining monopoly power, which in turn explains the correlation in conditions of perfect rationality and common knowledge of rationality. So the 'general fact' is, really, shorthand for all this 'stuff' you have to believe in order to believe the fact itself. Additionally, these studies make assumptions about the underlying *distributions* of profits, costs, capabilities, and so forth. As in *normal* distributions – Gaussian, that is. The trouble is, you can't observe those distributions, which means you have to *assume* them. So add *them* to the assumption base – to the set of stuff you have to believe in order to be able to 'know the fact.' We could go on (we won't). A question, though: What do you *do* about all this? Where should the mind go?

NNT's response: 'Stay as close as you can to reality' – that is, to facts that are as little as possible BEPSPs masquerading as facts. Okay, but, how do you do *that*? Well, here's a heuristic, one that's inspired by the abductivist's bootstrapping protocol: 'Seek the general assumptions embedded in the particular statement, then seek to refute that statement with *another* particular statement.' In other words, find the general assumptions embedded in what most people take to be 'facts' – that is, in objective, immutable beliefs that everyone believes everyone believes, which is why they end up in the ZOO – and then uncover the general assumptions embedded in those 'facts,' and then ask: 'What would have to be true if these assumptions were *false*?' 'False,' not 'true': that's Peirce's (second) contribution to the world's philosophical cuisine: *fallibilism* is the basic commitment to a stance that leaves open, indeed pursues, the possibility that even the staunchest beliefs may be false – by testing them. Against *predictions*, not explanations.

You want to turn this into a trading heuristic? Okay. Again, find the BEPSPs that function as the holy cows of common sense or consensus. (Example: 'Oil prices are going up.' Notice the ambiguity of the present perfect tense, which most analysts resort to in their reports; 'are going up' *really* means 'have been going up for the past n time periods, and we can think of reasons why they've been doing that, and we expect those reasons to keep holding, so there's no reason to change the assumption' – all of which is quite a mouthful, neatly summarized as 'are going up.') Then identify the general assumptions that are (hopelessly) embedded in the BEPSPs, and ask yourself: 'What would have to be true if any one of these assumptions were false?' Figure out what the distribution of value in the world would look like under those scenarios, and having done that, quietly buy inexpensive options on assets that *would* be valuable *if* the assumptions turned out to be false. (Notice the subjunctive: French speakers will have it a lot easier, as NNT might himself attest.) Those options will be cheap because most people assume that the assumptions are *true*, not false, so no one wants those options. Then *wait*. Sure, you'll lose the money you put up if the assumptions against which you bet turn out to be true. But that's just the cost of learning. It's the cost of making bets on the failure of beliefs that, though false, can 'hold up' for long periods of time before succumbing to the weight of the world. It's part of the operational expenses of the radical empiricist, and it's offset by the big-kaboom gains that come along with a play that works out.

The strategy's overall payoff depends, of course, on the frequency with which generally accepted assumptions are wrong in ways that impact the value of some asset. So it would be great, for the Black Swan hunter, if there were some treasure chest of assumptions that most people *systematically get wrong*: Gaussianity, linearity, and rationality, perhaps? If it turned out that some 'necessary illusions' (Nietzsche's contribution to finance theory) systematically survive refutation in most people's minds and that people consistently hold to them *because they must* – then, *then*, Black Swan hunting could be a bona fide sport, and the diamind its exemplary sportsman. And *this is just the insight* that allows the radical empiricist to outperform his deductinductivist colleagues.

You might ask: 'Why doesn't the application of just plain old Bayes's Theorem take care of the deductinductivist's problems?' In other words, why is it that (as NNT puts it) Bayes's Theorem is just 'not enough'? To recap, the Reverend Thomas Bayes was the man who gave us a simple algorithm for updating old beliefs in light of new evidence. That is, he gave us a way to calculate 'the probability of hypothesis H conditional on data D' in a way that depended on our probability for hypothesis H before data D was known; 'the probability of the data D given that hypothesis H was true'; and 'the probability of any hypotheses other than H that are consistent with D.' Not too shabby, for a mathematician, whom we might expect to be far less sensitive than many others to the 'messy stuff.' So, what's missing? Why does the abductivist, in the end, fare better in the intimate contest with himself for staying close to 'the world'? Think about that for a bit, before proceeding.

Here's what we'll do: we'll use Bayes's contraption to *look for a Black Swan*. Not *today* – no. Rather, we'll use authorial privilege to use Bayes's Theorem to look for a Black Swan in the times when people believed true the proposition 'all swans are white.' What happens if you believe that all swans are white? Well, you 'logically' (i.e., deductively) believe that 'if a bird is a swan then it's white.' And you believe *this* because (inductively), all the birds you have ascertained to be swans have thus far turned out to be white. So far, we're in deductinductivist Heaven: there's no anomaly to produce tremors in the edifice of knowledge.

Armed with such devices – and with Tom Bayes's trusty theorem – a zoologist of that gilded age goes to the field. She sees a bird. The bird is the size of a swan. It has a long, curved neck. It is black. She believes that 'all swans are white.' She believes it so strongly, in fact, that the belief is in her ZOO: it doesn't need to be *tested,* just as 'the force of gravity points downwards' doesn't need to be tested every time we do wind testing for a new airplane. It's part of the zoologist's *background assumptions*. She *is* a scientist, however. Not one of the mental rigour and incisiveness of Chekhov's Nikolai von Koren, perhaps, but, a scientist nonetheless. So she pulls out some hypotheses: 'This bird is a raven,' 'This bird is an egret.' Provided she is really interested in the bird in the first place. If she isn't, she may not even get close enough to the bird to be struck by its swanlike features. But suppose she is. She gets closer to the bird. She has several alternative hypotheses to consider ('egret,' 'raven'). No swan in sight – since it was excluded *ex hypothesis* (a sinister expression, and most telling). She picks the *most likely* hypothesis, given the data – 'egret,' say. A massive, fat egret. All is well. Bayes's Theorem was correctly applied. Black Swans continue to un-exist.

All because there is no *room*, in Bayes's Theorem, to update the set of hypotheses you begin with. 'Garbage in, garbage out,' the software programmer's adage tells us. And that's as it should be: if you *did* think of sneaking a new hypothesis into the denominator of Bayes's formula, then you'd have to *redo* all your prior probabilities. Redo all the work that got you to your current, deductinductivist state of bliss to begin with. Hard. Messy. Unpalatable.

Enter the radical empiricist, armed with Mr Peirce's diamind. He wants to get forever closer to facts that are as undistorted as possible by prior beliefs and assumptions. So he starts describing the bird,

Linnaeus-style. Long, curved neck. Wide beak. Wide wings. Song pattern. What have you. He makes a list of these observations. Hell, he might even structure these features as a tree – that would make things amazingly simple. But we'll suppose he doesn't, for the moment. When he's done, he considers the problem of *naming* the bird. This is as big a problem for him as for anyone else, to be sure. But he has a lot of fine-grained data to go on, which his deductinductivist colleagues do not have. This fine-grained data is problematic for all of the preceding hypotheses ('egret,' 'raven'), which he can produce as quickly as his colleague.

Now, our hypothetical radical empiricist *also* believes that 'all swans are white.' But the *way* in which he believes this *makes all the difference.* He believes it in a fallible way. The belief is not in his ZOO. It's alive and open for testing. So he can say:

> Suppose that 'all swans are white' is false. What would follow? Well, how about 'There exists at least one black swan.' And perhaps many more. Now suppose 'this is a black swan' is true – since it's suddenly made possible by the negation of 'all swans are white'? What then? How much of my fine-grained data is explained by *this* hypothesis? And more important, how much *more* of the fine-grained data is explained by this hypothesis than by any other hypothesis?

He has a 'match' – a good match, a *better* match than that provided by any alternative. So he makes a leap. An inference to the best explanation. (The denouement is well known: derided at first, he is later hailed as a great discoverer in academic circles. Exhausted by the mental effort required by the abductive leap, he starts to drink and carouse, gets fat, lazy, and tenured, and retires to the Ivory Tower, where he becomes a deductinductivist institution builder.)

Types of Models

One last tool in our toolkit for learning to speak mentalese: *models.* Think of models as tools for representing a salient part of the world. They can be pictures, but more often they're theories, equations, graphs, narratives, or bits and pieces of a narrative – you know, the stuff you build out of statements, our good old bricks. But not all models are the same, not all models work the same way, and not all models have the same payoffs to the user, so the mind is well advised to make, once again, several distinctions so as to be *choiceful* in its relationship to its own models.

To understand the music of models, let's spend a little time in the company of one of our diaminds: Charlie Munger, who is Warren Buffett's friend and partner and Wesco's chairman. Munger is deeply fond of both using the mind and analysing its misuses. That is, he thinks *and* he thinks about thinking, and he does both while *doing*. He understands (as very few do) the power of ideas as mediators of our interactions with the world, *alongside* their shortcomings – and in that regard, he's an authentic diamind. Indeed, he explicitly attributes his success to his own involvement with the workings of the mind – an involvement noted by those who've worked closely with him. In particular, they've noted his diverse and multidisciplinary 'mental models.'

The mind 'accesses' the world through mental models. It behaves like a large, dynamic, sometimes highly intelligent 'compression engine' (Figure 5.4) for the impressions the world leaves on the senses – impressions we routinely call 'data.' There are several layers of compression: from the inaccessible 'world' to the accessible sensory inputs; from the sensory inputs to the models embedded in our sensory apparatus; and from those 'perceptual' models to those cognitive or mental models – ideas, pictures, theories, mechanisms, input/output equations, structural equations, what have you – that we behold as mental models. However, Munger's mind functions not just as a great mechanical compressor – which would be a purely *M*-mode operation – but also as a monitor and executive of the compression process. That is, his mind understands the power of those ideas that live in the mind's 'penthouse' to shape attention, perception, association, communication, and action. As the old saying goes: 'Watch your thoughts, for they will become your destiny.'

Munger, like his partner Warren Buffett, sees himself as a pedagogue and thus an academic of sorts: 'I call [Berkshire Hathaway] the ultimate didactic enterprise. Warren's never going to spend any money. He's going to give it all back to society. He's just building a platform so people will listen to his notions … But you could argue that Warren and I are academics in our own way.'[1] Consequently, he's heeded the urge to make explicit some of his mental models – that is, compression schemata that make up the 'worldly mind.'

It's interesting that the most explicit of Munger's schemata is the one that deals with the mechanisms of human misjudgement (Figure 5.5). Here, Munger has essentially invented a personally useful social, cog-

Figure 5.4 The diamind as a data compression engine.

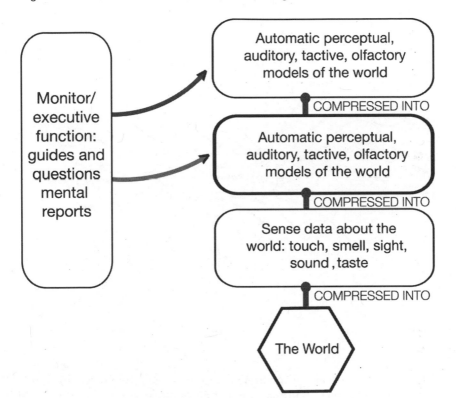

nitive, and neuro-psychology of human judgement and decision making, targeted at providing a set of stress tests for thoughts and ideas. He uses this map in either of two ways. *First,* as a BAT protocol when he audits his own beliefs about an opportunity. If his own beliefs 'pass' a test that checks for sources of bias and irrationality that many humans have been known to fall prey to, and if these beliefs point to an investment opportunity with abnormal returns, then chances are good that the underlying beliefs are valid and that the opportunity is real. *Second,* as a 'working model' of the compounding effects of well-known failures of rationality, which taken together *point* to opportunities arising from exploiting those failures. In the market as it's been constructed, *short-selling* assets whose value is predicated on false assumptions is itself an opportunity for positive gains. The big interaction effects that

Figure 5.5 Charlie Munger's personal psychology of human misjudgement.

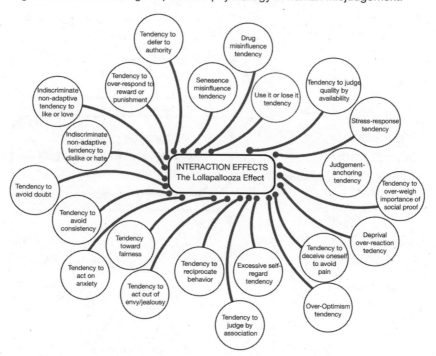

Munger carries on about can arise in either of these two ways: from using the map of irrationality as a belief acceptance test, or from using it as an opportunity generator.

Several things stand out about this mental map of misjudgement sources. First, the subtlety with which the tricky ideas about 'laws,' mechanisms, rules, and correlations is treated. He calls these 'tendencies.' Not rules. Not hard-wired mechanisms. *Tendencies.* A tendency is different from a rule – even a statistical rule – in that it's *corrigible.* You can work at it, purposefully, with the aim of reversing it. And you can sometimes succeed.

An example: Psychologists have smugly ascertained that humans just can't suppress thoughts. The prototypical experiment – one that got several people tenure in various places – involves asking some subjects not to think of a white bear. 'White bear thoughts' in this group is then compared with 'white bear thoughts in groups of subjects who have received no instructions.' From this, the 'humans cannot suppress thoughts' law. But once you realize that 'don't think of a white bear' is materially equivalent to 'think of something that is not a white bear,' which is logically equivalent to 'think of a non-white non-bear,' which is logically equivalent to 'think of a pink shoe,' or 'think of a black dog,' and so forth, you're in possession of a very good bypass mechanism for the 'law' in question.

So the 'law' isn't a law. It's a proclivity. A tendency. Perhaps a pointer to a mechanism that *relies* on laws but that isn't wholly *reducible* to them. Something that can be 'designed around' and thereby overcome. Munger is about ten years ahead of academic psychology, epistemologically speaking. And he knows it: 'Let's just say that high energy physics is now an alternative career path for most [psychologists].'[2]

Back to Munger's own toolkit of mental models of human misjudgement. What's striking about them is that they are, at the same time, both simple and deep. Charlie knows *this*, too: 'There is an old, two-part rule that often works wonders in business, science and elsewhere: (1) Take a simple, basic idea and (2) Take it very seriously.'[3] The words sound almost trivial until you dig a little deeper and review Figure 5.5. When you do, what they actually mean will hit you: the idea has to be both *simple* and *basic*. *Basic* means 'fundamental.' 'Fundamental' means 'having something to do with the foundation,' or the root.

So the 'tendencies' in Figure 5.5 are not, actually, just any old list. They are not the mere output of a book report on an introductory psychology text. (Indeed, Munger dares you to find an adequate treatment of 'envy' in such a text. If you can't, ask yourself *why not?* Then apply the 'tendencies' to arrive at a pretty good explanation, one that has to do with the psychology of psychologists.) They're the output of a highly skilled compression engine, one that has filtered long experience with counterproductive behaviours of the human mind down to this set.

They're also simple. They're one-liners. They refer to entities to which we have first-person access (selves, endowments, cash, other people). You don't need a PET scanner to generate observations that will make these words meaningful, but you *could* use a PET scanner to sharpen your understanding of them. Their simplicity is no accident, either. It has something to do with what Munger has called 'the ethos of the hard sciences,' which he believes is missing from psychology, economics, and sociology. That ethos has nothing to do with stating your 'theories' in terms of laws – that, in fact, is what he believes 'physics envy' in economics is all about.

Rather, it has a lot to do with insisting on immediate and sharp refutability. That's where simplicity helps you out. You need only three points along the trajectory of a planet to test the hypothesis that its orbit traces out a circle. You need four points to test the hypothesis that it traces out an ellipse. Not just refutability is at issue – as Karl Popper admonished – but also the *practicality* of the actual tests you perform in order to test a theory. And *that* is the marvel of the diamind: *it is able to think about thinking while thinking to the end of doing better.*

Okay, but everyone 'knows' vacuous truisms like 'the world is complex.' How, then, does simplicity help you generate explanations for complex phenomena? The key: *interactions*. Notice the lollapalooza box smack in the middle of Figure 5.5? It's the interactions box, which is where – and how – the myriad simplicities come together to generate complexity. It's also – very much so – an embodiment of what Munger calls the 'hard science' ethos: each law of physics, ranging from Newton's laws of motion, through Einstein's special relativity principle, to the Navier Stokes equations governing the flow of liquids, to the Maxwell equations governing the propagation of electromagnetic waves and their interactions with electrical currents, to the Boltzmann equations of statistical mechanics, to the Heisenberg matrix representation of quantum mechanics and the Schrödinger wave representation of quantum mechanics, is *simple*. Each takes, at most, one or two lines. No more. The complexity of the behaviours those laws explain – and hence the sophistication of the explanations they generate – arises from interactions: between the entities described by the models, and between the model's user and the model. And that is what 'solving the equation' is all about.

The following exercise will highlight the qualities of the 'deep tendencies.' *Build a stress test* for your thoughts out of the Mungerisms of Figure 5.5. If possible, to make it a useful test, make it a tree-structured classifier – that is, one you can perform quickly and recall in the presence of those influences (drugs, friends, painful memories, powerful people, etc.) that can pop up in your life and so easily distort the important faculty of reason.

What you'll notice, if you take this simple suggestion seriously(!), is that the twenty-three Munger-psychologisms are easily concatenable into a set of tests you can perform in real-time on your own thoughts. Thus they're both easily *falsified* and easily used as regulators for the all-important 'executive' monitor of the behemoth compression engine called 'mind' ... Which is precisely what you might expect from someone who once wrote a lecture subtitled 'practical thought about practical thought': ideas don't just represent –they *do*. They *do* in virtue of what they represent, but they also *do* in virtue of what they allow us to do *with* them ... Which is why they're both powerful and dangerous.

Now, what's remarkable about Munger is the following diaminded proclivity. He's taken by the ethos of the physical sciences, which he understands in a way that has nothing to do with 'popular wisdom' (he calls for increasing testability through axiomatic simplicity and for generating complexity through interaction effects). And at the same time, he's committed to adopting models and methods from other branches of academe – that is, to multidisciplinarity. A *non sequitur?* Hardly. Rather, it's an epistemological stance that's more sophisticated than the one currently in use in most social science departments today ... which looks sort of like the one in Figure 5.6. *That* figure, in case you're wondering, *was* the picture of human knowledge most consistent with the cutting edge of academic thinking ... *about seventy years ago*, when we had so few machines around – and consequently were so naive about their powers – that we saw much more in them than they could actually and eventually deliver. And that picture was one in which 'history' would be reducible to sociology and macroeconomics, which in turn would be reducible to psychology and microeconomics, which in turn would be reducible to biology, which in turn would be reducible to chemistry, which in turn would be reducible to physics, which would in time, given enough 'churning' and turning of the cranks of this massive compression machine, reduce everything.

Now, remember: if one field of knowledge reduces another, it means that the theories of the reduced field are all going to be explained away as special cases or direct consequences of the theories of the reducing field. So if you were to take this view of human knowledge and heed Munger's call for 'more fundamental' knowledge, you would focus on the 'penthouse' of science – just as you would focus solely on the 'penthouse' of thinking in the 'behemoth compression engine' model of the mind.

Yet whatever his sympathies for the mental tendencies of physicists, Munger's view of human knowledge is *not* that of Figure 5.6. Rather, he seems to *know* – intuitively if not explicitly – that at some point in the twentieth century, something happened to human knowledge and knowledge about knowledge along the way to certainty. And his 'worldly wisdom' – to be gotten by driving towards deep, diverse, and simple models from a large number of different disciplines *without* demanding that all models be logically compatible with one another – is

Figure 5.6 The unity of science: the early twentieth-century view of human knowledge about the world.

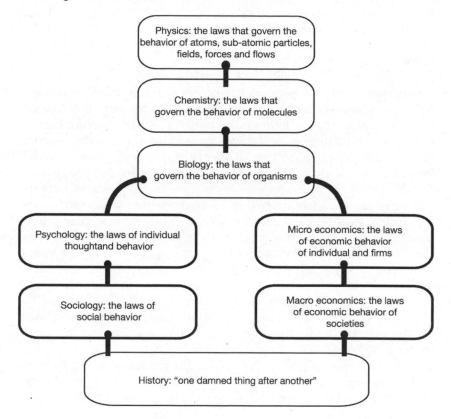

in fact one of the few stances towards knowledge that are consistent with the 'new picture' that has, in the meantime, emerged (Figure 5.7):

What he seems to know is this: the various academic disciplines are founded on models that are far from reducible to one another. In fact, they're likely *irreducible* to one another. Rather, each discipline contributes to the explanatory exercise of human science a family of models, which can be understood, at the core, by understanding the basic premises on which they rest. 'You do not have to understand all of celestial mechanics to understand the most important part of Laplace's contributions to physical science,' he admonishes.[4] And understanding *that* one idea is where most of the gold is.

Figure 5.7 The dis-unity of science and the worldly mind: the early twenty first-century view of 'human knowledge' and the basis of Munger's insight.

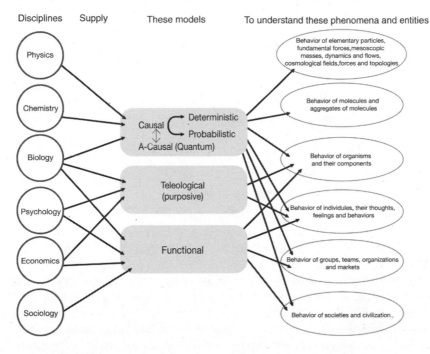

So it's useful to ask: Exactly *how* can we compress the fragmented and siloed knowledge of academe so that it becomes useful as worldly knowledge? What is the 'functional architecture' of worldly knowl-edge? Well, let's try breaking up *all* mental models into families that we can use to classify knowledge from various disciplines. This will help us create another one of those useful *trees* for parsing complexity into something simpler and more intelligible (Figure 5.8).

On one prong of the tree, we place *relational* models. Many of the models that structure perception are here. *Relational* means 'about rela-tions,' as in 'to the left of,' 'to the right of,' 'above,' and 'below' (visual models); 'higher,' 'lower,' and 'equal' pitch (auditory models); 'sourer than,' 'saltier than,' and 'sweeter than' (gustatory); 'more sulphurous than' and 'sharper than' (olfactory); and 'rougher than,' 'smoother than,' 'sharper than,' and 'blunter than' (tactile). This is a first cut at the first level of compression of 'world' by 'mind.' The resulting models map 'world' onto 'data' in an auditable way.

Figure 5.8 A tree-structured classifier for mental models.

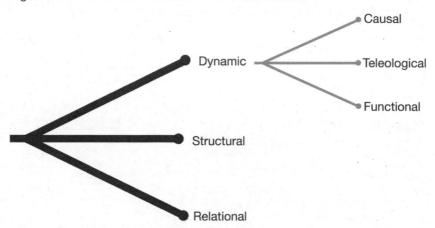

On another prong of the tree we place *structural* models. These are models that describe physical and logical structures ('a component of,' 'not a component of,' 'a subset of,' 'not a subset of') and so forth. You can use these models to describe pictures and other collages of sensory data in more detail and with greater clarity regarding inclusion and exclusion. They'll tell you that an organ system is part of an organism, that an organism is part of an ecological niche, that an ecological niche is part of an ecosystem. By 'part' we mean 'constitutive part': the part *constitutes* the whole, in that it's dependent on it, whereas the whole is dependent on the parts for its entitivity.

Both relational and structural models relate to the 'lower floors' of the 'compression engine.' They also, for the most part, 'live' in three-dimensional space. But they don't encompass the high-level abstractions that have been the glory of the human mind for 2,500 years. A third prong of the tree covers those abstractions – the *dynamical* models, which can be used to explain, predict, understand, analyse, and synthesize what happens to various entities in the world as it *goes forward* in time. Here, too, it's highly useful to make distinctions, as follows:

Causal models are the staple of most physical science – with the notable and recent exception of quantum mechanics, though quasi-causal models of quantum mechanical interactions are possible, courtesy of the special interpretations of Louis de Broglie and David Bohm. Causal models are based on the all-important cause-and-effect relationship: *if ... then ...* is their trademark. *If* you drop this pen from a height, *then* it will fall. *If* you drop a dog from a height, *then* it will fall. *If* you drop your neighbour from a height, *then* he will fall. You get the picture. Of course, going on and on about all possible objects that could fall is a terribly inefficient way to describe falling.

This is where Munger's drive towards the depth and simplicity of models helps a lot: far better to postulate a force (the gravitational one) and a set of objects (generic masses) and just say that a mass in a force field will accelerate at a rate inversely proportional to its weight. That was Newton's move (actually, that of d'Alembert before him), and it was – *note!* – perfectly consistent with Munger's basic principle: drive towards greater simplicity and more basic laws.

But causal models are not solely the domain of physics. When Didier Sornette uses sandpile dynamics to explain the stock market crash of 2008, or when a psychologist uses stimulus/response models to explain the automatic responses of humans in various circumstances, causal mechanisms appear in full force. When an economist posits that a preference is logically linked to a choice, he is – unwittingly – claiming a causal link between a mental event (a preference) and a physical one (a choice). Thus causal models are *everywhere*. When a neuropsychologist makes a claim about the brain processes that trigger certain automatic behavioural responses, she is making a model-based claim about the causal structure of human action and behaviour.

Teleological models are models that explain on the basis of individual purposes, of intentions. When we say that academics are self-deceived about the relative importance of explicit knowledge to the success of human enterprise, we're claiming they have an incentive to deceive themselves (increased ego gratification and fear of decreased ego gratification) that leads them to favour certain beliefs over others and to ignore or filter out information that suggests the contrary conclusion (the pain avoidance–induced self-deception tendency).

Economics is awash with intentional models. Game theorists explain market dynamics as processes of *tâtonnement* whereby self-interested actors play competitive and cooperative games with one another by adjusting their strategies sequentially up to the point where no single player can make himself better off by making a unilateral move – which is the concept underlying the Nash equilibrium. When agency theorists describe 'the firm,' they do so via a little model that represents shareholders as principals and managers as agents in contractual relationships that have been arrived at through negotiations by self-interested actors whose opportunity sets and opportunity costs are constrained by the 'market for corporate control' and the 'market for capital.' When a network theorist looks at humans and organizations, she sees 'ties' that proxy for to relationships that form a network in which the human or the organization occupies a position whose centrality is to be maximized by partnering with the right others.

Teleological models are not limited to social science theories of behaviour, of course. They arise every day in public discourse. Conspiracy theories regarding George W. Bush's Iraqi 'adventure' of 2003 have been based on a teleological model: a few 'people of influence' wanted to achieve control of the Middle Eastern nation and *conspired* to distort, filter, and otherwise modify information presented to the public in such a way as to engineer the outcome they wanted. And teleological models aren't just the stuff of social science and political discourse, either. When a biologist describes an amoeba, he often refers to what the organism *minimizes* or *maximizes* in behaving as it does. When a physicist writes down a Hamiltonian for a many-particle system, she assumes, in order to solve for the trajectories of the bodies vis-à-vis one another, that the system as a whole *minimizes* some figure of merit (such as the overall potential energy) and that it comes to rest in the minimum potential energy configuration. Similarly, when we use the double well to describe a feature of the diamind, we assume that the model describes a system that 'minimizes' that same objective function.

Finally, we have *functional* models. These are tricky, and we didn't have a good handle on them until people like Marx – inspired by Hegel and Feuerbach – came along and started to explain behemoth entities such as 'the economy' in terms of the *functions* of the various social and economic actors they encompassed. For instance, in a Marxian model of the economy the function of the workers is to add value to raw materials in excess of what can be added by the raw inputs themselves and by machines. The market as a whole *functions* to expropriate value from the workers and turn it into capital, whose function, in turn, is to replicate and multiply itself.

Once Marx started us thinking about functional explanations of human phenomena, the game was on and others followed suit. In the Austrian economics model (in contrast to the Marxian model), the *function* of a market is to increase the efficiency with which information is transmitted, credibly, from one remote location in the world to another. This is carried out through the price system, which functions to signal – in the absence of monopolies and other natural disasters – sudden demand and supply shocks from one corner of the world to another.

In neoclassical economics, the function of a market is to increase the overall welfare of the participants. The function of a business organization, according to an agency-theory view of such entities, is to maximally align the interests of the principals (shareholders) with those of the agents (managers and employees) who have been engaged to manage the business. Neuropsychological models assign *functions* to various parts of the brain and posit some kind of assignment of mental functions to brain loci. Models of computer languages assign *functions* to different parts of a computer language; they also assign functions to different modules and sublanguages, such as assembly-level languages. We don't speak of the workings of the mind in terms of causes and effects nearly as often as we speak of them in terms of the *functions* of various mental processes and procedures.

Now what exactly is 'diamind-like' about the ability to parse knowledge in terms of *models* rather than disciplines? It's precisely the fact that the mind is no longer beholden to 'ideology' and institutional cognitive commitments – a theme Munger has expanded on: 'Importation into many places of extremist political ideologies of the left and of the right ... had, for their possessors, made regain of objectivity almost as unlikely as regain of virginity.' To paraphrase: 'Importation into many *practices* of entrenched disciplinary cognitive commitments and ideas of the ontological, epistemological, and logical kinds ... had, for their possessors, made regain of objectivity almost as unlikely as regain of virginity.' Or, after one more iteration: 'Importation into many *practices* of entrenched disciplinary models and ways of knowing ... had, for their possessors, made regain of objectivity almost as unlikely as regain of virginity'.

It is not, in the end, surprising that Munger – the prototypical diamind – has made human thinking itself the subject of his most elaborate and well worked-out model – the model of human misjudgement, a model that's *reflexive* in that it always applies first and foremost to its user; *broad* in that it encompasses in simple and actionable form the core *automatisms* of human reasoning; and *deep* in that its component 'tendencies' can be used to generate connected explanations for large numbers of 'facts' and factoids about humans (Figure 5.9).

We find an echo of Munger's approach in the workings of another diamind – the physicist and (more important) *thinker* David Deutsch, one of the early and seminal contributors to the field of quantum computation.[5] Deutsch starts from this question: 'Is it possible, in this day and age of disciplinary fragmentation and specialization, to fulfill the idea of the Renaissance scientist and realistically hope to "know" every-

Figure 5.9 Munger's mind's eye: informationally broad and logically deep.

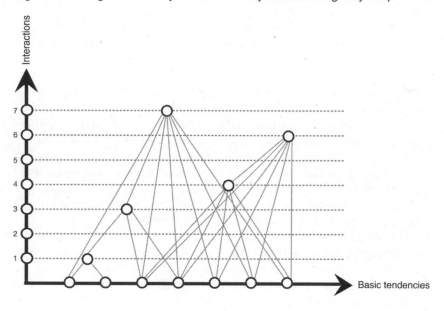

thing?' His answer: 'Yes,' if by 'know' we mean understand and by 'understand' we mean 'understand everything than can be understood.' For this, however, we need models that are *deep* – that cut to the deep explanatory models and mechanisms of the universe. In furtherance of this, Deutsch has developed a 'mental model map' that condenses phenomena to three basic classes (life, thought, computation) and that condenses disciplinary models to three basic families (quantum physics, theories of computation, theories of evolution). These mental models span teleological, causal, and functional forms and are held in check by a metamodel: 'epistemology.' On this point, Deutsch embraces Karl Popper's falsificationist approach, which insists that inductive reasoning is fatally flawed, that science makes progress by refutation rather than confirmation, and that truth – a local property of a theory – is radically different from certainty (i.e., the impossibility to doubt a theory or a model), which is an illusion that can be traced back to Plato.

In Deutsch's diamind, perhaps you recognize Munger's exhortation to drive towards deep and simple models, regardless of their ideological underpinnings, no matter how their explanations explain – whether by causal, teleological, or functional means. Evolutionary theory gener-

Figure 5.10 David Deutsch's diamind: one way to 'understand everything that can be understood.'

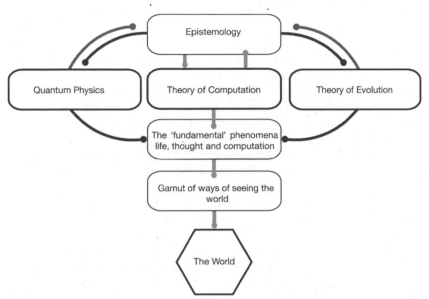

ates causal, functional, and sometimes teleological models. Quantum mechanics sometimes rests on causal models and is sometimes couched in teleological terms. The theory of computation rests on causal underpinnings of computation (the 'hardware'), on functional representations of structure (the 'assembly languages'), and on teleological representations of the designer of both the architecture and the higher-level languages used to represent the world. And epistemological metatheories posit that the all-important act of 'cognitive choice' underpins mental choicefulness about what to believe and how to believe it.

So, the drive towards 'simpler' and 'deeper' can pay off handsomely. It can facilitate the development of the 'worldly mind.' And yes, there's an even 'deeper' structure to Munger's model: the mind's proclivity to fall prey to *automatisms* borne of biology, the social and cultural milieu, and organizational and institutional influences. It's interesting that when asked to provide the one-sentence key to the secrets of his success, Munger says: 'I am rational.' And, what is rationality but the transcendence of the constraint and coercion of the automatisms of one's body and mind?

(More) Exercises for DIing Your Mind

Models, Models Everywhere. The following is a list of pairs of metaphors for entities we have first-hand experience with. Each metaphor is an incipient 'mental model' of that entity. The metaphors in each pair are not at first blush compatible with each other. Try to (a) *dwell* in the first metaphor by imagining yourself and your friends, tasks, and life in a world in which the metaphor is *literally true*; (b) likewise *dwell* in the second metaphor; then (c) *flip* between the two metaphors (the world may 'feel' different when you do the flip).

a Time is a resource. / Time is the dependent variable in a set of differential equations describing the instantaneous distribution and dynamics of energy in the Universe.
b The brain is a computer, the mind is the software that runs on it. / The brain is a biological organ that secretes the mind the way glands secrete hormones.
c Doing anything is choosing between doing that and doing something else. / Choosing is an illusion, doing is just behaviour that has causes we feel and effects we care about.
d Space is a three-dimensional continuum and is all there is. / Space-time is a four-dimensional continuum but we only have access to three dimensions.
e I am a body. / I am an embodied mind.
f Marriage is a business. / Marriage is a long love affair.
g My family is an instrument for my genes to replicate through time. / My genes are an instrument that allows my family to relate to one another meaningfully and empathically.
h An organization is an army. / An organization is a market.
i An organization is a large distributed information processing system. / An organization is a large network of contracts.

Thinking about Thinking while Thinking about Something That Matters

This last exercise is an augmented version of the 'very personal' exercise of the last chapter. Like the latter, it has two steps:

Step 1. Representation – Analysis. Record your own stream of consciousness as you think through a problem you face. Pick a different problem than you did for the exercise in chapter 4, unless you think you can make greater progress by dwelling inside the same problem space again. The only requirement is that the problem be meaningful to you.

Stream-of-consciousness rendition of your thoughts	Codification of your thinking in mentalese
Problem statement:	

In the left-hand column, record the stream of consciousness that comes to you as you apply yourself to your problem. *Edit nothing*, even if you believe you've strayed from the original problem statement. Make no effort, either, to sanitize or increase the coherence of your thoughts as you set them down on paper. If you have trouble writing as quickly as you think, record yourself and transcribe (or use transcription software to produce a record of your thinking). Oh yes: don't forget to stop – and to record carefully the *place* where you've stopped. Ideally, you should stop at an Archimedean point of your problem-solving process – a place that's either clearly a 'peak' (an answer, or *the* answer as far as you can tell) or a trough ('I've identified several non-answers but see a way forward'), a depression ('I've identified several non-answers and don't see a way forward) or a chasm ('I'm lost altogether,' or 'I'm working on the wrong problem').

In the right-hand column, use the description language introduced in this chapter to encode your stream-of-consciousness record on the left-hand side. Use the following coding system –

Problem. What is the problem statement in terms of current conditions and desired conditions? What would constitute a satisfactory point of conclusion or convergence in your thinking? Note that the problem can change as you journey down the stream of consciousness triggered by its statement. If it does, signal those changes in the left-hand column. Note also that the problem may break down into subproblems as you think through it. If this happens, specify each subproblem. Example: 'How to get X to do Y?' – a (perhaps *the)* prototypical managerial problem – will sometimes lead to 'How to persuade X to carry out action Y?' This in turn leads to 'Find the reasons I think X would think plausible for doing Y and figure out whether I can authentically put them forth, as well as the reasons X would find plausible for *not* doing Y, and see if I can refute or undermine them.' And so forth.

Problem difficulty class. Is the problem *easy* – that is, can you see your way to the solution, or a see the way you would get to the solution, having written down the problem statement? Alternatively, is it *hard* – that is, do you see 'fog' when you try to scrutinize your way to a solution? Encode each problem and each subproblem in terms of its perceived difficulty.

Type of solution. For each of the problem and sub-problem statements that have arisen, what type of solution are you searching for? Here, two distinctions are important:

- *Global versus local.* Are you looking for a solution that will help you deal with a *whole class* of situations (global) or with one particular situation alone (local)?
- *Stochastic versus adaptive.* Are you looking for a solution that will work, *on average*, in a large class of situations (stochastic), or for a solution you can *adapt* from one situation to another (adaptive)?

Type of solution-generating procedures. For the purpose of making this distinction, think of each of your thoughts in the stream-of-consciousness column as a step towards solving the problem. Yes, we know: some thoughts just seem random and unconnected to anything. Yet they *may* be useful: you may have subconsciously generated that thought for a purpose, even though you don't see what that purpose is right away. Now, what solution-generating procedure does your mind seem to be following? Is it deterministic (i.e., each thought is connected to the output of the previous thought), or probabilistic (i.e., some thoughts seem 'random' relative to the whole enterprise)? What happens to the random thoughts in the stream-of-consciousness transcript? Do they lead anywhere? Do they get overridden or shut down?

Next we have a variation:

Types of statements. This is a rich one. Take a pen to the statements in the left-hand column, classify them as 'more general' or 'more particular,' and assign some level of credence to them, ranging from 'certain to be true' to 'certain to be false' and travelling through 'possible,' 'uncertain,' 'probable,' and so on. If pressed for time, simply identify the statements that are *crucial* to your problem solving, but it is really best if you can comb through *all* the statements in the transcript. There are little miracles in every detail!

Types of models. Careful with this one – it's tricky. The question here is: Are there discernible models (images, metaphors, theories, dogmas, what have you) you can abstract from your own stream of consciousness (or of unconsciousness) that you can diagram or write down? List the models that appear in your record, then index them under the following headings: *relational* ('good is up, bad is down'), *structural* ('time is a resource'), *dynamical* ('the psyche is a hydraulic system for repressing uncomfortable thoughts and unacceptable urges and lusts'). Then index the *dynamical* models as *causal* (entities specified by their causal powers and connected by causal relations, such as the parts of an engine), *functional* (entities specified and connected by an overarching function of the whole), or *teleological* (entities specified by their *objective* functions or *goals*, with their connections specified by the *compatibility* or *incompatibility* of their goals, such as 'agents in a market'). Whew! – you might say after all this (we never said it was easy, just not impossible!). And now the *real* work begins:

Step 2. Reconfiguration-Synthesis. Now, working with the elements of your stream of consciousness as identified in the right-hand column, *reconfigure* your thinking by making point changes in your thinking processes (the reconfiguration step) and then working these changes back into a 'modified stream of consciousness' (the synthesis step). To this end, it might help to configure another sheet of paper as follows:

Speculative rearrangement of patterns of thought	Re-engineered twists and turns of thought relative to the original thought record

Now, remembering that analysis works forward and top-down and that synthesis works backwards and bottom-up, we'll *work backwards:* from statements to models to solution-generating processes to solution searches to problem types.

Statements. Remembering that the mind goes on autopilot with respect to accepting beliefs when it's in 'problem work-through' mode, define a belief acceptance testing (BAT) procedure and apply it to the statements you've isolated and analysed in terms of general/particular and true/possible/probable/false. For instance, for a general statement, a BAT procedure might be to think hard about any possible *dis*confirmation. Only one disconfirmation is necessary to vitiate a universal statement *because* it is universal. For a particular statement, a BAT procedure might take you to examining the source of the statement (so that the particular statement 'ROI is positive' is replaced by the particular statement 'X says that ROI is positive,' along with the general statement 'if X says something is true, then it is,' or 'X is credible'). Leave in place the statements that have survived your BAT procedure and replace the statements that have not with more precise or refined or limited versions that do survive your BAT. This process will enable you to see 'the general in the particular' and 'the particular in the general' – that is, the degree to which your acceptance of general statements depends on the truth of particular statements and the degree to which your acceptance of particular statements depends on the validity of general statements. Note: You will experience *fatigue* (yes, of the physical kind) because the identification of disconfirmation of anomaly and refutation makes brain burn through more glucose. (Alcohol can help momentarily but is not recommended; fresh fruit juice is better). You'll be tempted to regard the fatigue as an indication of the futility of the exercise; actually, it's an indication of its *usefulness.*

Iterate. Using the statements that have passed your BAT procedure, examine your original problem statement and modify it in light of the new statements/beliefs that you've accepted. Has the problem become easier or harder as a result of these changes?

Models. What modifications would you make to the models you've assembled as part of your reconstruction/analysis step in light of the new statements you'd accept as valid? Now, fasten your seatbelt: you're to *change* at least two of your *dynamical* models. For instance, change a *teleological* model (a person acting on the basis of beliefs and desires in order to satisfy a personal goal or objective) to either a *functional* model (a person acting so as to fulfil his or her social-role expectations and/ or obligations) or a *causal* one (a person acting in a way determined by his or her brain states).

Iterate. In your mind's eye, *flip* between the different models you've generated for any one phenomenon or behaviour. Go back to the problem statement as it now stands. What changes about the problem statement? What stays the same? If you 'like' any of the resulting new problem statements better than the 'old' problem statement, replace the old problem statement with the new problem statement. Repeat for as many different model changes as you can think of. Remember to always take time to *flip back and forth* in your mind's eye – much the way you did in the 'bi-stability' exercises in chapter 2. This will help you see the dependence of your 'problem' on your 'model,' and vice versa.

Solutions and solution-generating procedures. Now it's time to do the same for the solution types and the solution-generating procedures you've used. The goal here is to build up 'mental choicefulness' in the problem-solving process by *switching* between different kinds of searches. That is –

- *Global versus local.* If you previously searched for a global solution, flip to a local search. If you previously searched for a local solution, flip to a global search.
- *Stochastic versus adaptive.* If you previously searched for a stochastically optimal solution (a solution that works 'on average'), flip to an adaptively optimal solution search (one that optimally adapts to each particular situation), and vice versa.
- *Deterministic versus probabilistic.* If you previously searched in a deterministic fashion, introduce randomness to your search. This is tricky and bears a lot of thought. Humans do poorly with randomness, because it's precisely what they try to avoid as they engage in mental behaviour. One simple way to introduce randomness is to carefully isolate a few decision points in your search process and then flip a coin to decide which branch of the decision tree to take. A simple decision point is the one between 'thinking' and 'blinking' (you know, Gladwell-style). At any point in your thinking process you can decide to think further and more deeply, or you can 'just

blink' and go with a result you've either eyeballed or estimated by dead reckoning. Another decision point is the one between thinking further and *asking* someone else (and yes, that someone else can be Wikipedia.org or Google's various search engines). And obviously, there's also the choice to be made between blinking and asking. This is, then, a simple 'randomization' algorithm for introducing uncertainty to your problem solving and turning it from a deterministic process into a probabilistic one.

- *Iterate.* Flip back and forth between the different solution searches and solution search procedures, and examine the effects of each flip on your original problem statement. As usual, ask: Does the problem type change from easy to hard, or vice versa? Does a new problem statement arise that I 'like better' than the original? Why or why not?

Stop, at least for the time being. Record your observations. You'll be tempted to search for a natural end point to the process. There *is* no natural end point. The process is as much about generating new solutions as about generating new problem statements. As much about generating new solution search procedures as about generating new models. The 'natural' end point, then, is the point where *you* feel you have arrived in a better place: a better problem, a new insight into the solution space, a new solution type, a new model or concept, a new solution search procedure.

6 By Way of Conclusion: How Do We 'Know' All This Stuff?

We're at the end of this book and no doubt will face the same rhetoric that is levelled at all writers of 'business books': 'good stories' – if indeed they *were* good – 'but the willingness to draw such sweeping conclusions from so narrow a data set is itself surely one of the most embarrassing mental habits of business academics and consultants.' 'How can you' – the critic may go on – 'make such inferences about the relative success of diaminded ways of thinking after observing *only* successful diaminds – and not many of them, at that? How can you preach so broad an agenda for personal transformation on the basis of so few samples?' Remember that 'based on a sample of 1' is a common insult that strait-laced academics hurl at armchair academics – as well as at one another – to signal overextensions of what one may validly believe on the basis of what one knows, or *believes* one knows.

To all of that we would answer: It may be that our findings are preliminary and in need of elaboration and further analysis; but studies based on single cases need not preclude the sort of confidence that large-sample studies bring (at least, to the academic mind). Indeed, case studies based on single events *can* deliver levels of statistical validity that rival those of studies that include many different cases. How?

Let's say you believe you have built a better model for predicting weather patterns in the Greater Boston area. You've managed to predict with some accuracy the rainfall patterns in Massachusetts on different days over the past two months. Based on this predictive record, you receive a large number of requests from weather forecasters, who want to use your model to predict (or explain) all kinds of historical weather patterns – that is, *they want to give your model better statistical conclusion validity.* They like your model – they just want to make it more *reliable,* that's all.

You refuse them all politely and at the same time offer a 'better test' of your theory. 'Suppose' – you tell one of them over the phone – 'that I could predict not only whether it will rain tomorrow in Boston, but how much – in millimetres accumulation per square metre – it will rain between one and two p.m.? And' – you add with a wink no one can see – 'suppose I could also predict how much rain will fall in a precisely defined 1 square metre area at the intersection of Newbury Street and Massachusetts Avenue in Boston between 13:05 and 13:20 on 21 September 2010?'

The weather forecaster at the other end of the line would be right to be impressed by this narrowing of the boundaries of what constitutes a 'prediction': it *would* be impressive if the model were to accurately predict 90 per cent of these fine-grained features of a single case of rainfall – indeed, it would be every bit as impressive, if not more, than the ability of the model to predict more general characteristics of 90 per cent of all cases of rainfall in a given year. But why is this so? What is the psychological mechanism by which this persuasion happens?

The mechanism is all in the old 'degrees of freedom' argument that empirical researchers use when arguing for greater sample sizes: more individuals in the study sample, and more 'degrees of freedom' in the study, mean there are more ways a hypothesis could come out 'wrong.' The case study method we've described here, however, replaces the degrees of freedom provided by several different *cases* of rainfall with the degrees of freedom provided by different *features* of one case of rainfall. Precision in the description of a single case *compensates for* the sheer number of different cases. A painstakingly precise test of a detailed model against a richly described single case study *can* provide a measure of validity equivalent to the one provided by the test of a simpler model against a large set of 'thinly described' case studies; in which case 'based on a sample size of 1' is no longer an automatic blackball against a model or theory. And since validity is what we're really after – and reliability is only the proxy we use in the search process – why not go *for validity itself* from the very beginning?

The painstakingly precise case study method – PPCSM, for those who love acronyms – is our candidate for freeing validity from the shackles of reliability, for it recognizes that 'degrees of freedom' can be provided by careful studies of individuals as much as by studies of large numbers of individuals, in the same way that small numbers can provide perspectives onto infinity just as well as large numbers. The approach we've taken in this book is that of the highly precise forecaster in the above anecdote: we have aimed to provide descriptions of the cases we've studied that are rich enough to accommodate the testing of elaborate models of thinking and being – models that bring together many different features in the composition of a cognitive-behaviour portrait of the diamind in question. This approach is well suited to the study of cognition, perception, and behaviour 'in the wild' – of problem solving in the natural habitat of the problem solver, of perceiving and acting in the natural lighting and emotional landscapes of the perceiver and the actor – of which this book is an instance.

Now suppose that all social science were done in this way: painstakingly precise description of the sort that Zola had in mind when he declared his *Rougon-Macquart* cycle of novels to be 'social science.' From the preceding perspective, the chief contribution of the social sciences is less that they provide invariant 'laws of human behaviour' (they cannot, anyhow, straightfacedly purport to explain more than the behaviour of the subjects of their experiments – most often university students) than that they contribute precise, accurate, and pragmatically helpful description and design languages for representing and talking about human thought and behaviour.

What does 'pragmatically helpful' mean? It means, at the very least, 'actionable' – that you can *do* something tomorrow, something that is (a) different from what you would have done before you knew about the description, and (b) coherent with your understanding of it ... and perhaps a little more than that. The language of 'mental habits' we have introduced is helpful in this sense because it can be used to generate prescriptions that can plausibly lead to desired changes in the way one's mind routinely behaves. 'Use trees to structure your classifiers!'; 'Think of the complexity of the problem you're trying to solve while thinking about how to solve it!'; 'Flip among at least two different representations of a person, object, event, or phenomenon while thinking through problems involving said entity!'; 'If you can't easily do mental flips, think of this as a skill, not a trait, and invest in its development!' The prescriptions are actionable because the behaviours they prescribe are accessible: they're *things you could do starting tomorrow* – unlike changing your genes, or the socioeconomic status of your parental family, or the values and proclivities of your teachers. (And, yes, those factors *do* figure prominently among the explanatory variables of most standard social science models!)

After all this, you may still be sceptical. In particular, you may be wary of a sleight of hand that most scientists attempt, which involves producing prescriptive models, which they themselves then violate in the act of writing them down. The demand for *reflexive rationality* is rarely levelled at social scientists (curiously enough), even though we often use it in our everyday lives to figure out 'whether someone knows what he's saying.' For instance, is it rational to believe that most people are rational? If not, then is it rational to act rationally, or is it, rather, that a certain level of irrationality may be 'superrational' in some situations? Is it intellectually honest to make explicit claims about the intellectual honesty of one's research findings? Or may it be that intellectual honesty, like authenticity, must forever remain an implicit injunction in order for it to retain any value? Is it efficient to optimize your behaviours so that they're maximally efficient, if that optimization means you have to stop and think instead of talking, querying, speaking, and listening, among other things?

To our knowledge, no model in present currency in the social sciences stands up well to this kind of scrutiny. *Does ours*? In particular, in chapter 5 we 'went meta' on all models and argued for a view of models as logically deep representations that can be deployed quickly and adaptively to explain a broad range of phenomena. We argued for a mind that can use its own mental objects the way John McEnroe used to use his repertoire of shots to cope with a wide variety of opponents, court conditions, and levels of fatigue. We argued for a nimble mind – for a *dia*mind, that can at the very least flip between two different representations of the same situation. And we argued earlier that this kind of mind well describes some of the characteristics of a predictively astute individual, a Black Swan hunter. *But*, you might ask, do *you* have a deep model that can show the relationship between bi-stability and predictive prowess? Is *your* modelling technique up to the standard you're exhorting for others?

We *do* have such a model – a model as curious as it is versatile. In the statistical physics community, that model goes by the name of *stochastic resonance*.[1] The model predicts accurately that some bi-stable systems – such as the bi-stable 'double well' image of the diamind in chapter 1 – become *better* at detecting a signal embedded in noise if *additional* noise is injected into them (and what is a Black Swan if not a weak signal embedded in a whole lot of noise?). The mechanism for this phenomenon is based on the fact that a bi-stable system like the double well filters energy from the ambient noise into the regular or periodic signal that represents the 'Black Swan.' 'Intriguing,' you might say; 'but still, you're confusing the metaphorical with the actual. Surely you don't mean to suggest that the diamind can *actually* be represented by the double well device of Figure 2.2? Surely the neural circuitry underlying the workings of "mind" is going to be so much more complicated than something you can represent by a quartic potential, a double-well device? In which case, this is a nice story, but ...' To which we would reply: 'Good point. But what would *you* say if there was evidence that the *visual system* of a human creature, taken as a whole, exhibits this very phenomenon of stochastic resonance, and will therefore "see" a picture more clearly if we *add* noise to it?' Which is precisely what Simonotto, Riani, Seife, Roberts, Twitty, and Moss showed about twelve years ago.[2]

Precision and accuracy are equally important for making a theory or model pragmatically useful. By presenting the behaviour of our diaminds as snapshots, we've tried to bring description of a way of thinking to a precise enough level that it can be defined in a crisp, clean way – that we can just 'point to it.' In doing so, we have focused *your* attention on important mechanisms of the phenomenon of the diamind. Just as important, we've made it possible for you to perform thought experiments – *real* experiments – that can help you figure out the necessary and sufficient conditions for the production or annihilation of certain types of mental behaviour, and to ask, in a pointed way, 'What are the *constitutive* components of a *dia*mind?' It is only at the point where new models of mental behaviour and activity have taken shape – and not before – that 'normal science' approaches may become helpful, by helping us test hypotheses about the antecedents and consequents of the various components of a diaminded way of being. But *that* surely has not been our mission this time around.

Notes

Chapter 1

1 Mark Walker and John Wooders, 'Minimax Play at Wimbledon,' *American Economic Review* 91, no. 5 (2001): 1521–38.

2 Michel Foucault, *Discipline and Punish: The Birth of the Prison,* 2nd ed. (New York: Vintage).

3 Heinz Von Foerster, *Understanding Understanding* (New York: Springer, 1993), 35.

4 See Daniel Wegner, 'Ironic Processes of Mental Control,' *Psychological Review* 101, no. 11 (1994): 34–52.

5 Ralph Rosnow and Robert Rosenthal, 'Statistical Procedures and the Justification of Knowledge in Psychological Science,' *American Psychologist* 44, no. 10 (1989): 1276–84.

Chapter 2

1 Willard Quine and J.S. Ullian, *The Web of Belief* (New York: Random House, 1970).

2 Nassim Nicholas Taleb, *The Black Swan: The Impact of the Highly Improbable* (New York: Random House, 2007).

3 Malcolm Gladwell, *Blink: The Power of Thinking without Thinking* (New York: Little, Brown, 2008).

4 Scott Page, *The Difference* (Princeton: Princeton University Press, 2007).

5 This innocuous-looking dogma was put forth by Milton Friedman in 1953 in an oft-cited essay has been used for half a century as a boilerplate defence by mainstream economists against charges of intellectual dishonesty

of various kinds. Interestingly, the dogma has not itself been subjected to empirical scrutiny (even of the post-dictive type) – at least, not by econo- mists. But psychologists and behavioural decision theorists have un- covered ex-post-justification biases that seem to apply to scientists as much as they apply to lay persons. So …

6 You could even offer to *sell* your mathematician friend the option to make the bet in your stead and figure out his degree of belief in his own predic- tions from his willingness to pay for the right to·bet.

7 Milton Friedman, 'The Methodology of Positive Economics,' in *Essays in Positive Economics*, ed. M. Friedman (Chicago: University of Chicago Press, 1953).

8 Charles Munger, 'Academic Economics: Strengths and Weaknesses, after Considering Interdisciplinary Needs,' Herb Kay Memorial Lecture, Uni- versity of California at Santa Barbara, 2003.

9 Ibid.

10 Ibid.

11 Ibid.

12 Idem, interview in *Outstanding Investor Digest*, 13 March 1998.

13 Thomas Schelling, *The Strategy of Conflict* (Cambridge, MA: Harvard Uni- versity Press, 1960), esp. chs. 4 and 5.

14 Munger interview.

15 See Pierre Duhem, *The Aim and Structure of Physical Science* (Princeton: Princeton University Press, 1913).

16 Imre Lakatos, 'Falsification and the Methodology of Scientific Research Programmes,' in *Criticism and the Growth of Knowledge*, ed. Imre Lakatos and Alan Musgrave (New York: Cambridge University Press, 1970).

Chapter 3

1 Just to see that these are not 'mere words,' try, on your next trip, to keep a journal of meaningful events for the purpose of recounting them, later, to a close friend or family member. (Keeping a journal is a drag, but it does discipline the memory, so that what you think you remember and what you think you *should* remember come to coincide.) Then, on your next trip, repeat the exercise, but keep the journal of events for the purpose of recounting your experiences to *some other* very close friend, one whom you know to be significantly different from the first one, or whom you have a different relationship with. Compare, afterwards, not only the two journals and the kinds of things you paid attention to in your writing, but also the kinds of experiences you had on the two trips: the sights, smells, and

sounds you were connected enough with to remember vividly now.

2 Richard Feynman, *Surely You're Joking, Mr Feynman* (New York: Norton, 1985), p. 192.

3 Ibid.

4 Ibid., p. 193.

5 Ibid.

6 Friedrich Durrenmatt, 'A Monster Lecture on Law and Justice,' public address at the University of Berne, 1987.

7 Charles Munger, 'Academic Economics: Strengths and Weaknesses, after Considering Interdisciplinary Needs,' Herb Kay Memorial Lecture, University of California at Santa Barbara, 2003.

8 Walter Isaacson, *Kissinger: A Biography* (New York: Simon and Schuster, 1992).

9 Keith Oatley, 'Mental Models,' lecture, Desautels Centre for Integrative Thinking, Rotman School of Management, University of Toronto, 2008.

10 Philip Johnson-Laird, *How We Reason* (New York: Oxford University Press, 2006).

11 Robin Dunbar, 'The Social Brain: Mind, Language, and Society in Cultural Perspective,' *Annual Review of Anthropology* (2004): 163–81.

12 Keith Oatley and Maja Djikic, 'Writing as Thinking,' *Review of General Psychology* 12, no. 1 (2008): 9–27.

13 G. Shaw, R. Brown, and P. Bromiley, 'Strategic Stories: How 3M Is Rewriting Business Planning,' *Harvard Business Review* 76: 42–4.

Chapter 4

1 Willard Quine, *Ontological Relativity and Other Essays* (New York: Columbia University Press, 1969).

2 R. Sternberg, 'Intelligence and Non-Entrenchment, *Journal of Educational Psychology* 73 (1981): 1–16.

3 Douglas Hofstadter, *Godel, Escher, Bach: An Eternal Golden Braid* (New York: Basic, 1979).

4 Hilary Putnam, *Representation and Reality* (Cambridge, MA: Harvard University Press, 1993).

5 Colin Camerer, Teck-Hua Ho, and Juin-Kuan Chong, 'A Cognitive Hierarchy Model of Games,' *Quarterly Journal of Economics* (August 2004): 861–98.

6 George Zaslavsky, 'Stochasticity in Quantum Systems,' *Physics Reports* 80, no. 3 (1981): 157–250.

Chapter 5

1 Charlie Munger, 'The Psychology of Human Mis-Judgment,' public lecture at the Harvard Law School, May 1995.
2 Peter D. Kaufman, *Poor Charlie's Almanack: The Wit and Wisdom of Charles T. Munger* (Virginia Beach: Donning, 2005), c. 6.
3 Ibid., ch. 7.
4 Ibid.
5 David Deutsch, *The Fabric of Reality* (New York: Penguin, 1997).

Chapter 6

1 Bruce McNamara and Kurt Wiesenfeld, 'Theory of Stochastic Resonance,' *Physical Review A* 39, no. 9 (1989): 4854–69.
2 Enrico Simonotto, Massimo Riani, Charles Seife, Mark Roberts, Jennifer Twitty, and Frank Moss, 'Visual Perception of Stochastic Resonance,' *Physical Review Letters* 78, no. 6: 1186–9.

Annotated Bibliography

Much work in artificial intelligence has been devoted to building precise, tractable models of the fundamental mechanisms of thought and thinking. For an entertaining introduction, see

Douglas Hofstadter, *Godel, Escher, Bach: An Eternal Golden Braid* (New York: Basic, 1979)

and its philosophical sequel,

Douglas Hofstadter, *I Am a Strange Loop* (New York: Basic, 2007)

as well as the following collection of essays,

Heinz von Foerster, *Understanding Understanding* (New York: Springer, 1993).

Somewhat more technical, but no less interesting, is the collection of studies of computer models of basic mechanisms of thought to be found in

Douglas Hofstadter, *Fluid Concepts and Creative Analogies* (New York: Basic, 1993).

A less technical introduction to the micro-analytical processes of thinking, perceiving, and reasoning is

Marvin Minsky, *The Society of Mind* (Cambridge, MA: MIT Press, 1981).

For a more technical investigation of the basic problem of representing thinking processes in logical form, see

Murray Shahanan, *Solving the Frame Problem: A Mathematical Investigation of the Common Sense Law of Inertia* (Cambridge, MA: MIT Press, 1997).

No less technical but highly relevant to the problem of integration of knowledge states across several knowing agents is

RONALD FAGIN, JOSEPH HALPERN, YORAM MOSES, AND MOSHE VARDI, *Reasoning about Knowledge* (Cambridge, MA: MIT Press, 1995).

The symbolic information processing approach to modelling thought and language in cognitive science is well presented in

ALLEN NEWELL, *Unified Theories of Cognition* (Cambridge, MA: Harvard University Press, 1990).

More detailed application of symbolic information processing approaches to modelling thought can be found in

ALLEN NEWELL AND HERBERT SIMON, *Human Problem Solving* (Englewood Cliffs: Prentice Hall, 1972).

A modern approach to the same topic, buttressed by a general theory of cognitive 'work,' may be found in

JOHN ANDERSON, *The Architecture of Cognition* (New York: Erlbaum, 1996).

A detailed analysis of mental models (defined in specific ways) and their internal logic is to be found in

PHILIP JOHNSON-LAIRD, *Mental Models* (Cambridge, MA: Harvard University Press, 1990).

A high-level, less precise, but more inclusive review of the transdisciplinary roots of the study of basic mechanisms of thought is

PAUL THAGARD, *Mind* (Cambridge, MA: MIT Press, 1996).

Different types of *inference* have been studied from an analytical and computational perspective, as follows:

JOHN HOLLAND, KEITH HOLYOAK, RICHARD NISBETT, AND PAUL THAGARD, *Induction: Processes of Inference, Learning, and Discovery* (Cambridge: MIT Press, 1986)

JOHN JOSEPHSON AND SUSAN JOSEPHSON, *Abductive Inference: Computation, Philosophy, Technology* (New York: Cambridge University Press, 1994).

For a detailed account of the role of inference in discourse, dialogue, and reason more generally, see

Robert Brandom, *Making It Explicit: Reasoning, Representation, and Discursive Commitment* (Cambridge, MA: Harvard University Press, 1994).

There are several good textbooks on deductive logic, for instance,

Raymond Smullyan, *First Order Logic* (New York: Dover, 1968; reprinted 1995).

For a modern and more pedagogical exposition, see

Paul Tomassi, *Logic* (London: Routledge, 1999).

The problem of theory structure, choice, and validation is centrally treated from a falsification perspective in several works in the philosophy of science:

Karl Popper, *The Logic of Scientific Discovery* (London: Routledge, 1992)

and less famously but no less informatively in

Karl Popper, *Objective Knowledge* (London: Routledge, 1972)

in which an 'evolutionary' approach to the development of knowledge is advanced, as well as in

Karl Popper, *Realism and the Aim of Science* (London: Routledge, 1983)
Karl Popper, *Conjectures and Refutations* (London: Routledge, 1984).

An alternative view on the role of theory in science is to be found in

Thomas Kuhn, *The Structure of Scientific Revolutions* (Chicago: University of Chicago Press, 1962).

For an 'integrative' view of Kuhn and Popper – disavowed by both – see Lakatos's essay in

Imre Lakatos and Alan Musgrave, *Criticism and the Growth of Knowledge* (New York: Cambridge University Press, 1974).

An elaboration of Lakatos's position on the role of theories and other mental objects and the ultimately 'empirical' foundation of even the most self-evident concepts and theories is

IMRE LAKATOS, *Proofs and Refutations* (New York: Cambridge University Press, 1970).

The 'revisions' that Kuhn saw fit to make to his 'paradigm'-based theory of scientific evolution is to be found in

THOMAS KUHN, *The Road Since Structure* (Cambridge, MA: MIT Press, 1990).

An inductivist counterpoint to the rationality of various choices among beliefs is to be found in

RUDOLF CARNAP, *Logical Foundations of Probability* (Chicago: University of Chicago Press, 1962).

Modern updates on the Bayesian inductivist perspective on choosing among beliefs and validating them can be found in

JOHN EARMAN, *Bayes or Bust* (Cambridge, MA: MIT Press, 1992)
EDWIN JAYNES, *Probability: The Logic of Science* (New York: Cambridge University Press, 1999).

Modelling (including modelling the way we model) as a craft and as a science is well represented by several works in the various basic social sciences. In economics:

DAVID KREPS, *Notes on the Theory of Choice* (Boulder: Westwood, 1988)
DAVID KREPS, *Game Theory and Economic Modeling* (Oxford: Oxford University Press, 1990)
MARTIN OSBORNE AND ARIEL RUBINSTEIN, *A Course in Game Theory* (Cambridge, MA: MIT Press, 1994)
ARIEL RUBINSTEIN, *Modeling Bounded Rationality* (Cambridge, MA: MIT Press, 2003)
ARIEL RUBINSTEIN, *Lecture Notes in Microeconomics* (Princeton: Princeton University Press, 2006)
AMARTYA SEN, *Rationality and Freedom* (Cambridge, MA: Harvard University Press, 2002)
JÖRGEN WEIBULL, *Evolutionary Game Theory* (Cambridge, MA: MIT Press, 1996).

In sociology:

JAMES COLEMAN, *Foundations of Social Theory* (Cambridge, MA: Harvard University Press, 1990)

JON ELSTER, *Nuts and Bolts for the Social Sciences* (New York: Cambridge University Press, 1989)

CHARLES LAVE AND JAMES MARCH, *An Introduction to Models in the Social Sciences* (New York: Harper and Row, 1967).

In psychology:

HERBERT SIMON, *Models of Thought*, 3 vols. (New Haven: Yale University Press, 1979)

HERBERT SIMON, *The Sciences of the Artificial* (Cambridge, MA: MIT Press, 1996).

If you are interested to see how modelling in physics proceeds, by comparison, see

RICHARD FEYNMAN, *The Feynman Lectures on Physics* (Reading: Addison-Wesley, 1964).

For a 'classic' and pedagogical account that stresses intuitions and that buttresses equations and theory with pictures throughout, see

CHARLES MISNER, KIP THORNE, AND JOHN WHEELER, *Gravitation* (San Francisco: Freeman, 1970).

Cross-disciplinary accounts of modelling and the architecture of explanatory theories and mental models include

YANEER BAR-YAM, Y., *Dynamics of Complex Systems* (Reading: Addison-Wesley, 2003)

JOHN CASTI, *Reality Rules: Picturing the World in Mathematics* (New York: Wiley, 1992)

NEIL GERSHENFELD, *The Nature of Mathematical Modeling* (New York: Cambridge University Press, 1999)

DEAN KARNOPP AND RONALD ROSENBERG, *System Dynamics: A Unified Approach* (New York: Wiley Interscience, 1975).

Much can be learned about the informational and computational properties

of various models and the structure and dynamics of problem statements and
solution procedures from

THOMAS COVER AND JOY THOMAS, *Elements of Information Theory* (New York:
    Wiley, 1991)
DAVID FOGEL, *Evolutionary Computation: A New Approach to Machine Intelligence*
    (Piscataway: IEEE Press, 2005)
MICHAEL GAREY AND DAVID JOHNSON, *Computers and Intractability: A Guide to
    the Theory of NP-Completeness* (New York: Freeman, 1979)
JURAJ HROMKOVIC, *Algorithmics for Hard Problems* (New York: Springer, 2003)
DAVID MACKAY, *Information Theory, Inference, and Learning Algorithms* (New
    York: Cambridge University Press, 2003)
CHRISTOS PAPADIMITRIOU, *Computational Complexity* (New York: Cambridge
    University Press, 1994).

The following is a highly biased sample of applications of modelling approaches to practical situations and predicaments encountered in various
fields:

ZBIGNIEW MICHALEWICZ AND DAVID FOGEL, *How to Solve It: Modern Heuristics*
    (New York: Springer, 2004). (Engineering, computer science, economics,
    operations research)
MIHNEA MOLDOVEANU, *A Science Too Cruel for Words: The Interventional Use of
    Representational Models of Human Ways of Being* (Forthcoming, 2009; mimeo
    available from the author). (General management, management consulting,
    investment and trading strategies)
GEORGE POLYA, *How to Solve It*. Princeton (Princeton University Press, 1957).
    (Pure and applied mathematics)
JOHN STERMAN, *Business Dynamics: Systems Thinking and Modeling for a Complex
    World* (New York: McGraw Hill, 2000). (Business logistics, operational strat-
    egy and process design)
NASSIM TALEB, *The Black Swan* (New York: Random House, 2007). (Trading,
    investment strategies and manoeuvres)

Index